The Short Oxford History of France

D0220460

Revolutionary France

The Short Oxford History of France

General Editor: William Doyle

AVAILABLE NOW

Old Regime France
edited by William Doyle

IN PREPARATION, VOLUMES COVERING

France in the Central Middle Ages 900–1200
France in the Later Middle Ages 1200–1500
Renaissance and Reformation France 1500–1648
Modern France 1880–2000

The Short Oxford History of France

General Editor: William Doyle

Revolutionary France

1788–1880

Edited by Malcolm Crook

OXFORD
UNIVERSITY PRESS

OXFORD

UNIVERSITY PRESS

Great Clarendon Street, Oxford OX2 6DP

Oxford University Press is a department of the University of Oxford.
It furthers the University's objective of excellence in research, scholarship,
and education by publishing worldwide in

Oxford New York

Auckland Cape Town Dar es Salaam Hong Kong Karachi Kuala Lumpur
Madrid Melbourne Mexico City Nairobi New Delhi Shanghai Taipei Toronto

With offices in

Argentina Austria Brazil Chile Czech Republic France Greece
Guatemala Hungary Italy Japan Poland Portugal Singapore
South Korea Switzerland Thailand Turkey Ukraine Vietnam

Published in the United States
by Oxford University Press Inc., New York

First published 2002.

British Library Cataloguing in Publication Data
Data available

Library of Congress Cataloging in Publication Data
Data appllied for

ISBN 978-0-19-873187-0

Typeset in Minion
by RefineCatch Limited, Bungay, Suffolk
Printed in Great Britain
on acid-free paper by the
MPG Books Group, Bodmin and King's Lynn

General Editor's Preface

During the twentieth century, French historians revolutionized the study of history itself, opening up countless new subjects, problems, and approaches to the past. Much of this imaginative energy was focused on the history of their own country – its economy, its society, its culture, its memories. In the century's later years this exciting atmosphere inspired increasing numbers of outsiders to work on French themes, so that, more than for any other country, writing the history of France has become an international enterprise.

This series seeks to reflect these developments. Each volume is co-ordinated by an editor widely recognised as a historian of France. Each editor in turn has brought together a group of contributors to present particular aspects of French history, identifying the major themes and features in the light of the most recent scholarship. All the teams are international, reflecting the fact that there are now probably more university historians of France outside the country than in it. Nor is the outside world neglected in the content of each volume, where French activity abroad receives special coverage. Apart from this, however, the team responsible for each volume has chosen its own priorities, presenting what it sees as the salient characteristics of its own period. Some have chosen to offer stimulating reinterpretations of established themes; others have referred to explore long-neglected or entirely new topics which they believe now deserve emphasis. All the volumes, however, have an introduction and conclusion by their editor, and include an outline chronology, plentiful maps, and a succinct guide to further reading in English.

Running from Clovis to Chirac, the seven volumes in the series offer a lively, concise, and authoritative guide to the history of a country and a culture which have been central to the whole development of Europe, and often widely influential in the world beyond.

William Doyle

University of Bristol

Contents

List of contributors

ELINOR ACCAMPO is Associate Professor of History and Gender Studies at the University of Southern California. She is author of *Industrialization, Family Life and Class Relations: Saint Chamond 1815–1914* (1989), co-author of *Gender and the Politics of Social Reform in France, 1870–1914* (1995), and a contributor to *The New Biography: Performing Femininity in Nineteenth-Century France* (2000). She is currently writing a biography of French feminist and birth-control advocate, Nelly Roussel (1878–1914).

MALCOLM CROOK is Professor of French History at Keele University. He has published extensively on the history of France from 1750 to 1850, most notably *Toulon in War and Revolution: From the Ancien Régime to the Restoration, 1750–1820* (1991), *Elections in the French Revolution: An Apprenticeship in Democracy , 1789–1799* (1996), and *Napoleon Comes to Power: Democracy and Dictatorship in Revolutionary France, 1795–1804* (1998). He is currently working on a history of electoral culture in France from 1789 to 1889, *How the French Learned to Vote*, and has recently become editor of the journal *French History.*

ROBERT GILDEA is Reader in Modern History at the University of Oxford and Fellow of Merton College. Among his numerous publications are *Barricades and Borders: Europe 1800–1914* (1987 and 1996), *France 1870–1914* (1996), The *Past in French History* (1994), and *France since 1945* (1996 and 2001). His latest book, *Marianne in Chains: In Search of the German Occupation*, will be published in 2002.

MICHAEL HEFFERNAN is Professor of Historical Geography at the University of Nottingham and editor-in-chief of the *Journal of Historical Geography.* His recent publications include *Geography and Imperialism, 1820–1940* (1995) (with Morag Bell and Robin Butlin) and *The Meaning of Europe: Geography and Geopolitics* (1998). He is currently working on a book of essays on the history of geography in Europe and North America since the eighteenth century.

THOMAS KSELMAN is Professor of Modern History and a Fellow of the Nanovic Institute for European Studies at the University of Notre Dame (Indiana). He is the author of *Miracles and Prophecies in*

Nineteenth-Century France (1983) and *Death and the Afterlife in Modern France* (1993), and the editor of *Belief in History: Innovative Approaches to European and American Religion* (1991). He is currently editing a collection of essays on the history and legacy of Christian Democracy, and writing a series of essays on Catholic–Jewish relations in modern France.

PETER MCPHEE is Professor of History at the University of Melbourne. He has published widely on the history of modern France, notably *A Social History of France 1780–1880* (1992), *The Politics of Rural Life: Political Mobilization in the French Countryside, 1846–1852* (1992), and, most recently, *Revolution and Environment in Southern France: Peasants, Lords and Murder in the Corbières, 1780–1830* (1999). His current research project is an exploration of the impact of the French Revolution on daily life.

PAMELA PILBEAM is Professor of French History at Royal Holloway, University of London. Her latest book is *French Socialists before Marx: Workers, Women and the Social Question in France* (2000). Her other books on France include: *The 1830 Revolution in France* (1994), *Republicanism in Nineteenth-Century France 1814–71* (1995), and *The Constitutional Monarchy in France 1814–48* (1999). She has also published *The Middle Classes in Europe, 1789–1914* (1990) and is currently writing *The Fame of Illusion: Madame Tussaud and the History of Waxworks*.

Introduction

Malcolm Crook

Revolutionary France, 1788–1880: Exemplar or exception?

'Dangerous rioting', wrote Louis-Sébastien Mercier in the 1780s, 'has become a moral impossibility in Paris.' The eternally watchful security forces in the expanding French capital, he added, 'make the chance of any serious rising seem altogether remote'. Mercier was not alone in his optimism. Towards the end of the eighteenth century the realm of France was generally regarded as a well-ordered, prosperous, monarchical state. Few contemporary observers predicted that this apparently favourable situation was about to alter so dramatically, though historians have naturally been preoccupied with the search for tensions fermenting beneath the surface of what would soon be known as the Old Regime. For there can be few periods of history as momentous or exciting as the hundred years in France that began with the Revolution of 1789 and ended with the establishment of the Third Republic after 1870. The intervening decades witnessed four major upheavals, in the 1790s, 1830, 1848, and 1870–1, which brought numerous changes of government and a whole variety of regimes in their wake: no less than three republics, three monarchies, and two empires emerged in the ensuing search for stability. France became a vast political laboratory, experimenting with a dozen constitutions, and inventing the modern doctrines of liberalism, nationalism, and socialism, not to mention the concept of Revolution itself.

From the storming of the Bastille in 1789, to the crushing of the Paris Commune in 1871, revolutionary France astounded and appalled in equal measure. The political vocabulary was enriched by the coinage of terms like Left and Right, from the places occupied by radical and conservative deputies in the National Assembly, or words such as Terror, from the political violence that so disfigured the Rights of Man. Time itself was changed and months from the revolutionary calendar, denoting crucial events in Thermidor or Brumaire, were also added to the lexicon. Leading actors like Mirabeau, Danton, and Robespierre became household names of international renown or loathing, while the arrival of Napoleon Bonaparte brought to the stage a colossus who bestrode not just France but the whole of Europe. Even after Napoleon had been consigned to his island prison on Saint Helena the upheaval continued unabated. The revolutionary passion play was re-enacted and the repertoire extended so frequently in the nineteenth century that France in general, and Paris in particular, were regarded as the epicentre of an upheaval destined to change the entire world.

France, which had acted as a great focus for the Enlightenment prior to 1789, now seemed to represent humanity in general. The cosmopolitan eighteenth century thus concluded with a French Revolution that proclaimed the universal Rights of Man and the Citizen and proceeded to export the ideals of Liberty, Equality, and Fraternity to most of the European continent and beyond. Even though much of this influence was extended through conquest, during the long wars that accompanied the Revolutionary and Napoleonic decades, many of those in the annexed territories and sister Republics shared the convictions of their 'liberators'. During the years that followed, revolutionary France continued to provide a model to which radicals of all shades aspired.

Of late, however, these developments have been less favourably assessed, their costs more negatively calculated. Indeed, France has come to be seen as an exception rather than the exemplar, its bloody path to the modern world less instructive than the grand revolutionary narrative might suggest. Yet, as this volume will demonstrate, these critiques have only served to enhance the ongoing debate among historians about its course and consequences. Not only has much of the most original writing on history emerged in France over recent decades, but a good deal of it has illuminated French history during the century of revolution.

In the first two chapters of this book, Malcolm Crook and Pamela Pilbeam seek to show just how and why France acquired its reputation as a hotbed of subversion. The accompanying analysis will be conducted in a critical fashion, for while many looked to France for inspiration, the model often failed to live up to expectations. Whatever the rhetoric of freedom, the power of the French state resisted democratic control. As Alexis de Tocqueville argued long ago, continuity with the state-making efforts of the Old Regime monarchy was as much in evidence as change. The revolutionaries might have begun by replacing royal administrators with elected officials, but they were soon appointing their own agents and it was upon these fresh foundations that Bonaparte built his imperial bureaucracy. The corps of centrally appointed prefects endured whatever the nature of the regime in power, stability at the administrative level compensating for the chronic instability caused by the series of upheavals that ensued until 1880.

A major reason for the longevity of this conflict was the entanglement of religious divisions with the political struggle, an issue explored by Thomas Kselman in his contribution. In 1788 an anxious Louis XVI was apparently reassured by one of his ministers that, unlike seventeenth-century England, religious quarrels were not involved in the crisis he was facing. Yet it was not long before altar, like throne, was being fundamentally challenged in France. The schism between Church and state may have resulted from miscalculation on the part of the revolutionaries, but their inability to grasp the spiritual dimension, or at least to consign it to the private sphere, had disastrous consequences. Under Napoleon there was more of a truce than a solution to the breakdown in relations, which ebbed and flowed during the nineteenth century, as a clerical and religious revival occurred. Religion, whether Christian or civil, played a vital role in the political war that was waged up to and including the creation of a Third Republic.

Religious aspects found little place in the narrative of revolutionary France that was shaped by Marxism and which accorded priority to social and economic dimensions of the upheaval. If the French Revolution was above all a 'bourgeois revolution', then the hundred years that followed witnessed the prolonged struggle of the bourgeoisie to consolidate and defend the gains initially made during the 1790s. On one side progress was threatened by the old aristocratic and clerical elites, which remained unreconciled to the Revolution and conducted a desperate rearguard action to reverse it. On the other, bourgeois hegemony encountered growing resistance from the rural and urban popular classes who resented the creation of a free market economy and fought hard to retain their peasant culture and communities, or artisan skills and crafts, in face of the relentless onslaught of capitalism. The eventual triumph of the bourgeoisie was perforce a protracted affair, only completed after 1870 with the advent of the Third Republic.

Whatever the recent criticism, it would be wrong to completely discard an interpretation that has inspired some notable investigations into social and economic aspects of French history. For most of those who led the Revolution of 1789, like subsequent upheavals, were wealthy non-nobles, while much of the dynamic of the Revolution evidently came from the discontent of the lower classes. Yet in the 1950s and 1960s a number of awkward questions began to be raised concerning the nature of the elites which emerged from the revolutionary struggle. Evidently the old nobility showed a greater durability than was once acknowledged, though they survived as wealthy landowners rather than as privileged aristocrats. Moreover, the fortunes of the bourgeoisie were subject to close investigation and found seriously wanting in capitalist terms. In a famous inaugural lecture, Alfred Cobban demonstrated that it was the professional rather than the commercial middle class who led the revolutionary assemblies. Part of Elinor Accampo's brief is devoted to an exploration of the cultural as well as the material development of these groups.

The extent to which the French Revolution fostered the forward march of capitalism has also proved a major bone of contention. The relatively sluggish growth of the French economy in the nineteenth century was seized upon by critics of the Marxist interpretation as evidence that, in both long and short term, the upheaval retarded rather than advanced economic growth. Yet recent studies have highlighted development rather than stagnation, a matter which Peter McPhee judiciously examines in his chapter on town and country. Cash-crop farmers were responding creatively to market opportunities in just the same way as urban craftsmen catered for rising consumer demand. Revolutionary France was not so much backward as different in the route it took towards industrialization. There were positive advantages to be derived from the gradual rate of economic development, which certainly contrasts with the frenetic pace of political change.

In 'revisionist' interpretations of French history between 1788 and

1880, best exemplified by the work of François Furet, economic and social aspects have been omitted in favour of politics and ideas. According to this approach, the attitudes and assumptions represented by the prevailing political culture were not simply a reflection of changes at the material level; rather they possessed a dynamic of their own. The age of revolution in France thus lasted for a century until the ideals of liberty and equality, masses and market, were finally reconciled under the Third Republic in 1880. One might style the revisionist interpretation 'Whig-Republican', for it shared with Marxism a similar trajectory and an aura of inevitability concerning the eventual triumph of the Republic. Critics have suggested that the real terminus of modern French history resides in the Bonapartist synthesis of authority and democracy, a heritage which haunted the nineteenth century, and has found a more recent incarnation in the Fifth Republic. Yet this is to confuse short-term recourse to dictatorship with the more enduring qualities of the liberal Republic which has been re-established today as strongly as it was a century ago.

These days the so-called 'cultural turn' is raising some searching questions regarding grand narratives of any description. Issues of gender, national identity, ethnicity, and colonialism have undermined some of the French claims to universalism as a consequence. One of the outstanding paradoxes of French development has certainly been the long delay in awarding full citizenship to women on the same basis as men. A full century elapsed between the arrival of universal manhood suffrage in 1848 and the advent of the female franchise in 1946. Some historians have gone so far as to assert that revolutionary France was constructed 'against women' rather than simply 'without them'. Elinor Accampo suggests that this assertion is somewhat exaggerated, though the evolution of gender relations was a halting one because of, as much as in spite of, the periodic posing of the woman question in the heat of the revolutionary moment.

The notion of the Republic 'one and indivisible' has also been challenged of late and the claims of peripheral regions, which occasionally threatened to undermine the central government, are explored by Robert Gildea. Whilst historians are prone to talk of France prior to 1789 as a unified entity, it was in fact a patchwork quilt to which pieces were still being added in the eighteenth century. Few contemporaries had bargained for the uniform, national framework that was imposed upon them after 1790. Inevitably the business of fashioning French citizens to fit the unitary state was a long-term process. Yet to regard identity as requiring absolute allegiance to one community rather than another is probably mistaken. Many people were able to juggle a variety of affiliations, to nation, region, town, or village, during the decades of revolution in France. It was possible to speak both patois and French, indeed to be simultaneously peasant and French.

In contemporary France, at the turn of the twenty-first century, the problem of identity has been raised in an even more acute fashion by the presence of inhabitants who do not share the same religious or ethnic background as the majority. As Mike Heffernan demonstrates, this represents the legacy of an empire that was being constructed during the nineteenth century. France, a maritime as well as a continental power, had always displayed global ambitions, even though these were frequently thwarted. Yet a contradiction became apparent between the ideals of the Revolution and its practice in the wider world. Rights of citizenship were eventually extended to blacks and colonial slavery was abolished in the 1790s, but it was soon reintroduced by Napoleon. The definitive abolition of slavery in 1848 did not deter Republicans from consolidating the work of the Second Empire which, unlike the First, did seek to expand French territory outside Europe. The Third Republic might highlight the benefits of exporting French culture beyond the seas, but this civilizing mission was often no more than a thin veil for colonial exploitation.

The paradoxes as much as the achievements of revolutionary France continue to both inform and interrogate the present. In 1989, just as the bicentenary of the French Revolution was being celebrated, Communist regimes were collapsing in eastern Europe. The fall of the Berlin Wall was naturally compared to the storming of the Bastille in 1789 and Liberty once more appeared to triumph. Yet the French experience should have offered a salutary warning that the process of upheaval is not so easily consummated, that reconstruction is usually a protracted and painful process, and that stability is hard to restore. The 'end of history' has not arrived after all and revolutionary France still has much to tell us.

The survey of those momentous years that follows cannot claim to be comprehensive in its coverage, but it does seek to raise vital questions about the nature of this period, as well as attempting to address them. The issues explored during the French century of upheaval included the competing claims of liberty and equality; the extent of government authority; the recognition of individual rights; the practical implications of popular sovereignty; the justification of violence to secure political objectives; the place of the Church in society; the definition of nationhood; and relations between the sexes, to name but a few. In all these respects a revolutionary France that was both exemplar and exception remains profoundly instructive, illuminating debates that remain just as relevant today as they were from 1788 to 1880.

1

The French Revolution and Napoleon, 1788–1814

Malcolm Crook

Introduction

Revolutions only occur when regimes disintegrate. The French monarchy was not overthrown in 1789; it had already begun to collapse a year earlier when it proved incapable of reform. The revolutionaries thus occupied as much as created a political vacuum, which they sought to fill with a new order. Yet it was far more difficult to build than to destroy and 1789 merely marked the beginning of a decade of upheaval that was only brought to a temporary halt with the advent of the Napoleonic dictatorship at the turn of the new century. Although it profoundly shaped the nature of nineteenth-century France, even the Bonapartist regime turned out to be something of a stopgap. In political terms Napoleon created another option, rather than a definitive solution. The events of 1815, when he staged his famous, but short-lived, Hundred-Day return, only served to restart the revolutionary cycle that would dominate French political history during the decades to come.

This chapter, like the one that follows, will focus on a political narrative so as to provide a foundation for the thematic chapters that follow. Yet it is not intended to serve up a potted version of events which have attracted a vast amount of interest over the past two centuries and which, as the bicentenary of 1989 demonstrated, remain deeply controversial. The chronological outline will instead contain an interpretation aimed at explaining why the *Ancien Régime* (as it quickly became known) collapsed, why a liberal alternative proved unsustainable, and how Napoleon was finally able to restore a semblance of stability. A revolution is best defined as a loss of the monopoly of authority by a single source of power, in this case the eighteenth-century monarchy. A revolution ends when a new centre of power triumphs over the various contenders for supremacy. Constitutional monarchy, democratic republic, and liberal republic were all tried and found wanting in the 1790s because there was no consensus on accepting them as a political framework within which differences could be resolved. The Terror of 1793–4 did enforce a degree of unity, but it was never envisaged as a long-term solution. The Bonapartist dictatorship secured a considerable, yet not enduring measure of consent. Napoleon abdicated in 1814, when he was overturned by a combination of external defeat and internal upheaval, of the sort that had brought down the various alternatives attempted during the preceding quarter of a century.

The collapse of the Old Regime

If the monarchy was collapsing before it was overturned, there are good reasons for seeking explanations within its own structures. Leadership was certainly lacking. The king, Louis XVI, was a well-intentioned but weak individual, incapable of offering the firm resolve that the crisis of the late 1780s required. Yet much more than personal deficiencies were at issue, for the difficulties that the French monarchy faced were deeply rooted in the system of government and the nature of society. To describe the king as 'absolute' is misleading, for limitations were as evident as strengths. Even the notion of 'administrative monarchy' is flawed, for whilst there were few formal checks on royal rule, in practice the machinery of government was extremely rudimentary. Both at the centre and in the provinces, where intendants were nominally in charge, bureaucratic resources were limited and administrators were obliged to rely upon the cooperation of semi-autonomous bodies such as estates and municipalities in order to function. A good deal of government business, above all taxation, was effectively contracted out, exposing the crown to pressure from vested interests.

The most obvious shortcoming lay in the crown's inability to raise sufficient revenue to meet its responsibilities, especially to fund expenditure in the military domain. Hostile contemporary commentators naturally made great play with alleged waste at court, castigating a spendthrift queen Marie-Antoinette in particular. In reality the major burden stemmed from the demands of a global foreign policy, which committed France to a battle for maritime hegemony against Britain as well as a continental struggle more latterly waged alongside the Austrian Empire than against her. When these twin strategic strands were disentangled, France succeeded in defeating her British imperial rival in the American War of Independence, a conflict mostly fought at sea that was concluded in 1783. Yet this proved a Pyrrhic victory, since France made few colonial gains and the price the monarchy paid was impending bankruptcy.

Finance minister Calonne made a last-ditch effort to retrieve the situation by reform, hoping that a package of fiscal and administrative measures he devised in 1786 would receive a seal of approval from a specially convened Assembly of Notables. This in itself was a telling development which, in the absence of debt repudiation, demonstrated how the deficit encouraged democracy, or at least compelled the crown to consult. The monarchy was not strong enough to simply impose change, yet rather than giving their consent the Notables demanded further concessions, among them the calling of an Estates-General. According to the opposition, this long-defunct representative body, which had last met in 1614, was the only suitable forum for the consideration of significant reform of the sort that Calonne was proposing.

The monarchy inevitably jibbed at this demand for wider consultation, but the subsequent attempt to force through reform in 1788 was scuppered by some violent resistance in the provinces as well as at Paris. These events have been called an 'aristocratic revolt', but 'pre-revolution' seems a more appropriate term, since the campaign against alleged 'despotism' was socially diverse and initiated a number of developments that marked the beginning of Revolution.

The recall of the dormant provincial estates in Provence, for example (a gesture aimed at restoring some measure of legitimacy to the discredited government), produced an eruption of hostility between more and less privileged sections of this antiquated gathering. A similar dispute arose at the Estates of Brittany, but in the Dauphiné, clergy, nobles, and commoners presented a united front that prefigured the abolition of the corporate orders and the emergence of a national assembly. The prospect of political reform was, therefore, beginning to unleash social conflict between nobles and non-nobles, and also within their ranks, revealing divisions among those hitherto united in their opposition to the crown.

Clearly, change could not be determined from above and any changes would reshape the monarchy itself, as well as its administration. The 'absolutist' regime (to call it a 'system' is misleading since there was little that was systematic about it) was riddled with contradictions that rendered the task of reform virtually impossible. The myriad of overlapping jurisdictions constituted a formidable obstacle to innovation, and offered endless means of resistance in the name of 'liberty' under which the forces of conservatism and tradition frequently masqueraded. It was impossible to legislate for the whole country and enlightened reform of local government aimed at greater uniformity, such as L'Averdy attempted for the municipalities in 1764, could simply end by encouraging still more diversity. The *parlements*, which registered royal edicts in the provinces, were able to insert a substantial spoke into the wheels of government, even though their short-lived abolition from 1771 to 1774 demonstrated that they could be overridden in extreme circumstances. Ironically, tough action from the centre only brought howls of protest about despotism: the crown was impaled on the horns of an insoluble dilemma, torn between challenging vested interests, on the one hand, and attempting to work through the established order, on the other.

Of late considerable stress has been laid on the emergence of a 'public sphere', constituted by press, pamphlets, salons, and academies, which exposed politics to public debate beyond the confines of ruling circles. To be sure, court factionalism continued to wreak havoc with government policy, which was plagued with ministerial instability as a result. Yet this battle for influence was now played out in a more open fashion and under the gaze of far more people, not least in the capital, Paris, which was threatening the political supremacy of Versailles, where the king was ensconced. The opposition, or rather opponents of the royal government, now had access to potent means of expression and a debilitated crown was unable to prevail over a hostile barrage of print, especially since censorship had practically ceased. There was no alternative but to continue with the process of consultation. When, in July 1788, the calling of the Estates-General was agreed for the following spring, the era of monarchical sovereignty founded on a denial of the representative principle was symbolically closed.

What would replace it was unclear. The fateful decision to recall a body that had last met in 1614 solved nothing in this regard. Rather it served to deepen divisions among opponents of the crown. A struggle for power ensued, but the triumph of the eventual victors was far from preordained. It is oversimplifying to depict the confrontation as turning from a political struggle against the monarchy into a class war between nobility and bourgeoisie. The lines of battle were by no means sharply drawn and the demand for a constitutional monarchy remained paramount, yet a social dimension was becoming more apparent. The *parlements* had already drawn attention to the fact that a uniform land tax, such as royal ministers were mooting, would jeopardize the whole principle of privilege on which the existing social order rested, for it carried implications of greater equality. This same issue was crystallized by the conflict over the precise structure that the forthcoming Estates-General should take.

Since an absence of fixed regulations characterized most monarchical institutions, it was by no means certain exactly how elections to the Estates-General had taken place in the past. However, it was widely believed that clergy, nobility, and third estate had chosen delegates separately and in roughly similar numbers. Once assembled they had continued to meet in different chambers and unanimity was required for decisions to be made, even if these were not binding on the king, who was seeking advice not receiving instructions. Such a prospect was anathema to many observers, nobles as well as educated wealthy commoners among them, who demanded a doubling of representatives for the third estate and voting at the Estates-General by head rather than according to order. It was in fact a clergyman, the Abbé Sieyès, who provided the most famous case for change in January 1789, with his pamphlet *What is the Third Estate?*, declaring that the commons should be 'something' rather than nothing. Indeed, he argued that the third estate, which comprised all inhabitants who were classified as neither clergy nor nobles, and thus constituted more than 90 per cent of French society, should be 'everything'.

Sieyès also proposed what should be done in the event of deadlock at the Estates, which duly occurred when leading conservatives and those favouring change failed to agree, while the king proved incapable of offering a lead. In mid-June the deputies of the third estate decided to break the deadlock regardless of the other two orders; as true representatives of the people they turned themselves into a National Assembly. A few days later, on 20 June, having been locked out of their usual meeting place, they gathered in an indoor tennis court and took an oath not to disband until France was set on a firm constitutional basis.

The Revolution of 1789

It was one thing for 600 men, who were mostly middle-class professionals from the provinces, to declare they wielded sovereign power, quite another to secure acceptance for their self-proclaimed status. Members of the clergy, mainly parish priests, followed by some liberal nobles, did soon join the National Assembly, but the king riposted with a royal session to which all deputies were summoned and where he ordered them back to their separate chambers. It was Mirabeau, a dissident nobleman from Provence, who boldly declared that the nation would not be dissolved, even at the point of a bayonet, yet fellow revolutionaries certainly feared that force would be used against them. Even though their continuing resistance brought an immediate climb-down from Louis XVI, who now recognized the National Assembly, there seemed little doubt that this was only a temporary reprieve, as troops were gathering at Versailles and around Paris for an impending show of force.

That the National Assembly survived and went on to restructure France from top to bottom was the result of popular intervention in the summer of 1789. Since the decision to convene the Estates-General had coincided with a poor harvest in 1788, it was to be expected that disturbances would occur the following spring. Yet to suggest that the mobilization of peasants and townspeople in 1789 was merely a familiar response to the scarcity and high price of food-stuffs would ignore the impact of elections to the Estates. A rough estimate would suggest that a half of all adult males, and in rare instances a few females, had taken part in preliminary rounds of voting and the associated business of drawing up *cahiers de doléances*, listing their grievances. This procedure was accompanied by unprecedented political and social unrest in many parts of the king-dom. At Marseille and Toulon, for example, the 'people' rioted as the electoral assemblies were meeting, in order to force their concerns on to the agenda. These disturbances were calmed, but by no means dispelled, as the deputies began to meet at Versailles. Impatience at the lack of political progress, as a result of the stalemate in June, was already erupting in fresh violence when the dismissal of the popular minister, Jacques Necker, on 11 July 1789, seemed to herald instead the prospect of violent counter-revolution.

The celebrated uprising in Paris, where the fall of the Bastille on 14 July came to symbolize the people overthrowing monarchical despot-ism (though there were only a handful of prisoners inside the fort-ress), crushed the court's plans for a comeback and brought the king to heel. Not only was the National Assembly preserved, at the same time its mandate was extended. Chaos in the capital was accom-panied by the similar dismantling of royal control in towns all over France. As at Paris, so elsewhere, municipal committees took over from established oligarchies. Above all, the constitutional revolution was consolidated as a result of rural upheaval in which peasants vented their wrath against seigneurial authority. The only feasible way to rein in this vast insurrection was by a bold declaration that the feudal system was abolished in its entirety, though hated dues were subject to redemption payments on the part of the peasantry. On the same, memorable night of 4 August, many other features of pre-revolutionary France were also swept away in a heady atmosphere of altruism, as well as desperation. The deputies' long list of sacrifices, comprising individual, corporate, and provincial privileges, amounted to a 'death certificate' for the *Ancien Régime*, a term coined to describe the preceding era that was so unceremoniously consigned to the past.

When, later in August, the National Assembly set out its vision for a new France, in the Declaration of the Rights of Man and the Citizen, it was evident that those in charge were committed to a major transformation of both state and society. To be sure, the *cahiers* of 1789 had collectively laid out a broad agenda for change that was often far-reaching in nature. Yet few envisaged such a radical programme of humane, liberal, egalitarian, and uniform measures, which contained the germ of still more revolutionary ideas and for which a new political discourse was being invented. The social and cultural implications of this unanticipated and unprecedented Revolution were already challenging the constraints imposed by a huge, diverse, and still predominantly traditional country. Great expectations had been aroused among the victors of 1789, matched by profound loathing on the part of the vanquished. In these circumstances compromise would be difficult to achieve.

An impossible monarchy, 1789–1792?

There were few, if any, advocates of a Republic in 1789. Contemporary political wisdom assigned a monarchical framework to large states like France, while Louis XVI's eventual acquiescence in the events of 1789 earned him some renewed popularity. Yet the king had been humiliated in October when, after a mass protest at Versailles in which women played a leading role, he and his family were obliged to return to the capital city, virtual prisoners of the Revolution. On account of suspicions regarding his real intentions, Louis was granted only limited powers in the parliamentary monarchy that emerged over the next two years. Historians like François Furet have consequently argued that the ideology of national sovereignty contained no place for a king. The political edifice cemented by the Constitution of 1791 was thus a logical contradiction, condemned to failure. According to this interpretation, deputies in the National Assembly were driven by their revolutionary discourse not simply towards a Republic, but also in the direction of an authoritarian democracy that already prefigured the Terror. The sovereignty of the people, it is argued, would brook no opposition to its undivided will.

Yet this view is not borne out by the many areas of agreement and lasting successes of the assembly's efforts, such as the new administrative and judicial systems—the departments created in 1790 are still with us—not to mention constant efforts to achieve political compromise. It also ignores both the threat of counter-revolution and the pressure from peasants and urban workers, for whom the immediate gains of 1789 seemed largely illusory. The plots of discontented provincial nobles like La Rouërie, the continuing protests of urban workers over unemployment, or peasant refusals to pay taxes, were much more than figments of the revolutionary imagination.

The king himself provoked the severe limitations on his power by the ambivalent attitude he displayed towards the Revolution. Regarding himself as a prisoner in Paris he attempted to flee the country in June 1791, but the so-called flight to Varennes ended with his arrest, not far from the north-eastern border, in the town of that name. It was a testimony to the monarchist convictions of most national deputies that he was later reinstated, though the episode had further damaged his position and heightened suspicions of his conduct, especially among the people of the capital. Meanwhile, the refusal to create a second parliamentary chamber as a check on the first was reinforced by the early emigration of numerous nobles, including the king's two brothers, which seemed to confirm their intransigence at the Estates-General. These princely émigrés were soon joined by many aristocratic military officers, who threatened armed intervention and sought to join hands with counter-revolutionary elements inside France. Though no grand scheme existed to subvert the Revolution there were a whole series of plots which sustained a climate of insecurity and nourished a conspiracy mentality. In these circumstances it was understandable that the deputies would err on the radical side when deciding to award the king no more than a suspensive veto, to establish a single legislative assembly and to abolish all titles of nobility.

The moderate disposition of the deputies was more accurately reflected by the restrictions they placed on the suffrage. In fact, the taxpayers' franchise employed under the constitutional monarchy was a relatively generous one by late eighteenth-century standards and there were few immediate demands for universal male suffrage, let alone the extension of the vote to women. The real barrier to democracy lay in the indirect nature of all elections above the municipal and cantonal level, which were conducted by electoral colleges in each of the newly established departments. The tax threshold for these second-degree electors, who were required to spend several days voting in the chief town, was set at a higher level, while the qualification for eligibility as a national deputy imposed a barrier which less than half a million Frenchmen could cross.

The qualification for second-degree electors was briefly abolished in 1792, but indirect elections remained the rule throughout the revolutionary and Napoleonic periods. Only the ill-fated Constitution of 1793 made provision for direct election. The intention was clearly to base the new regime on an élite of wealthy property-holders, the so-called notables, who quickly took charge of the plethora of new, elective administrative and judicial bodies that were established after 1790. Though former nobles were relatively thin on the ground, well-heeled, well-educated men monopolized election not only to the national assemblies that sat during the next two decades, but they also ran local government at departmental level, save for a short spell in 1793. Even the larger towns, often the scene of municipal revolutions in 1789, returned notables to the helm in the first round of local elections in the spring of 1790.

It thus appeared that an 'aristocracy of wealth' was replacing the old 'aristocracy of birth', much to the chagrin of some urban radicals, who protested that the Revolution had changed too little for the mass of the people. Yet, in so far as unrest continued during the relatively 'quiet year' of 1790, it was a result of economic disruption in the cities and rural dissatisfaction with redemption payments for seigneurial dues (which was later abandoned to appease the peasants). At the same time the freshly granted freedoms of publication and association did facilitate the gradual emergence of radical movements. There was a veritable torrent of pamphlets and often-ephemeral newspapers, such as the famous *Ami du peuple* edited by Marat, or the *Patriote français* of Brissot. Equally important was the creation of a network of political clubs, many of which were affiliated to the Jacobin Club in Paris (named after the former convent in which deputies to the National Assembly had begun to meet). By the summer of 1791 almost 1,000 of these clubs had been established and in some places rival associations were set up, especially after more moderate members quit over Jacobin hostility to the king following his flight to Varennes.

In these circumstances there is no doubt that a stable, constitutional regime would be hard to sustain, since a culture of consent is not easily created to replace a tradition of submission. The consolidation of a liberal monarchy would surely take a good deal of time and patience, not to say trial and error. In the event, the necessary breathing space was cut short by the onset of two major problems, one internal and the other external: the rupture with the Catholic Church and the war with other European powers. Neither of these were inevitable, though tension with the Church, a fundamental institution of the Old Regime in France, like friction with traditional monarchies elsewhere in continental Europe, was certainly growing in 1790.

Yet in 1789 it had appeared that religion was on the same side as the Revolution, when numerous parish clergy hastened to join the National Assembly. Aristocratic bishops were rather less sympathetic, the worldly Talleyrand a notable exception. Priests in general were disturbed by toleration for Protestants and Jews, the abolition of monasticism, and the sale of ecclesiastical property (to help solve the national deficit which revolutionary changes could not conjure away). However, the depth of their misgivings only became fully evident when wholesale church reform was proposed in the Civil Constitution of the Clergy. So anxious were lay deputies to deny any hint of separate status for 'citizen priests' that they rejected pleas for a church council to discuss the legislation. Instead, keen to pave the way for the sale of clerical property, they imposed an oath of allegiance to these new arrangements, which was to be sworn by churchmen at the beginning of 1791. Contrary to expectations, those who refused the oath, the refractory clergy, were only just outnumbered by those who took it, the jurors, though the latter would be reduced by retractions during the months that followed. Clergy in areas that were more committed to the Church were encouraged by their parishoners to refuse the oath and then proceeded to lead their flocks into opposition against an apparently godless regime. The counter-revolution was thus baptised and received popular support for the first time.

Internal opposition was soon matched by the threat from abroad. Yet, once again, it had initially seemed that European peace might prevail, notwithstanding the international challenge that the revolutionaries had issued to the old order everywhere with their universal Declaration of Rights. The continental monarchs were content to make threatening noises for the most part, though these were inevitably treated more seriously in France than they truly warranted.

It was the revolutionaries, with little opposition in the Assembly, who actually declared war on the Habsburg Emperor in April 1792. The Austrians were soon joined by the Prussians, and the allied enemies made early successes against a French army weakened by the emigration of most of the officer corps. Military conflict introduced a fatal dialectic into the Revolution, encouraging radicalism as a means of self-defence and turning dissenters into traitors, who deserved short shrift; the king himself would be an early victim of this increasingly intimidating atmosphere.

A democratic republic, 1792–1794?

By the summer of 1792 France was being invaded and Paris itself, a mere 200 kilometres from the north-eastern border, was cruelly exposed. The capital was in turmoil, its *sections* or neighbourhood assemblies meeting incessantly to debate means of responding to the crisis, its radicals reinforced by the arrival of determined volunteers (the *fédérés*) from all over the country. The Legislative Assembly sought to moderate demands from the streets and to pull the nation together, but it was impossible for the deputies to prevail over the organized and armed force of artisans and shopkeepers who self-consciously adopted the name *sans-culottes* (working men wore long trousers, not the knee-breeches which attired their social superiors). It was they who effectively decided the deposition of the king in the bloody events of 10 August, when the Tuileries Palace was stormed and Louis XVI and his family were obliged to seek refuge in the assembly hall. It was these same individuals who carried out the September Massacres, breaking into prisons in order to purge the capital of the alleged enemy within, all the better to resist the advancing Prussian army. Small wonder that the domination of Paris over the Revolution, which endured for the following two years, was equated with anarchy by many friends of the Revolution, as well as by its bitterest opponents.

As a result of this 'second revolution', which overturned the Constitution of 1791 along with the king, it was decided to elect a new parliament, to formally establish a Republic instead. Elections at the beginning of September 1792 remained indirect, but at the primary stage there was virtually universal male suffrage. Despite a disappointing turnout, the National Convention was vested with unprecedented authority, not least because until a new constitution was devised (and ratified by the people), its members would play an executive as well as legislative role. Indeed, having proclaimed the French Republic on 21 September, one of its first tasks was to act as a judicial body too, as the king was tried in the Convention for his crimes against the Revolution. There was little doubt that he would be found guilty, but his fate was less certain. There were those who favoured a referendum on his punishment, while others sought a reprieve, which was only narrowly defeated. On 21 January 1793, Louis XVI was taken out and beheaded.

Yet the prospects for a brave new world under a democratic Republic were extremely bleak. As the Revolution became more radical, so its opponents grew more numerous and more varied. Some historians have coined the expression 'resistance to the Revolution' to describe this growing internal upheaval, or civil war, because to call it Counter-Revolution both suggests a degree of unity that it did not possess and a common objective to restore the *Ancien Régime* that was far from being the case. Revolutionaries might see a single conspiracy at work, but urban opponents in towns like Lyon, Marseille, Bordeaux, and Toulon had nothing in common with peasant insurgents in the Vendée, or in the *massif central*. For the former it was the nature of the Republic that was at stake and a perceived threat to property on the part of lower-class 'anarchists' who had seized control in a period of crisis, while for the latter it was hatred of townspeople and the fate of the Church that was more important. Such contradictory aims, and the failure of even like-minded groups to coordinate their efforts, help to explain why the infant Republic was able to overcome the resistance of literally millions of its people. The much feared collaboration of internal insurgents and foreign foes also failed to materialize: only in the isolated case of Toulon, where rebels surrendered the Mediterranean naval base to the English fleet, was the possibility exploited, though this bridgehead was soon allowed to collapse. The allied enemies of the French Republic were as mutually antagonistic and inefficiently organized as the native insurgents.

Yet the National Convention in Paris was no more united than its various opponents, as acrid debate over the fate of the king had demonstrated. Girondins and Montagnards represented ill-defined parliamentary factions that inhibited the formation of coherent government policies. Unity was only achieved forcibly, by means of a purge of Girondin deputies from the Convention at the end of May 1793, an event which once again involved pressure from the Parisian *sans-culottes* and only served to exacerbate provincial resistance to the capital. During the summer months, as a consequence of this anarchy, the whole fate of the Revolution hung in the balance. Though the hasty completion of a new constitution, that of 1793, and the accompanying referendum, certainly helped to assuage misgivings on the part of many supporters of the Republic, there was no possibility of this ultra-democratic document being put into operation. It was instead suspended until circumstances might permit, though when that time came it was considered too extreme. The only means of saving the Republic was, in fact, recourse to wholesale coercion. And though the series of emergency measures that became known as the Terror may have succeeded in the short term, it was only at the price of crippling the nascent democracy with a burden of mob rule and draconian repression.

The Terror was embraced piecemeal, and by all groups in the Convention. In the spring of 1793 a Revolutionary Tribunal was established to punish political crimes, a Committee of Public Safety was created to coordinate government activity, and representatives on mission were dispatched to the provinces to supervise local authorities. Even then it took the summer crisis of invasion and uprisings before a wide-ranging Law of Suspects facilitated the incarceration of thousands of opponents and, in October, Terror became 'the order of the day'. Now heads began to roll from the guillotine, not simply at Paris, where the most famous victims—Marie-Antoinette and prominent, anti-montagnard politicians such as Brissot—met their end, but all the more so in the provinces. Repression in the urban centres of the Midi was ferocious—'Lyon no longer exists' exulted Fouché after the ending of the revolt there—but the level of violence in the Vendée acquired a momentum of its own as both sides committed unspeakable atrocities. Nobles and priests may have been over-represented among the thousands who perished, but the vast majority comprised ordinary peasants and artisans.

If the Terror was slow to gather speed and was essentially targeted against those who rebelled against the Republic, then it was also relatively short-lived. The final spasm in the spring of 1794 is hard to explain, more a settling of political scores than a defensive reflex, though the renewed venom of so-called 'revolutionary justice' ultimately served to hasten its demise. Robespierre was certainly not responsible for the bloody phenomenon, but he had become so closely associated with the Terror, as its apologist rather than its architect, that his removal from power was a vital prelude to its conclusion. The relative facility with which he and his allies were overthrown in the events of 9 Thermidor (according to the new republican calendar, or 27 July 1794 old-style) demonstrates that his authority was not institutionalized in the way that Bonaparte's would later become. Deputies in the Convention reasserted their dormant influence to regain control of the major government committees and then proceeded to dismantle those emergency measures that had enabled particular individuals, especially those 'on mission' in the provinces like Claude Javogues, to use and sometimes abuse the great authority vested in them. It was also significant that the overthrow of Robespierre was a parliamentary affair; the *sans-culottes* were spectators rather than instigators on this occasion.

The influence of the popular movement was now rapidly dwindling. The extraordinary circumstances in which the Terror was established had seen ordinary people enjoying unprecedented authority at the local level, as members of municipal councils, revolutionary tribunals, and watch committees, for example. As the wealthy became suspect of wavering in their loyalty to the Republic, and either withdrew or were removed from office, representatives on mission had little choice but to replace them with persons from a more humble background. Moreover, the period saw some experiments with social projects of an economic and educational nature well in advance of their time. There was also an imposition of price controls, the so-called 'maximum', which for a while curbed inflation caused by the disastrous experiment with paper money (the ill-fated *assignats*), and helped regulate the supply of necessities.

The period was also noteworthy for a kind of cultural revolution. The introduction of the republican calendar, for instance, which remained officially in force until 1806, was part of an onslaught on Christian traditions which saw the closure of churches and the abdication or execution of thousands of priests. Dechristianization represented the climax of hostility to the Church that had been growing since 1791 and perhaps had its roots in the anticlericalism of the Enlightenment. Yet the severity of the onslaught was utterly unanticipated and took many politicians by surprise. Efforts to supply a religious alternative, such as the Cult of the Supreme Being, celebrated in Paris in June 1794, at best failed to evoke much enthusiasm, and at worst provoked derision.

The explanation for this radical, even curious, phase of the Revolution, which has distressed and perplexed so many admirers of its earlier years, should primarily be sought in the exceptional circumstances of war and counter-revolution. The Terror was above all a war-dictatorship. The French people were mobilized in unprecedented numbers—the *levée en masse* of August 1793 put perhaps three-quarters of a million men on to the field of battle—and they had to be organized and rewarded. A gargantuan effort was required and, in this respect at least, the endeavour was crowned with success: by the spring of 1794 the territory had been cleared of invaders and it was the French who now went over to the offensive. It was no coincidence that as the military pressure eased, within and without, moderate deputies in the National Convention were able to seize political control and begin to shift the Republic away from its violent, if egalitarian course.

A liberal republic, 1795–1799?

Parliamentarians gave no thought to reviving the monarchy after 9 Thermidor, not least because the National Convention, which remained responsible for the government of France, was a regicide body. On the other hand, the Thermidorians, as the now-dominant deputies became known, certainly wished to curb the democratic as well as the anarchic features of the Terror and return to a more liberal regime. Proposals were initially made to revise the Constitution of 1793 but, in the wake of abortive uprisings by the Parisian *sans-culottes* in the spring of 1795, a fresh document was devised instead. In some respects this third constitution of the revolutionary decade looked back to its predecessor of 1791 but, in an effort to correct some of the shortcomings of that first attempt at a revolutionary settlement, there was also a good deal of innovation. Those historians who end their accounts of the Revolution at this point, or who merely record a succession of failures after 1794, have badly misjudged both the practicality and the originality of the republican experiment which took place over the next five years.

The Constitution of 1795 established an executive Directory from which the period has taken its name. There were five directors, one of whom was to be replaced each year, in an obvious attempt to avoid dictatorship, either collective or individual. Directors were elected by, but distinct from, the two parliamentary bodies, a Council of Five Hundred and a Council of Elders, the latter containing 250 deputies all aged over 40. The single-chamber legislature was thus abandoned, though the checks and balances introduced by the new system might frustrate rather than preserve its liberal objectives. Equilibrium was equally sought in the reintroduction of restrictions on the franchise: the basic right to vote was awarded to all male taxpayers, but severe limitations were placed on eligibility to office and membership of the departmental electoral colleges. As Boissy d'Anglas put it: 'We must be ruled by the best.' Yet there was little protest in the Convention, where Thomas Paine was an isolated radical who defended the ideals of manhood suffrage, despite his recent spell in prison during the Terror.

The new constitution contained another novelty, as a Declaration of Duties was added to the Declaration of Rights (from which the entitlement to education and poor relief, like the sanction for insurrection, was now removed). Like its predecessor in 1793, the Constitution of 1795 was put to a popular vote, or plebiscite, and massively approved, albeit on a low turnout. More worrying for its authors was the hostility aimed at the accompanying 'decree of the two-thirds', which stipulated that a majority of the new deputies for the new legislature must be recruited among existing members of the National Convention. Fearing that the departmental electoral colleges would choose reactionary politicians, and thus call their constitutional labours into question, the Thermidorians were anxious to remain in office and ensure the immediate survival of the Directory. However, the 'two-thirds' rule was overwhelmingly rejected in some parts of the country and opponents in Paris staged an uprising on 13 Vendémiaire, Year IV (5 October 1795). The insurrection was crushed without too much difficulty, by troops under the command of a youthful Napoleon Bonaparte, but the episode was indicative of changing opinion within the capital, where middle-class protesters rather than *sans-culottes* had taken to the streets.

Though they were tarred with the brush of royalism, these rebels were essentially conservatives who demanded more guarantees for property and public order than the Thermidorians seemed capable of offering. A monarchical restoration was certainly attractive to many of the notables, and a good many ordinary people too, but committed royalists lacked a credible candidate for the throne. After the death in 1795 of Louis XVI's infant son (technically Louis XVII following the execution of his father), the former king's brother, the émigré Comte de Provence, became the royal pretender. At this point the old jibe that he had learned nothing and forgotten nothing from the recent past rang completely true, for he promptly issued an uncompromising declaration from Verona (where he was in exile), which promised a return to traditional kingship. Nonetheless, conservative elements were reluctant to rally to the Directory, especially as the next round of partial elections, in 1797, offered them the prospect of adding to their gains in 1795 and acquiring a majority in the legislative councils. Since publications and associations were allowed some latitude, they campaigned hard and won most of the seats on offer.

In face of this 'royalist' resurgence, defenders of the Republic resorted to illegality. The army was called in to support a purge of right-wing deputies on 18 Fructidor (4 September 1797), which was repeated at the local level; recently elected departmental and municipal personnel were also removed from office. A 'Fructidorian Terror' followed, in which there was a crackdown on returned émigrés and refractory priests, while press censorship was once again applied with a vengeance. The Constitution had clearly been violated, and many historians would argue that the experiment with a liberal Republic effectively ended at this point. However, more than two years would elapse between 18 Fructidor 1797 and 18 Brumaire 1799, when another *coup d'état* brought Bonaparte to power. Enough political space remained for two more rounds of elections to take place, in which the major threat to the Directory emanated from a Jacobin revival. Radicals had not entirely disappeared and in 1796 'Gracchus' Babeuf organized an ill-fated conspiracy that was celebrated by posterity, but easily overcome at the time. However, renewed repression of 'royalists' encouraged old Jacobins to re-emerge, re-establish clubs, and successfully contest the annual elections. In the spring of 1798 adverse electoral results were annulled by the executive even before left-wing deputies had time to take their seats, but the following year virtually all of the elections were allowed to stand. Fortified by a resolute Jacobin minority, the deputies reasserted their will over the government, though in choosing Sieyès as a Director they were admitting a staunch advocate of constitutional revision to the highest office in the land.

When the first set of Directors had taken office in 1795 they were under no illusions about the magnitude of the task they faced and their survival for more than four years might be seen as a triumph in itself. The legacy of civil war in 1793 was painfully apparent in the enduring hostility between those who had fought each other, and lost loved ones in the process. No sooner was the official Terror brought to an end in 1794 than an unofficial 'White Terror' began to erupt in those areas which had been stricken by violence. Former terrorists were hunted down and killed, or massacred in the prisons of Lyon and Marseille where their earlier excesses had landed them. Several thousand were slaughtered in this sporadic sectarian violence which continued intermittently after 1795. How could such bitter opponents be encouraged to acquiesce in the electoral triumph of the other side, still less sit down at the same table together? It was a vain search in the Midi, or at Paris, for moderate men who had no past atrocities or dubious associations to live down.

Yet, given more time, the halting experiment with political pluralism might have evolved in a more positive direction. Certainly the state's finances and administration were put in better shape under the Directory. Liberated from the controls imposed in 1793 and 1794, and with the assistance of some better harvests after 1795, the economy was also beginning to recover. Though growth was benefiting the rich to a far greater extent than the poor, everyone gained from the return to metallic currency and the curbing of inflation. Directorial deputies were also aware that the regime required a republican culture to secure its future and much effort was put into education, especially at the secondary level. On the other hand, a campaign to promote the republican calendar and a set of revolutionary festivals proved largely counter-productive.

The failure of the Directory to make peace with the Church crippled its efforts to restore general stability. In 1795 the link between Church and state was formally severed and people were free to worship as they wished. There was an immediate rush to reopen churches and recall priests, but the halt to persecution was only temporary. Refractory clergy, who had rejected the earlier reform of the Church, were especially resented and came under renewed legislative pressure in the wake of the Fructidor purge. Yet even constitutional clergy, led by the indomitable Abbé Grégoire, who were keen to work with the Republic, found a relationship difficult to establish. The Directory was, in fact, committed to secularizing public life and felt that religion was a private and individual matter to be shut out of the public domain. Processions and bell-ringing aroused particular ire among republicans, but disaffected the faithful who regarded this as an insensitive attack upon tradition. Meanwhile, the attempts to impose the *décadi*, the tenth day of the republican week, rather than Sunday as a rest day, like the refusal to recognize religious holidays, was a major bone of contention. Above all, the absence of a religious settlement put a potent weapon in the hands of royalists who promised to restore altar as well as throne.

Ironically, the great military success enjoyed by the Directory also contributed to its undoing. Whatever the difficulties at home, enemies abroad were overcome: Spain and Prussia made peace in 1795 and Austria followed suit in 1797; only Britain, secure as a naval fortress, remained at war. In the Low Countries and the Rhineland territory was annexed, expanding the Republic to ninety-nine departments, while a series of sister republics was created in the Italian peninsula. To be sure, the loyalty of many of the new citizens was dubious given the fiscal sacrifices they were obliged to make, but more worrying was increasing political reliance of unpopular politicians on the victorious republican army. Troops were used to enforce the purge of parliament in Fructidor 1797. In view of the breakdown of law and order in many parts of the country they were increasingly employed on a regular basis to maintain law and order, to supplement an ineffective gendarmerie or militia. Indeed, many towns were in a state of siege, and military tribunals were employed to punish criminals instead of unreliable civilian courts. Soldiers' allegiances were stronger towards their generals than the discredited deputies and army leaders began to nurture political ambitions of their own.

In the end it was a change in the fortunes of war that brought down the Directory, just as it had determined the fate of previous revolutionary regimes. The dogged effort to defeat Britain, rather than seek an accommodation, produced the expedition to Egypt in 1798. Yet the opening of a new front only served to revive a hostile coalition against France, which now involved Russia and Turkey as well as Austria. The consequence was fresh disasters and the threat of invasion, which had similar internal repercussions to those experienced before. On the one hand, with the introduction of conscription in 1798 there was widespread resistance which, in the west of France and the Belgian departments, amounted to a general uprising. On the other hand, the crisis prompted calls for emergency measures that recalled the Terror and struck fear into many hearts. By the summer of 1799 the situation was being mastered, but it had encouraged some politicians to redouble their search for a longer-term solution to a decade of instability that seemed to have no end in sight.

Bonaparte comes to power

With hindsight the Bonapartist outcome has acquired an aura of inevitability, but at the time a modified version of the Directory appeared much more likely. When Sieyès began plotting a *coup d'état* Bonaparte was marooned in Egypt and thus excluded from the political conspiracy being hatched in Paris. Of course, military support would be required to accomplish the constitutional revisions that were envisaged, as had been the case with preceding coups. But Sieyès was actually canvassing other generals when Bonaparte unexpectedly returned from the eastern Mediterranean and imposed his involvement despite misgivings on the part of the former clergyman. Nonetheless, force was to be kept to a minimum, ideally not to be employed at all, and this would limit the role intended for Bonaparte after the coup had been conducted.

Revision of the Constitution of 1795 necessitated a complex and lengthy process that would take years rather than months to achieve. In the circumstances legality could not be preserved, but the conspirators hoped to obtain parliamentary sanction for their efforts. Deputies would be invited to respond to the (fabricated) threat of an insurrection in Paris and (equally contrived) resignations from the executive directory. However, the concern to preserve a semblance of legality would necessitate some protracted manoeuvres rather than an incisive surgical operation. It was far from representing a classic example of a political takeover. On the second day of the coup, which had begun on 18 Brumaire (9 November 1799) when the councils agreed to transfer their session from the capital to nearby Saint-Cloud, suspicions were aroused and opposition was beginning to organize. Ironically, Bonaparte's ill-judged intervention, in an attempt to has-ten approval for change, ultimately served to strengthen his hand in the affair. His menacing speeches to the legislative councils provoked the very use of outright military force that it was hoped to avoid: deputies were obliged to flee after they had verbally and physically assaulted the general in an effort to secure his arrest.

The use of bayonets, which Mirabeau had vowed to resist in 1789, proved decisive a decade later, though the coup remained bloodless. A rump of deputies was subsequently reassembled to register the edicts which replaced a defunct Directory with a Provisional Consulate and nominated two legislative commissions from the suspended councils to draw up a fresh constitution. There was little adverse reaction to the events of Brumaire. The conspirators had taken their precautions in Paris and disseminated some carefully conceived propaganda, which turned the resistance of some sixty deputies to good effect as evidence of a real subversive plot. The outcome of this latest upheaval went further than those which had already occurred under the Directory, but two of the three provisional consuls had already been directors, while the third possessed impeccable revolutionary credentials, and a new constitution was promised to regularize the changes. There seemed little reason, as well as little stomach for a fight, though an enthusiastic response was similarly lacking. The public would wait and see what emerged from the promise to create a more viable Republic.

Bonaparte seized the opportunity to become master of the fluid situation in which power was once more up for grabs. Dismissing Sieyès's proposal that he fill a largely nominal role as head of state, the general imposed himself as First Consul in the Constitution of 1799 that was issued a month after the coup. His two associates in the Consulate, as the new regime was known, were capable individuals, but their position was clearly a subordinate one. This was recognized by contemporaries who responded to the question 'What is in the new constitution?', by replying, 'There is Bonaparte'. Unlike its three predecessors this relatively brief document dispensed with the Rights of Man as a preface. And if virtually universal male suffrage was restored by the abolition of any fiscal requirement for voters, then its importance was negated by the government's choice of deputies from a list of elected candidates. Indeed, the initial nominations to Legislative Body, Tribunate, and Senate (a constitutional watchdog which would actually be used to authorize changes by decree) were made long before the first round of elections was held in 1801.

Precedent was followed when the constitution was submitted to a popular vote at the turn of 1800 (though the advent of the new century was masked by continuing use of the revolutionary calendar). Few negative verdicts were recorded, but the referendum was significant because it revealed a cynical attitude towards the will of the people and their apathy towards the new regime. Both these factors were hidden from view for almost 200 years until Claude Langlois demonstrated that only half the official number of voters had actually turned out. Bonaparte's brother, Lucien, had simply doubled the figures when a disappointing response became apparent. Though the level of support undoubtedly improved when subsequent consultations were held to endorse further changes to the regime, the practice of manipulating the results continued. Still, the process served to justify the emergent dictatorship, which was gradually installed over the next four years.

The authoritarian turn was characterized by censorship of the press and restrictions on individual freedom, as well as by electoral fraud. Of course, *liberté* had enjoyed a chequered career over the past decade and it was more surprising that French politicians had persisted with the liberal project for so long than that they were now prepared to abandon it. Edmund Burke, the British critic of the Revolution, had predicted in 1790 that it would all end in military dictatorship. Most revolutionaries were prepared to make their peace with Bonaparte and cooperated in his service in order to achieve the political stability they all desired. The second and third consuls offer a good example of the consular *ralliement*: Cambacérès was a regicide, while Lebrun was a royal servant under the *Ancien Régime*. To be sure, these diverse revolutionaries were handsomely compensated for swallowing their principles, yet it was not simply self-interest that motivated them, as the First Consul tended to believe. Men of talent were also anxious to be associated with a system that successfully tackled many of the problems left unresolved after a decade of Revolution.

The firm government provided by administrative innovations, for example, brought stability to the local authorities. The decentralization of the early years of the Revolution had occurred by default as much as by design for, having wrenched autonomy from the collapsing monarchy, local politicians were reluctant to surrender it to the new regime. One important aspect of the Terror was an effort to reimpose a degree of control from the centre, which was not entirely relaxed after Thermidor. Though little attention has been paid to them, the directorial commissioners, who were attached to local bodies after 1795, were predecessors of the prefects created in 1800. The latter, however, had far greater authority and fewer rivals to contend with, for though elected councils were retained at departmental, arrondissement and municipal level, they met infrequently. The prefectoral corps thus exemplified one of Bonaparte's guiding principles: authority from above, confidence from below. Judges, like administrators, had been elected during the 1790s, but in future they too would be nominated by the First Consul. More famous was the completion of the work of codifying the law, a project begun in the 1790s, but now brought to fruition as the Code Napoléon. Law and order was a priority for the Consulate, with 'brigandage' high on the list. Regular justice was incapable of dealing with violent crime, so exceptional measures were maintained, perhaps amounting to a 'security state'.

Bonaparte was certainly willing to resort to severity when he considered it necessary: the ruthless punishment of Jacobins wrongly accused of plotting to blow him up with a bomb, the 'infernal machine' that exploded in Paris in 1800, is a good case in point. Yet reconciliation was also a characteristic of the Consulate, especially in the religious sphere. Many of the intelligence reports received by the Consulate rightly suggested that the religious issue was a key factor in opposition to the Republic. The First Consul himself had no particular commitment to the Catholicism of his upbringing, but he was realistic enough to acknowledge its importance to others. A new pope, Pius VII, was elected just as Bonaparte came to power and contacts were soon made with a view to reaching some sort of settlement. Whereas the revolutionaries had bypassed the papacy, it was now the focus of negotiations that came to fruition in the Concordat of 1801. A number of features of the Civil Constitution of the Clergy were retained, notably the state's responsibility to remunerate the clergy, but bishops would be nominated by the First Consul rather than elected by the laity. Above all, the Church acknowledged the secularization of its pre-revolutionary property: purchasers of *biens nationaux* could rest assured that their gains were guaranteed in perpetuity.

Nonetheless, Bonaparte was well aware that the Concordat would alienate many republican supporters, not least in the army. This explains why promulgation was delayed until after the Peace of Amiens brought a brief armistice with Britain. Though the general had secured his position at home in the spring of 1800, he still needed to prove himself on the battlefield, where the second coalition remained at war with the French Republic. Victory at Marengo, a close-run thing, was as essential to the foundation of his authority as the coup of Brumaire. Peace with Austria followed in 1801 and then with Britain twelve months later. The summer of 1802 was thus a propitious moment to enhance Bonaparte's authority. The ten years of his initial mandate seemed ungenerous in view of what had already been achieved and so the Life Consulate was devised. Bonaparte would be Consul as long as he lived and was also given the right to nominate a successor. This step towards a revival of the hereditary principle would be followed two years later by the Empire.

A republican empire?

On 2 December 1804, a great coronation ceremony was held in Notre-Dame, in the presence of the Pope, but significantly Napoleon crowned himself as a testimony to his self-made status. The renewed outbreak of war with Britain demanded a hereditary safeguard for his regime, though the Emperor still lacked an heir. Napoleon I, as he became known after his coronation, had promised to end the Revolution and he succeeded in this regard for longer than any of the preceding regimes. One obvious explanation resides in his monopoly of military force, as commander of the armies during a period of persistent warfare and much attendant *gloire*. Yet to label his regime a military dictatorship begs many questions, not least because the imperial government was administered by civilians and much of the revolutionary heritage was maintained. The authoritarian system over which Napoleon presided was accepted by the bulk of the French people, who had massively endorsed the imperial regime of 1804 in another plebiscite. Instead, the particular blend of tradition and innovation that characterized the Napoleonic era has been summed up by Annie Jourdan under the challenging title of 'republican empire'.

Yet this First Empire was a rather barren period where reform within France was concerned, hardly surprising in view of the amount of attention which had to be devoted to external affairs and defending the bloated territory. Government control over the political sphere was inexorably tightened, with the abolition of the second parliamentary chamber (the Tribunate) in 1807 and the increasing use of the Senate to rule by decree. In 1808 the creation of the Imperial University gave the government a monopoly over secondary and higher education, a system that remains renowned for its centralization.

While liberty was further restricted, equality was simultaneously threatened. The advent of the Empire brought the return of a full-blown court with all its pomp and ceremony. In 1808 a Napoleonic nobility emerged and a series of revolutionary politicians were awarded titles—Sieyès, for example, became Comte—which many wore uneasily. The titles carried no privileges, but there was an attempt to merge them with the Old Regime nobility, most of whom had returned from emigration and were becoming more prominent as servants of the state. This was evident in the prefectoral corps, where most imperial recruits were of noble origin, while in the municipality of Marseille, for instance, Baron de Montgrand who was nominated as mayor in 1809 had last served before 1789. Birth was once more becoming an important criterion for promotion, and beneath the frippery and foppery of the Empire something of an aristocratic reaction can be discerned. The return of the old nobility also meant a preference for older men and, it would seem, less critical ones than former revolutionaries.

This trend was exacerbated after 1809 when Napoleon married the Habsburg princess Marie-Louise and finally succeeded in obtaining an heir. Yet it was significant that when rumours circulated of Napoleon's death in Russia there was no thought of creating a regency for his infant son. The increasingly frantic efforts to underpin a 'fourth dynasty' bore testimony to Napoleon's realization that, unlike other monarchs, he could not retain authority once he had been defeated.

However, for a long time defeat on the continent seemed a distant prospect. In 1810 the Empire reached its maximum extent, with the borders stretching from Rome in the south to Hamburg in the north, not to mention those parts of the Spanish and Italian peninsulas, Germany and Poland, which were satellite states under French control, or ruled by members of Napoleon's own family. War had resumed on the continent in 1805, though the period of peace with Britain had ended even before the Empire was proclaimed. Defeat at Trafalgar ended any hope of maritime supremacy for France, and thus any realistic hope of vanquishing the British, but Napoleon continued to steamroller his continental opponents. He took out the Austrians at Austerlitz and the Prussians at Jena, before concluding peace with the Russians at Tilsit in 1807.

Inevitably, as in the 1790s, the impact of war, and especially military defeat, remained the crucial factor in determining the future of the Empire. As long as European conflict continued, the threat of overthrow persisted, and from the ill-fated invasion of Russia in 1812 onwards the day of reckoning drew closer. By 1814 France once again faced invasion and resistance to Napoleonic rule grew stronger, if insufficient to seal his downfall by itself. Napoleon was obliged to abdicate and exiled to Elba. His Empire collapsed and France ended with less territory than he inherited when he came to power in 1799. It had been a marvellous adventure, but a million Frenchmen had lost their lives in the process, not to mention millions of other Europeans.

Conclusion

When Louis XVIII took possession of the vacant throne in 1814 he was content to leave most of the existing personnel in place. He resisted pressure from the small, hard core of émigrés who, having remained in exile with him until the bitter end, were demanding a greater reward for their loyalty. It is often said that Louis succeeded to the throne of Napoleon, maintaining structures as well as individuals from his predecessor. Indeed, the prefects, like the Napoleonic Code, are still with us 200 years later. As Alexis de Tocqueville argued long ago, the revolutionaries effectively completed rather than overturned the state-building begun under the Old Regime. Yet the ideological legacy of the Revolution could not be conjured away by means of such continuity. Before long the Hundred Days of 1815 would not only rescue the tarnished reputation of a triumphantly returning Napoleon, but also reveal the persistence of apparently exorcized revolutionary demons. This extraordinary event demonstrated just how far the memory and mentality of the Revolution had seared into the French consciousness. At the same time, this unexpected resurgence of popular radicalism dramatically set the scene for the century of upheaval that would follow.

2

Upheaval and continuity, 1814–1880

Pamela Pilbeam

Introduction

The French are prisoners of the cascade of revolutions they have experienced since 1789. Nineteenth-century French revolutions are always interpreted as continuations of 1789. For French republican historians, most notably in recent years François Furet, repeated revolutions were stages in the emergence of a republican state. For socialists, revolutions were the consequence of the social and economic deprivation of the poor and would cease when, through reform or revolution, a more equal society was achieved. For liberals or less ideologically committed commentators, revolution occurred either as a consequence of individual misjudgement or when political and economic crises, which might have been manageable separately, coincided.

Revolution still remains a significant marker in the discourse between Left and Right. Unlike Britain, where taking to the streets is regarded as an outrage against civil order, most French recognize, albeit with varying degrees of enthusiasm, the right of the citizen to protest. Indeed, the Constitution of 1793, much revered by later republicans, explicitly acknowledged the right of rebellion. Yet, despite repeated revolutions in the nineteenth century, continuity was a striking feature of France's administrative, judicial, fiscal, financial, religious, and educational structures. Economic and social changes were gradual. The French population was static after the 1850s.

In this chapter we shall address two questions: why was France so effervescent in these years? And what did these disturbances actually signify? Many of the fundamental conflicts touched on in these pages, notably to do with religion, class, and gender, will be developed in subsequent chapters. The period 1814–80 was punctuated by revolutions, violent changes of regime and prolonged episodes of popular disorder. The two most significant were those of 1830 and 1848. Both provoked a change in the regime. Whereas the fighters on both occasions were Parisian artisans, the governmental revolution came about because the economic grievances of workers coincided with conflict and stalemate within the ruling élite. On neither occasion, nor indeed in September 1870 when Louis-Napoleon was deposed, did the élites actively seek revolution, indeed the memory and mythology of 1789 meant that property-owners, with rare exceptions, were anxious to avoid upheaval. Why were argumentative members of the educated élite unable to negotiate political compromises and what part did their failure contribute to the fall of successive regimes?

The outbreak of revolution in 1830

The apparent catalyst for the Three Glorious Days (the July 1830 revolution) was a quarrel between king and parliament (1829–30) over how much notice the king should take of the views of the majority in parliament when choosing governments. Liberal historians used to argue that nineteenth-century political instability was an inescapable legacy of the conflicts engendered by the 1789 revolution. Contemporary liberal historians, such as Furet, Rosanvallon, and Tombs still conclude that the Restoration was 'impossible'. It is true that the Bourbons were restored by France's enemies after they defeated Napoleon in 1814. However, the political settlement was a compromise between the new king and Napoleon's notables. Louis XVIII was careful to retain all of the Emperor's officials who would join him, along with the administrative, judicial, legal, and fiscal institutions devised during the revolutionary years. The main innovation was the Constitutional Charter that provided a parliamentary framework to restrain monarchical authority. Legislative power was to be shared by the hereditary monarch, an elected Chamber of Deputies and a nominated, subsequently hereditary, Chamber of Peers. The precise details of their power-sharing were left vague. This was to be problematic later, but it left space for compromises to be struck.

This equilibrium was shaken when Napoleon escaped from exile in Elba and successfully called on many of his former servants to return to the Imperial colours. The Allies resumed the war and Napoleon was exiled to the distant Atlantic island of Saint Helena. In 1815, the attempt to defend the Empire by former Bonapartists and republicans united in 'federations' opposed by ultra-royalists, often former émigrés, drew the battle-lines for conflicts which bubbled up repeatedly throughout the subsequent Second Restoration. Those former Imperial servants who had agreed to serve the monarchy in 1814, and then responded to Napoleon's demand for allegiance in 1815, remained permanently and acrimoniously excluded from office during the Second Restoration. They formed the nucleus of left-wing opposition to the Bourbons. The virulence of their opposition was sharpened by the White Terror, a campaign of revenge exacted by ultras, as the extreme right-wingers were known, during the early months of the Second Restoration.

Did the circumstances of the Hundred Days and the Second Restoration make the Bourbon monarchy an impossible regime? The institutional framework created during a quarter of a century of revolution remained intact. Louis XVIII terminated the reprisals of the White Terror inflicted by the ultras and dissolved the ultra-dominated *chambre introuvable*, the right-wing Chamber of Deputies elected in the immediate aftermath of Napoleon's second defeat. While Louis XVIII was in control of government and aimed for the centre ground the system remained workable. Rival hostile political groups emerged, but they lacked structure or definition. There were ultras on the Right who treasured an idealized myth that traditionally France had been, and ought to be, run by a harmonious trio of king, Church, and nobles, although they had no single vision of how it could be resurrected. An amorphous majority of deputies in the centre wanted a viable constitutional monarchy, but they also lacked an agreed blueprint for its operation. Finally, there was a small, diffuse left wing, noisily loyal to the 1814 Charter, whose members were variously labelled 'independents' and 'doctrinaires', until they settled on the term liberal. All were committed to making the new system work and competed for influence. There were only a few minor, left-wing outbursts, including a short-lived rebellion in 1816 in Grenoble, home of the republican Rey.

In 1820 the political compromise was upset by the chance murder of the Duc de Berry, eldest son of the future Charles X (Louis XVIII was childless). The ultras asserted that the killer was a liberal and launched a sustained bid to reclaim the political power they had lost in 1816. The ensuing polarization of politics was to lead to revolution in 1830. A new electoral law was pushed through parliament in 1820 that gave a second vote to the 25 per cent of the 100,000 voters who paid most tax. Electoral lists and elections were also manipulated to smother the Left. In defence the Left was forced to reinvent itself. In 1821 some grouped themselves in the *charbonnerie*, an offshoot of the Italian *carbonari*, a secret society which revered the principles of 1789 and adopted the symbols and ideas of radical freemasonry. A number of small conspiracies were uncovered, all centred on various army units. Government repression and the decision to occupy the under-employed army to defend the conservative Spanish royal claimant against his liberal rival in 1823 snuffed out this form of opposition.

Political conflict thus focused on parliament. The 1814 constitution had restored Catholicism as the state religion. Clerical influence in education was promoted, from primary to higher levels. Young, newly recruited priests were deployed by the clerical hierarchy, which had ultra-royalist political sympathies, to evangelize France. A week's missionary activity in a chosen area would climax with a church service asking forgiveness for the sins of the Revolution. In 1824 Charles X became king and he was crowned the following year with 'medieval' pomp in Reims cathedral. Henceforth, the aspirations of the ultras, particularly the secret clerical Congregation, one hundred-strong in the Chamber, knew no bounds. A law against sacrilege was passed, horrifying the anti-clerical Left, which had withered to a mere nineteen seats in the 1824 election. They were even more shocked when a state loan was raised to indemnify those émigrés who had lost land during the Revolution.

Ultra success caused those with a stake in the survival of revo-lutionary principles to rally as a liberal opposition. In 1827 François Guizot, who had been removed from his Chair of History at the

Sorbonne as a result of clerical pressure, headed a liberal electoral committee in Paris. Its stated aim was simply to ensure that those who were entitled to vote appeared on the electoral lists and that elections were conducted fairly. Membership of electoral lists, which had shrunk by 20 per cent due to government manipulation of the tax returns which qualified individuals for the suffrage, was soon restored to previous levels as local groups informed voters of their rights.

Anxious that liberal pressure was eroding his majority, chief-minister Villèle held and lost a general election at the end of 1827. Royalists and liberals were equally matched with about 180 seats each, while ultras were reduced to about sixty. Charles appointed a concili-atory centre-right government, headed by Martignac, and made one of the liberal leaders, Royer-Collard, president of the Chamber of Deputies, but Martignac was unable to please either liberals or ultras and resigned in August 1829. If Charles had followed what had become accepted practice he would have appointed a left-of-centre government, because the liberals had won most of the 100 or so by-elections occasioned by irregularities and duplicated nominations. Instead he allowed himself to be persuaded by his ultra friends that liberals represented a revolutionary threat and appointed an ultra government which, from November, was headed by the Prince de Polignac, his close companion and, like him, a former émigré. As the annual recall of parliament was postponed liberal newspapers organ-ized petitions to refuse to pay taxes unless they were approved by parliament. When Charles reopened parliament in March 1830 with a speech critical of the liberals, the assembly responded with an unprecedented vote of no confidence in the government. Charles prorogued the assembly and in May called another general election in which, predictably, the liberals secured a majority with 274 seats.

The king had manoeuvred himself into a corner, unable to make a right-wing government work and totally unwilling to countenance a liberal ministry. After several weeks of hesitation the king published four ordinances on 26 July 1830. The first ordered the liberal news-papers, which were blamed for the political conflict, to cease publica-tion. The other three dissolved the new assembly and called a fresh election in which the most wealthy 25 per cent of the restricted elect-orate determined the outcome.

Did this political conflict provoke the revolution that ensued? The short answer is no. Undoubtedly the 1789 Revolution had left a legacy of irreconcilable division and suspicion, but there were plenty of opportunities for compromise, even after promulgation of the four ordinances. The liberal deputies, who eventually assumed leadership of the revolution, were reluctant to defy the ordinances and only did so when the position of the king had been made untenable by artisan revolt. The July 1830 revolution really began with an artisan insurrection in central Paris. Artisan demonstrations had become common since the onset of economic depression in 1827, but they spiralled out of control when the publication of the ordinances provoked liberal journalists and printers to join and direct this form of protest.

The political crisis of 1848

In August 1830 the quarrel within the political élites was patched together when the liberals invented an Orleanist monarchy. No attempt was made to address the grievances of artisans and peasants, nor to include any but the most wealthy sections of the middle class in political decision-making. In 1848 political conflict was not between the king and the majority in parliament, but between the king's government, which had the support of parliament, and a movement for parliamentary reform, the Banquet Campaign. This attracted the support of only about a quarter of the deputies, but was spearheaded, as in 1830, by a handful of left-wing newspapers, especially *La Réforme*. The extension of the right to vote had been a perennial topic of debate in parliament. In 1839 and again in 1847, when proposals to enlarge the electorate and/or reshape constituency boundaries were rejected by the assembly, reform banquets were organized throughout France. Participants paid 4 francs a head for food and drink, and were treated to rousing reform speeches at the end of the meal. Over 100 banquets were held in the months before parliament reassembled in January 1848. They added a little spice to the rather dull political debates of the July Monarchy, but the Banquet Campaign itself would never have toppled Louis-Philippe. The reformers were very divided in their aims, which ranged from modest franchise reform to universal manhood suffrage. A few wanted the state to take the initiative to solve the social and economic problems which were accompanying industrial growth, while an even smaller number were sympathetic to the demands of early socialists that the state should provide for the unemployed. This was a very relevant issue because in 1848 France was beset by an economic crisis similar to the one that accompanied the Revolution of 1830. However, just as in 1830, only a tiny number within the élite wanted to link the economic crisis with the political debate.

It was the last-minute decision to make such a connection that brought revolution in February 1848, just as it had in 1830. The reformers planned a banquet in central Paris and, for the first time in this campaign they announced that a march of workers and students would precede it. Alarmed by the potentially explosive fusion of economic and political grievances, the government banned the banquet. The organizers, including the radical deputy Ledru-Rollin, editor of *La Réforme*, cancelled the banquet, but the march went ahead. It was the government's failure to control the march that led to the change of regime.

Can one conclude that in 1848 political conflict was responsible for revolution? Undoubtedly, as in 1830, opposition leaders profited from revolution. In 1830 the organizers of electoral committees and liberal newspaper editors took charge, while in 1848 the banquet leaders and left-wing journalists set up the new Republic. However, on neither occasion were the issues under political debate before the revolution insoluble, nor did government critics have an agreed agenda. In 1848 the tiny minority of radicals who declared a democratic republic could not agree on whether state-initiated social reform was the answer to the escalating economic crisis. In April 1848 universal manhood suffrage returned a National Assembly with former monarchists, both Orleanists and Legitimists, in an overwhelming majority. Their subsequent decision to close the temporary workshops which were providing a living for over 100,000 unemployed led to a workers' rebellion in Paris, the June Days. In the election for a president in December 1848 Napoleon Bonaparte's nephew, Louis-Napoleon, romped home, leaving the republican candidates standing. The Second Republic was progressively emasculated as the old monarchist élites reasserted control at central and local level. With their support an Empire was substituted for the Republic in 1852 after Louis-Napoleon's *coup d'état* in December 1851. The old élites may not have loved the new emperor, but their fear of popular unrest united behind him large numbers of those who supported the rival Bourbon and Orleanist monarchies and were unable to agree on a single, royalist candidate.

Empire to Republic, 1870–1871

Political conflict played no part in the collapse of the Second Empire. By 1869 Louis-Napoleon had done much to transform his regime into a parliamentary system. His critics were a vociferous, but mutually antagonistic minority. In 1869 thirty republicans were elected to the legislative assembly and only eighty Bonapartists were returned. The power of the assembly was extended, but it should be noted that the use of plebiscites was retained. The constitutional changes of 1869–70 were subsequently confirmed by 7.3 to 1.5 million votes. The republicans were not a substantive threat to the regime and they supported the emperor's decision to declare war on Prussia in the summer of 1870 to curb her ambitions in Germany. The French high command was so confident of victory that battalions were issued only with maps of German, not French, territory. The Second Empire collapsed because Louis-Napoleon was captured at Sedan and the Prussians were soon in control of northern France. Three days later a Republic was declared in Paris by a minority of motley republicans. It would be more than a decade before a secure republican system was established.

Political conflicts thus surrounded the main nineteenth-century revolutions, but in each case there was room for negotiation. One has to examine other factors in order to analyse the outbreak of these revolutions, and the other numerous, smaller-scale rebellions that occurred like the Paris Commune of 1871.

Social factors in revolution

Until the 1970s all republican historians, not only the Marxists, would have unanimously stressed economic and social factors in the outbreak of revolution. Since then emphasis has been on ideas and, above all, political culture. Artisans and peasants play little part in Furet's *Revolutionary France, 1770–1880*, for example. Yet nineteenth-century, middle-class observers had no doubt that urban unrest was the work of a lawless section of the 'popular classes'. Social scientists, liberals, and socialists, described a society irremediably torn apart by social conflict, between what socialists like Auguste Blanqui called the 'proletariat' and a small, wealthy élite (exploitative in the view of socialists) in charge of government. Socialist accounts of the 1830 revolution, such as those of Cabet and Blanc, gendarmerie reports, novels, newspapers, and political tracts all emphasized that towns were lawless, peopled with 'dangerous' classes. These were not artisans as such, it was asserted, but down-and-outs, who lived at the margins, involved in street theft and other criminal activities. The educated élite was convinced that such individuals formed a major element in revolutionary crowds, as documented in the memoirs of the conservative liberal, Alexis de Tocqueville. Novelists and playwrights thrilled the upper classes with tales of this urban sub-proletariat, which was depicted as a race apart, threatening the norms of civilized society. The novels of Eugène Sue (*Les Mystères de Paris*) and Victor Hugo (*Les Misérables*), crammed with such characters, were serialized in the new popular newspapers, such as Émile de Girardin's widely circulated *La Presse*. Queues formed outside newspaper offices to snatch the latest episode and even sober, old-fashioned political broad sheets, such as *Le Constitutionnel* were obliged to fill their columns with tales of urban degradation and degeneration.

However, police and government prosecutors' reports of insurrection indicate that the actual street-fighters were not drawn from a criminal underclass. The active force consisted of what contemporaries called the *classes populaires*, more respectable artisans and peasants. Successful revolutions, in 1830, 1848, and in 1870–1, were fought by artisans in central Paris. Studies of those who manned the barricades in 1830 reveal that the majority were skilled artisans, tailors, craftsmen in the luxury metal industries, and cabinetmakers prominent among them. They were settled workers, mostly Parisians, or from neighbouring departments. Many were family men. By 1870–1 workers in newer suburban industries were also involved and women took part alongside their men. However, this was not evidence of the 'class war' so feared by contemporaries like Alexis de Tocqueville, or welcomed by Karl Marx. Artisans were not a united 'working class' and turned to street demonstrations and barricades only in extreme circumstances, when the ruling groups paid no attention to their pressing needs.

Urban geography and revolution

Artisan riots and demonstrations always alarmed governments, wherever they took place, but successful revolution was always Parisian-based, focused on the central districts where the homes and workshops of artisans were intermingled with the centres of government and the newspaper industry. A unique feature of nineteenth-century revolutions was the barricade, thrown up across a street by neighbours allied in rebellion. Barricades were often coordinated by the local café owner and defended by whole families. They were constructed from the railings that surrounded trees, upturned carts, market stalls, tables, and other luckless pieces of furniture, while paving stones were prised up to heave at the soldiers. A barricade was a drawbridge raised by a street to symbolize its protest. In 1830, 1832, 1848 (twice), and 1871 numerous barricades were erected in the central worker districts of Paris, making them more or less a no-go area, depending on how well fighting was progressing in nearby streets which housed government buildings. The barricade itself was purely a holding operation. For a revolution to succeed the incumbent government had to admit defeat or be overrun on its own territory at the Tuileries Palace, the Chamber of Deputies, or the Hôtel-de-Ville.

The political geography of the nineteenth-century city was a distinctive one. Workshops and the homes of workers existed in streets adjacent to the homes of the political élite and government offices. Nearly all streets were very narrow, making defensive barricades child's play and cavalry charges almost impossible. A few isolated grand avenues existed, but large-scale town planning and the separation of the different social groups and activities into distinct districts was only present in the dreams of utopian socialists before the 1850s. Rapid urban growth contributed to a feeling of lawlessness and lack of control. Paris swelled from three-quarters of a million inhabitants in 1815 to 1.5 million by mid-century as migrants, who traditionally came to work in the building and allied trades during the winter months, decided to remain all year. Police records show that such migrants rarely manned barricades, but some pursued radical politics. Socialist affiliations are recorded in the memoirs of the stonemason Nadaud, the draughtsman Perdiguier and Suzanne Voilquin, who was a needlewoman.

Violence and political volatility were endemic in nineteenth-century cities, and the situation was made worse because governments commanded scant resources to maintain what they called 'public order'. In 1830, 1848, and 1870 the failure of the regime to hold the loyalty of vital elements of their armed defenders was crucial in toppling those in power. The Minister of the Interior appointed police commissioners throughout France, but they were few in number and could do no more than arrest individual urban criminals. The commissioners were answerable to Paris directly and not to the local prefect. Prefects would call on the volunteer militia, or National Guard, to control riots, demonstrations and more widespread unrest. The Guard was an invention of 1789 and always betrayed its revolutionary origins when it was caught in a tight corner, sympathizing with revolutionaries in Paris in July 1830, in Lyon in 1831, and 1834, and again in Paris in February 1848. The desertion of the National Guard was absolutely crucial in the collapse of both the Bourbon (1830) and Orléans (1848) monarchies. Indeed, the revolt of the Paris Commune in March 1871 was organized and led by National Guard battalions.

National guardsmen were crucial to revolutions partly because the institution was held to embody the spirit of 1789. After 1814 their officers were habitually retired (and discontented) veterans of the Imperial armies. After 1830, when the members elected their officers, as they had done in the early 1790s via a form of quasi-universal suffrage, most of those chosen were republican dissidents, with the result that some battalions had to be dissolved by the government because they might prove unreliable in a crisis. On the other hand, the Guard was quintessentially middle class, composed of shopkeepers and craftsmen, with a sprinkling of professional men. They had to provide their own uniform and weapons and received no pay. In 1830 and 1848 some must have turned out on the barricades mainly to protect their own shops and workshops from looters rather than to promote upheaval.

The last line of defence against revolution was the army, organized after 1814 on a departmental basis. Its members consisted of upper- and middle-class officers, who were volunteers and usually college-trained, and youthful, rank-and-file conscripts, who served for three years. An annual contingent was chosen by lot, but better-off families could buy substitutes for their sons. The composition and organiza-tion of this army led to problems when it was used to restore law and order. Regiments were stationed in the chief town of each department and their senior officer was answerable directly to the Minister of War. His relationship with local officials, especially the prefect, was rarely relaxed. His men were mostly drawn from the area and for a variety of personal, emotional, financial, and other reasons, their relations with local people were often strained.

In the period of prolonged foreign peace that did not end until the Crimean war broke out in 1854, opportunities for rapid promotion were non-existent. Colonial service in Algeria might have offered better prospects, but men were moved there as a punishment rather than as an incentive. Under Napoleon a man from the ranks might rise from NCO to a commission, but after 1815 he would remain an NCO. The lack of financial rewards, or possibilities for promotion might propel non-commissioned officers onto the insurrectionary side of the barricades. In the revolutions of both 1830 and 1848 the decisive factor in the change of regime was the desertion of NCOs and their men to the revolutionaries. Their motives seem to have been in part political; the Restoration army was obliged to retain the services of large numbers of Imperial soldiers. A Bonapartist trad-ition survived the dissolution of Imperial regimental structures and was reinforced by the boredom of life spent in small provincial towns with no enemy to fight. As a consequence the *charbonnerie* of the early 1820s was staffed by discontented NCOs and aged junior commissioned officers. The same sort of military personnel also constituted an important element in the republican clubs of the 1830s.

Nineteenth-century revolutions were thus the product of a num-ber of factors: political, social, and economic conflicts, short and long term; the vulnerability of central Paris to insurrection; and, above all, the defection of the National Guard and sections of the regular army. What did revolutions signify? Revolution often brought alterations, not just in the personnel, but also in the form of government. It is necessary to ask exactly what was signified by the shift from Monarchy to Republic to Empire, and back to Republic, as well as by the impact of Socialism. Consideration should also be given to the institutional changes that followed the arrival of different forms of government, and whether revolution substantially influenced the composition of the ruling élites.

Monarchy

Since the republican regime adopted in 1870 became permanent, the dominant republican historiography has assumed that a Republic was the only suitable regime for post-revolutionary France. The monarchical institutions established in 1814 were thus no more than a temporary stopgap. Yet the Restoration monarchy was very different from its *Ancien Régime* predecessor. It was based on a negotiated deal between king and élite that resembled the British constitution more than any of the revolutionary models. Two Chambers shared legislative authority with the king. There was a Chamber of Peers, whose members were nominated by the king, some for life, some hereditary. A second chamber had been rejected in 1789, but the most innovative feature in 1814 was the directly elected Chamber of Deputies. About 100,000 adult males aged over 30, out of a population of 31 million, qualified as voters by paying at least 300 francs a year in direct tax. Those eligible for election, of whom there were roughly 15,000, had to be 40 years old and pay 1,000 francs in annual tax. Although all fiscal matters had to be approved by the deputies, this was a constitutional, rather than a parliamentary regime. The Constitution stated that ministers were to be responsible, but it did not specify to whom, and it was possible for the king to rule by decree in an emergency. In 1830 the Bourbon monarchy was abolished, not because a dominant element in the political élite was hostile to monarchy as such, but because the ambiguity of these two provisions was exploited by the ultras in a rearguard action to remain in power against the wishes of most voters.

After the July Days of 1830 the liberals were forced into real innovation; they chose a new dynasty. Moved by utilitarian considerations, they made Charles X's cousin, the Duc d'Orléans, king of the French people. He was described, at first in admiration, then ironically, as the republican, bourgeois, king of the barricades. The most conservative liberals, such as the Duc de Broglie, asserted (amazingly) that Louis-Philippe had a hereditary claim to the throne. It is true that he would probably have been Regent for Charles X's under-age heir when the elderly Bourbon monarch died. The more right-wing supporters of the deposed king refused to swear an oath of allegiance to Louis-Philippe and became known as Legitimists. They regarded those who invented the new monarchy as successors to the brief, unsatisfactory experiment in constitutional monarchy during the Revolution that had collapsed in August 1792.

The Orleanist monarchy was no more of a parliamentary regime than its Bourbon predecessor. The new constitution of 1830, revised on a single afternoon in August with no debate, abolished the right of the monarch to rule without parliament, but set up no formal controls over his choice of ministers. The right to vote was extended to 25-year-olds and 200-franc taxpayers, which only increased the electorate to 166,000 men. An annual payment of 500 francs in direct tax was still required from members of the Chamber of Deputies. However, it is true that the electoral principle was extended to all local councils and that the minimum numbers for an electoral college brought the tax qualification for municipal voters down to 80 francs or less, in practice enfranchising over 2 million men. In local elections in some villages half the adult male population was qualified to vote.

Louis-Philippe worked hard to invent an Orleanist monarchy. Endless paintings were made of him in National Guard uniform, but to no avail. In 1848 he was accused of failing to pay sufficient attention to demands for parliamentary reform and holding on to a government too long. Both were unfair charges, because the Guizot-Soult government, set up in October 1840, had an increased parliamentary majority, and proposals for parliamentary reform had been decisively defeated in parliament.

Louis-Philippe was deposed and once he had left for exile in Britain, assertive and influential Orleanist and Legitimist political groups emerged under the Republic and Empire that followed. Yet when the opportunity came to reconsider monarchy after 1870 it proved impossible to restore either the Legitimist claimant, the Comte de Chambord, or the Orleanist Comte de Paris. Former Legitimists and Orleanists gradually transformed themselves into conservative adherents to the Third Republic, more anxious to preserve their own power than that of a distant and unpromising potential king. Despite the royalist rhetoric of de Bonald and de Maistre, the survival of monarchy between 1814 and 1848 had far more to do with the preservation of social order than the principle of divine right.

If enthusiasm for monarchy waned, did the emergence of feasible alternatives explain subsequent political changes? We need to consider first Republicanism, then Bonapartism, both of which had been tried out in France during the revolutionary decades.

Republicanism

Despite the rhetoric of republican historians there was nothing inevitable about France becoming a republic in the nineteenth century. The First Republic (1792–1804) left no agreed template for the future, but instead a conflicting set of quasi-democratic, oligarchic, and authoritarian models. The most-enduring legacy, never forgotten, by its enemies and moderate republicans alike, was the rule of the Jacobins and the accompanying Terror (1793–4). From 1799 ambitious republicans served Napoleon, convincing themselves that this general, who ran the best public-relations machine, had in fact saved the Revolution. In 1814, with similar fleetness of foot, many threw in their lot with Louis XVIII. That a republican myth survived was mainly due to Napoleon's Hundred-Day return and the subsequent exclusion of former revolutionaries from office. At this stage Republicanism was a luxury to be debated in cafés by unemployed former Imperial officials and a few old Jacobins. Although some of the liberals who jostled for power during the 1830 revolution had republican leanings, none thought a republic a practical possibility and salved their consciences by claiming that if such a regime were declared, the Great Powers would intervene a third time to restore the Bourbons.

Yet in February 1848 no alternative to a democratic Republic was even considered. Had a republican movement matured in the intervening years as sympathetic historians tried, and still try, to persuade us? After the July Days of 1830, radicals were instantly dismissive of the new monarchy, which was accused of smuggling away the artisan revolution and ignoring the social problems caused by economic change. Clandestine republican clubs accordingly sprang up. The Amis du Peuple and the Société des Droits de l'Homme, were based on a neo-Jacobin model popularized by Buonarroti, survivor of Babeuf's Conspiracy of the Equals in 1796. Their leaders were often sons of the men of 1789; most had taken part in the *charbonnerie*.

The response of the Orleanist, or July Monarchy, was to use judicial procedures to repress the clubs and their associated newspapers, such as the *Tribune*, and outlaw even the use of the term republican. By 1835 the regime had imposed stricter censorship than the Restoration and the republican clubs folded. This was partly the consequence of repression, but also because there was no consensus on what a Republic ought to be. Members in the clubs of the early 1830s had talked vaguely of votes for all. Some early socialists were also republicans. However, on the eve of upheaval in 1848 there were only six committed republicans in the Chamber of Deputies. The editors of *Le National* and *La Réforme*, who took the lead in the declaration of a Republic, had diverging views of what a republic entailed, the contingent from *La Réforme* insisting vaguely that social reform should accompany political change. The voters were certainly not convinced that a republic was the answer. The new Constituent Assembly, voted in by 84 per cent of the 9 million male electors in April 1848, contained only a minority of genuine republicans, although all those elected called themselves republicans. These triumphant conservatives were soon able to dismantle the Second Republic. They played on fears that the demands of socialists and *démocrates-socialistes* (social radicals who won a substantial number of parliamentary seats in 1849) for government action on poverty and unemployment would threaten the fabric of society. After Louis-Napoleon's *coup d'état* in December 1851, a popular movement in central and southern France to defend the Republic emerged too late.

Republicans were persecuted throughout the Second Empire and, perhaps unsurprisingly, showed little enthusiasm to devise an agreed republican alternative. The transformation of the Empire into a more liberal parliamentary state thus owed more to impetus from within imperial ranks than to republican opposition. A new Republic was declared in September 1870, but it took the bloodshed of the Paris Commune (March–May 1871) and the best part of the ensuing decade for politicians to negotiate a viable and broadly acceptable republican framework.

Bonapartism

A sentimental affection for Napoleon survived 1815, sustained by his followers who had been stripped of civil or military jobs after the Hundred Days. Their sons often maintained the tradition. Republican and Bonapartist sympathies were closely intertwined, reinforced by the popular belief, cultivated by Napoleon, that he had 'saved' the Revolution. When Napoleon died in 1821 Bonapartism was a romantic memory of battles, flags, medals, and songs. His son, the 'little eagle' lived his short life an Austrian and in 1830 no one considered him a possible ruler. It was Louis-Philippe and one of his ministers, Adolphe Thiers, who revived Bonapartism, hoping that their own reputations would be enhanced by their reverence for the Emperor. Napoleon was honoured in Paris, with the July column and the Arc de Triomphe, and at Versailles, where the focus of Louis-Philippe's restoration of the palace were art galleries groaning under the weight of massive canvases which lauded imperial victories. In 1840 Napoleon's remains were brought back to France and, with due ceremony, placed in Les Invalides in central Paris.

Neither king nor minister gained credit for their nurturing of memories of the Emperor. The eventual beneficiary was his nephew, Louis-Napoleon, whose *Napoleonic Ideas* developed the myth that Napoleon had been a constitutionalist, thwarted by war-mongering foreign powers, while *The Extinction of Poverty* convinced some that both Bonapartes were sympathetic to the underdog. Two abortive attempts to raise the garrisons of Strasbourg (1836) and Boulogne (1840) showed that people were content merely to treasure Bonapartist memories passively. However, in June 1848 Louis-Napoleon was elected to the Assembly in his absence in the department of the Seine, though he was not allowed to take his seat until the autumn after another by-election. When he made a fumbling, tentative maiden speech, conservative politicians were reassured that he did not pose a threat to the Republic. However memories, myths, the popular appeal of his name and the support of former monarchist deputies such as Thiers, helped him secure a runaway victory in the presidential election held in December 1848. Above all, his election represented the defeat of radical and socialist republicanism and in particular the demise of General Cavaignac, who had put down the workers' rebellion in June. Louis-Napoleon seemed a pliable figurehead to the old monarchist élites, a means of resurrecting royalist values at a time when traditional monarchy was truly impossible.

As President and then Emperor Louis-Napoleon tried to revive the glories of Bonapartism with minimum military effort. He ultimately destroyed his own creation when his foreign minister Gramont pursued the illusion of power by engaging in war with Prussia. Louis-Napoleon's uncle had also played at sham constitutionalism with plebiscites that meant little and assemblies that carried no weight. In contrast to the old élites who surrounded him, Louis-Napoleon likewise presented himself as a democratic despot, restoring universal male suffrage which the conservatives had abolished in March 1850 and reintroducing plebiscites. The directly elected parliamentary assembly made little contribution to the Second Empire. A system of official candidatures for aspiring deputies ran in tandem with plebiscites (which offered no more choice than those of his uncle) to give authentication to Louis-Napoleon's legislative programme. Few republicans stood in imperial elections and those who were elected were excluded because they refused the oath of loyalty. The most important cities in France refused to sanction the imperial regime: in 1852 over two-thirds of the voters abstained in substantial towns such as Strasbourg, Bordeaux, Saint-Étienne, Sedan, and La Rochelle.

In 1859 some republicans began to regard Louis-Napoleon more tenderly after he fought with the Piedmontese against the Austrians, in a war which led to Italy becoming a united country and the almost total elimination of the territorial authority of the papacy. Louis-Napoleon cemented the reconciliation by encouraging exiles to return. Republicans were no more in accord about their preferred political system than before and in 1864 the number of republican deputies rose only modestly to a total of eight. Meanwhile Louis-Napoleon was taking his first trembling steps towards liberalism. In 1860 the Assembly was allowed to make an annual address detailing its legislative plans, its debates were published and the Assembly could question ministers. A year later the government gave up the practice of raising revenue outside the budget voted by the Assembly. In 1864 worker associations and strikes were made legal. In 1867 press censorship was relaxed and political meetings permitted. In 1869–70 the liberalization of the Second Empire was acclaimed by plebiscite.

Under the direction of Louis-Napoleon autocracy gave way to a constitutional system not unlike that of the monarchies earlier in the century. It was buttressed by the illusion of democracy, a mass (male only) electorate, and plebiscites. Louis-Napoleon had always been somewhat of a disappointment to out-and-out Bonapartists and this transformation of his regime must have confirmed their fears.

Socialism

Socialists began to exercise an influence during the middle decades of the nineteenth century but the fear they aroused among conservatives vastly exceeded their power. The term 'socialist' was first used by Pierre Leroux in 1832, although social reformers who can be considered early socialists were active much earlier. These included the revolutionary communist Babeuf, who organized the abortive Conspiracy of the Equals in 1796; Charles Fourier, who dreamed of setting up autonomous profit-sharing communes in which women would be 'liberated' by the disappearance of traditional marriage and the nuclear family, but who never succeeded in launching a viable experimental *phalange*; and lastly Saint-Simon who drew up plans for government by those who took an active part in running the economy, the 'industriels', pushing aside the 'idlers', who simply lived off their investments. The followers of Saint-Simon formed a Saint-Simonian sect, an odd mixture of government engineers, doctors, and their womenfolk, plus a number of women workers in the textile trades who wanted to liberate women and workers. Their self-proclaimed leader, Prosper Enfantin, alienated much sympathy when his recommendation of trial marriage resulted in a number of tragic suicides. Those who broke away from Enfantin began to call themselves Fourierists, although they no longer attacked marriage. They still emphasized the idea of autonomous communities, but they began to pin their hopes on persuading the state to acknowledge its responsibility for organizing labour through an expanded public works' programme.

Louis Blanc gave a different meaning to this idea in 1840, in his book entitled *The Organization of Labour*. Blanc hoped to solve the social question, the problem of unemployment and poverty, by asking the state to act as a 'banker to the poor', through repayable loans to social workshops or artisan cooperatives. However, the most popular of the socialists before the 1848 revolution was Étienne Cabet. He founded an artisan newspaper, *Le Populaire*, which in the early 1840s made extensive investigations into worker problems. He also established a workers' organization, the Icarians, which attracted up to 100,000 artisans, men and women, who hoped that the evidence collected by *Le Populaire* would bring about reform in working conditions, wages and job security. Cabet wrote one of the most popular utopian socialist books, *Voyage in Icaria*, which in two volumes described a perfect communist state, in which all property was held in common and money was superfluous. On the eve of the 1848 revolution Cabet was involved in plans to set up an experimental community in Texas.

Other socialists, such as Philippe Buchez and Ange Guépin, helped create producer cooperatives in France. A number of women also participated in the Saint-Simonian and Fourierist movements, including Jeanne Deroin, Eugénie Niboyet, Pauline Roland, and Suzanne Voilquin. In 1832–3 they ran their own newspaper, *La Femme libre*. George Sand and Flora Tristan were female activists who stood outside these movements. Tristan publicized a version of Fourier's plans for *phalanges*, but her major scheme, the Workers' Union, was based on Robert Owen's idea for a consolidated union of all workers. She died in 1844 during a national publicity tour. All of these socialists hoped that the 'social question' that dominated so much debate at the time, could be resolved by moral reform. A combination of education and secular religion would facilitate the replacement of nascent capitalism with a form of cooperative association, either of workers, or of whole communities. Before 1848 almost none of them expected to change the existing political system, although the tireless revolutionary Auguste Blanqui did organize an abortive insurrection in Paris in May 1839.

The declaration of the democratic Second Republic seemed to offer new possibilities and most of the socialist writers took advantage of the early optimism of the first half of 1848. Cabet, Blanqui, and Raspail ran workers' clubs in Paris which each had up to 6000 members. Blanc was made secretary of the Provisional Government and president of the Parliament of Industry, a consultative assembly of Parisian workers and their employers. Blanc, Buchez, and

Considérant were leading figures in the Constituent Assembly elected in April 1848. Deroin, Niboyet, and Roland ran a women's club and founded a newspaper, *La Voix des femmes*, which demanded education for women, improved working opportunities, crèches for working mothers, the right to divorce, and votes for women.

None of their hopes was realized. The Constituent Assembly was stacked with conservative monarchist notables who were appalled by the high profile of radicals and socialists and conducted a spirited and successful campaign to defend the traditional dominance of the élite. Blanc was forced into exile after the June Days, although he had nothing to do with the Provisional Government's national workshops, or the June rebellion against the decision to close them. Cabet retreated to Texas. Having failed to have a 'right to work' included in the 1848 constitution, Considérant also became involved in experimental communities in America. Deroin and Roland were imprisoned when their 'association of associations' of more than 100 artisan cooperatives was forcibly closed by the government. Roland was deported to Algeria and died shortly after her release. Deroin went into exile in London, where she remained until her death in 1894.

The Second Empire ran a campaign for the systematic persecution of socialist and republican critics, but socialists began to regroup in the 1860s. Ideas for worker cooperatives, as well as schools and evening classes for artisans and their children, were gradually replaced by faith in international brotherhood. The Paris Commune in 1871 briefly raised the standard, only for its brutal repression to delay the reappearance of socialism. After the Communards were granted amnesties in 1879 small socialist groups were formed which expressed loyalty to the old utopian and revolutionary traditions, but despite their radical rhetoric, they were principally involved in getting members elected to the new democratic parliament. Trade unions were only legalized in 1884.

The durability of the French state

France experienced more violent changes of regime and more variations in its the governing system than any other European country
in the nineteenth century, but the ship of state seemed to possess a
self-righting mechanism. On no occasion did revolution seriously
threaten the institutional infrastructure that had been established
during the Revolutionary and Napoleonic decades. The names of
organizations changed, the imperial courts of law became royal or
republican, but the judicial system and Codes of Law remained
unaltered. The financial and fiscal arrangements determined at the
beginning of the century also subsisted. The administrative framework, from council of state to postmasters, via prefects, was tinkered
with; briefly, in the spring of 1848, prefects were renamed commissioners. However, attempts by ultras to raise the issue of provincial
autonomy in 1816, like proposals in the 1860s to press the case for
municipal liberties in Paris and other cities, did nothing to break the
centralized mould.

Throughout these years revolution did little to unseat dominant
political groups. There used to be a Marxist-style mythology that the
1789 Revolution elevated a bourgeois élite to replace the landed aristocracy. There is no doubt that middle-class professionals, particularly civil servants, lawyers, and doctors, gained official appointments
and political influence during the 1790s. 'Aristos' were persecuted,
but the term was interpreted in more of a political than a social sense.
Emigrés risked the sequestration of their land, but in 1814 nobles still
owned 20 per cent of the land in France, compared to 25 per cent in
1789. Napoleon successfully reintegrated old, and not so old, noble
families to run his Empire, while creating new titles and the *Légion
d'honneur* with which to reward them. In 1814 the richest, most
influential families in many parts of France remained landed nobles,
especially in their traditional strongholds of southern and western
France. They retained much of this pre-eminence until at least 1880.

During the Restoration Charles X, his ultra-royalist supporters,
and writers like de Bonald and de Maistre, dreamed of resurrecting a
'traditional' France ruled harmoniously by king, Church, and nobles.
In reality, prior to 1789 nobles and wealthy non-nobles had both

competed for influence. Tall tales were woven around the 1830 Revolution, notably to the effect that the landed aristocracy had been elbowed aside by bourgeois groups. In fact, both before and after 1830 a significant proportion of members of parliament held noble titles, though numbers were declining. In the Chamber of 1821, for instance, 58 per cent of deputies were nobles, in 1827 40 per cent, and in 1840 the figure was still over 30 per cent. However, there were many types of title, from those going back four centuries and to more recent inventions; in 1840 forty-five deputies sported bogus noble credentials.

In 1827 60 per cent of voters and 73 per cent of parliamentary candidates listed themselves as landowners, as did 31 per cent of deputies in 1829 and 23 per cent in 1831. What did this mean? Little more than that France was predominantly an agricultural country and that, in the absence of income tax, land was the overwhelming component of direct taxation. In 1829 only 14 per cent of deputies were businessmen and this had slipped to 13 per cent ten years later. The most often cited occupation, before and after the so-called 'bourgeois' revolution of 1830 was that of public servant. Around 40 per cent of deputies throughout the period of the constitutional monarchy held official appointments. There was no great difference in the social composition of parliament, or indeed of officials, before and after the 1830 revolution. The defining characteristic of deputies was not social, but political. In 1830 the ruling élite split over the role of the Bourbon monarchy and the Catholic Church, but the division was far from permanent. The notables who invented the new Orleanist monarchy were not irreligious and the vast majority was determined to preserve the political dominance of the rich.

For a short time in 1848 it appeared that the introduction of adult male suffrage might democratize politics, but the election to create a Constituent Assembly for the Second Republic soon dispelled any such notions. Less than half of the 853 deputies elected were genuine republicans. The majority were wealthy Legitimist (150) or Orleanist (300) notables, who had sat, or would have qualified for, the parliaments of the constitutional monarchy. Moreover, some 700 of these deputies paid more than 500 francs a year in tax. There were only eighteen workers and six foremen among them. The socio-professional composition of the first French parliament ever elected by direct democracy was reminiscent of its predecessors earlier in the nineteenth century: 325 lawyers, 160 landowners, 99 army officers, 65 industrialists, 53 businessmen, and 53 doctors.

Nor did the political composition of the ruling élite immediately alter when France became a Republic once again after 1870. Analysis of the 650 deputies elected to the first assembly in February 1871 reveals 400 monarchists, 20 Bonapartists, 80 assorted independents, and a mere 150 republicans, including 43 radicals elected in Paris. Most deputies were still being recruited from the predominantly rural landowning notables who had run France throughout the century. However this was an unusual election, held when much of the country was occupied by German troops and many voters were more anxious to end the war than support the republican regime. During the decades that followed, consolidation of the Third Republic and further economic change ensured that more middle-class and republican politicians gradually took control.

Conclusion

This chapter has considered the significance of revolution in nineteenth-century France. In conclusion we must ask why insurrection ceased to be the common currency of French politics after the rebellion of the Paris Commune in 1871 and what, if anything, revolution had achieved.

During the Franco-Prussian war, which ended with the loss of Alsace-Lorraine in March 1871, Paris was under siege. The peace terms appalled the Parisians, especially members of the National Guard who had been at the heart of so much determined resistance. The attempt of the national government, based at Versailles, to take possession of cannons purchased by Parisians for their own defence provoked a National Guard and worker revolt. This was followed by the declaration of a Paris Commune, or independent municipal government, in March 1871, an event which recalled the extremism of the French Revolution. Thiers, head of state after the elections of February 1871, refused all negotiation with the Communards, who represented various strands of socialist and neo-Jacobin thinking. In the last week of May 1871, which became known as 'bloody week', Paris was retaken street by street and many public buildings were set on fire as barricades fell. Over 20,000 rebels were killed, along with just 900 government troops. Another 40,000 Communards were arrested, of whom hundreds were condemned to death or deported from France. Worker resistance was broken. Paris remained in a state of siege until 1878.

Why did the Paris Commune fail to inspire a national revolution as Parisian revolutions had done in 1830 and 1848? A number of other transient communal rebellions did occur elsewhere, at Marseille or Lyon for example, but the Communards were primarily concerned with Parisian autonomy. In fact, the transformation of the political geography of the capital in the 1850s and 1860s had destroyed many of the old, radical, artisan strongholds in central Paris, permitting Thiers the free use of troops to conquer the rebellion. The building of the rail network, its focus on Paris and the central location of a network of major termini, track, and extensive marshalling yards, all fragmented the densely populated and formerly radical districts, as artisans were forced out into distant suburbs to live and work. Railway construction provided an opportunity to demolish much broader swathes of worker housing than was strictly necessary, in order to make the capital safe from revolution. Wide avenues flanked with banks, large department stores and all the paraphernalia of a developing consumer society, cut through the narrow streets, lanes and courtyards, making it far more difficult to erect barricades and defy authority, as the bloody defeat of the Commune of 1871 showed.

During the century successive governments had been sensitive to the repeated failure of army and National Guard to defend the status quo. In 1840 the Thiers government initiated the building of a ring of forts around the capital to reinforce central garrisons, aware that in 1830 there were insufficient troops to hold the city. The growing rail network gave further guarantees that Paris would be defended; in June 1848 the new lines were already in use to transport soldiers and national guardsmen to Paris to defeat the rebels. During the 1870s the National Guard itself was dissolved.

Nineteenth-century revolutions were always closely associated with high food prices and shortages. In the last quarter of the century, however, wheat from America's prairie states and the Russian steppes helped to eliminate this problem. Equally, the gradual transformation and dilution of artisan structures reduced the contribution of traditional radical elements, often recruited among tailors, weavers, printers, cabinetmakers, and so on. Popular unrest lost its leaders. New organizations, including trade unions, had strongholds outside the centre of capital cities and interests that were of an economic rather than political nature, a factor that made regimes more secure throughout Europe. Although the largest trade union in France, the Confédération Générale du Travail, was in constant conflict with employers, and the early years of the twentieth century witnessed some violent confrontations with the government, the republican system itself was no longer threatened.

Democratic institutions and mass education also contributed to dampening enthusiasm for revolution. In 1880 France was unique in being a secular and democratic republic. The Third Republic was based upon a legislative assembly elected by universal male suffrage and proclaimed itself a thoroughly parliamentary regime. True, it remained dominated by wealthy, educated élites, but voters were persuaded that the opportunity for consultation existed, and the need to take to the streets was thereby removed. Compulsory primary schooling also seemed to be a panacea, offering educational and employment opportunities as never before. Huge armies of blue- and white-collar workers grew up to run the railways and the burgeoning bureaucratic organizations of the centralized state. The age of revolution seemed to be over.

Yet was the nineteenth century really such an age of revolution in France and, if so, what did the upheaval signify? Profound episodes of popular unrest were the product of long- and short-term economic problems. Those who erected barricades were more intent on securing the sympathy of opposition politicians for immediate objectives than taking charge of government. Having profited from periods of political volatility, those who took control then turned their backs on revolution and invariably tried to minimize change. On each occasion the 'revolutionary tradition' of the 1790s was honoured and its symbols, flags, and songs were dusted and apprehensively toned down. Each revolution was rather like a geological eruption, indeed contemporary observers such as de Tocqueville often compared the days before the outbreak of revolution, in 1830 and 1848, to being poised on the edge of a volcano. A revolution was thus the expression of the relief of tension. Seemingly cataclysmic, its occurrence prevented a far more severe and intense shock in the future as French society slowly adjusted to the strains and stresses of modernization. In 1889 the centenary celebrations rejoiced in a bowdlerized version of 1789 which attempted to smooth away the political divisions of the previous century. That attempt continues today.

3

State and religion

Thomas Kselman

Introduction

In both the 1780s and the 1870s France was on the eve of seismic shifts
in its religious landscape. In 1789 the French Revolution inaugurated
a decade that saw the assertion of religious liberty as a basic right in
Article 10 of the Declaration of the Rights of Man, the Catholic
Church assaulted by a republican state, and a series of liturgical
experiments designed to sanctify the nation as a divine object. The
consolidation of the Third Republic in the late 1870s was followed by
a decade in which the French state passed laws that severely undermined the power of the Catholic Church over education and family
life. As in the 1790s, these changes were enacted in the name of freedom of religion and conscience, values Republicans believed were
inimical to Catholicism. Once again Republicans linked their attacks
on Catholicism with the promotion of alternative symbols and rituals
aimed at generating a nation unified around a common set of values
and beliefs.

The fact that the leaders of the Third Republic felt obliged to act
aggressively against Catholicism a century after the Revolution suggests the failure of the religious reforms of the 1790s. Catholicism
survived and in some ways flourished in the nineteenth century,
while the religious experiments of the revolutionary regime were
apparently ephemeral. Nonetheless, the Revolution was a pivotal
moment in the history of religion, for neither Catholics nor the heirs
to the revolutionary tradition ever forgot the religious conflicts that
divided France so bitterly and violently. Over the next century both
drew on their memories to try to construct a French society that
would reconcile the sacred and the secular. For most Catholics this

meant a regime in which their religion was accorded a central place in public life and private morality; for their Republican opponents it meant freedom of religious choice, the restriction of Catholicism to the private sphere, and a citizenry whose moral code combined respect for family and property with a love for the nation which protected and nurtured them.

Historians have long been familiar with the significance of the Catholic Church in the revolutionary era and its role in the political battles of the nineteenth century, and no treatment of French religion in this period can ignore the ways in which fears and hopes generated by the Revolution echoed through the century. One of the chief consequences of the Revolution was to embed religious conflict deeply and inextricably into the political debates that divided France, thus helping to produce the bitter hatreds that accompany arguments cast in terms of God against Satan, Good against Evil. The passage of the laic laws of the 1880s and the separation of Church and State in 1905 suggested to Republicans a historical pattern in which reason finally triumphed in its struggle with fanaticism; for Catholics these measures were added to the list of national sins dating to the Revolution, crimes that could draw down further punishment from an angry God. Dechristianization and secularization are the terms commonly used to describe the end results of this combination of revolutionary trauma and structural change, processes through which Catholicism substantially lost its ability to shape public policy and private beliefs. The religious history of modern France, according to this line of reasoning, can be summed up nicely in Max Weber's words as the 'disenchantment of the world'.

For all its rhetorical power, however, this vision of inevitable decline provides only an incomplete sense of the role of religion in nineteenth-century France. Beyond the politically charged debates over Catholicism lay a realm of religious experience that grappled with perennial human problems. Confronted with sickness and death, with threats to their families and communities, French men and women turned to Catholicism, but also to other sources of supernatural help, for relief and consolation. The Revolution, which abolished the official Catholic monopoly over religious life, opened up new space for choice and experimentation that produced innovative liturgies that responded to both personal and collective needs. Instead of restricting ourselves to the language of conflict and decline we need to think of religion in France in the century following the Revolution as characterized by pluralism, voluntarism, and experimentation.

The French Revolution as religious trauma

The Revolution that began in 1789 destroyed a religious as well as a political regime, and served as the seedbed for the religious alternatives that were available to the French in the nineteenth century. Religious issues were central to the Revolution, first of all in attempts to reform Catholicism, as exemplified by the Civil Constitution of the Clergy (July 1790), and then by experiments designed to replace Catholic 'fanaticism' and 'superstition' with beliefs and rituals more suited to a nation that enshrined liberty, equality and fraternity as its holy trinity. The religious innovations of the Revolution were not mere adjuncts to a political programme, but integral parts of a rapidly evolving agenda aimed at a regeneration that was simultaneously political and religious. Such a connection was noticed by Alexis de Tocqueville, when he wrote that 'the ideal the French Revolution set before it was not merely a change in the French social system but nothing short of a regeneration of the whole human race. It created an atmosphere of missionary fervor and indeed assumed all the aspects of a religious revival.'

The religious aspirations of the Revolution follow a model inherited from the Old Regime in which the Catholic Church was intimately tied to the French monarchy in both theory and practice. The links between Church and polity started at the top, but they reached deeply into popular culture as well. Bishop Bossuet's claim that the Bourbons ruled as a result of divine will was repeated endlessly throughout the eighteenth century, and was accepted without question by Louis XVI, whose pious devotion to the Catholic Church was both simple and sincere. Catholicism was integrated into life at the lowest level as well, with weekly assistance at mass each Sunday the general rule. It was the parish priest who kept the official register of the population, who officiated at the rites of baptism, first communion, marriage, and extreme unction that marked the major transitional moments of life, and who heard the annual confession which permitted people to receive the Easter Communion demanded of all Catholics. It is not a simple matter to move from evidence of sacramental observance to conclusions about religious belief, a topic about which historians disagree, but for the vast majority of the population the sacraments had salvific as well as social functions. Catholicism legitimized the monarchy and sacralized key moments in the lives of both individuals and communities. It also claimed to open the way for individual souls to save themselves from the terrors of hellfire and to gain instead a life of eternal bliss, a view of the afterlife overtly rejected by only a small minority of urban intellectuals.

The ubiquity and strength of Catholicism in the eighteenth century are evident, but even before the Revolution disruptive religious currents were making an impact on French society. Catholicism was by no means monolithic and, in the course of the eighteenth century, it had been riven by a series of major conflicts. The most public of these divided a dissident Jansenist minority from an orthodox majority defended by Jesuit spokesmen, a dispute that lasted throughout the eighteenth century. On theological grounds Jansenists minimized the role of free will in the face of God's sovereignty, while their Jesuit opponents, who were expelled from France in 1764, emphasized human capacity and a more indulgent deity. This theological debate provoked pastoral troubles when orthodox bishops attempted to deny the sacraments to Jansenists, actions that generated resentment against the clergy, especially in urban areas. A second and related set of tensions divided Gallicans, who insisted on the independence of the national Church, and ultramontanes, who were more respectful of papal authority. When the Revolution swept away the Gallican Church of the Old Regime it paved the way for the triumph of ultramontanism in the nineteenth century, when French Catholics came much more under the sway of Roman authority. A third fault line divided the lower clergy, who staffed parishes and were responsible for ministering to the faithful, from the upper clergy, who were more likely to be drawn from the privileged aristocracy. Finally, the clergy were distinguished from ordinary parishioners by their sacramental role and their education, a split that would help fuel the anticlericalism of the Revolution and the century that followed.

A glimpse of some erosion in the cultural authority of Catholicism can also be observed in royal decrees in the 1780s that granted religious minorities some modest civil rights they had formerly been

denied. The 500,000 Protestants (roughly 2 per cent of the population), who had been officially proscribed since the revocation of the
Edict of Nantes in 1685 had managed to survive, with Calvinists concentrated in the south and Lutherans in the east. In 1787 an Edict of
Toleration permitted them to register births, marriages and deaths
with royal judges, although it stopped short of permitting them the
right of public worship. Through the issuing of *lettres patentes* in 1784
the French monarchy also revised the status of the 40,000 Jews who
lived in France. Jews were still regarded as a distinct nationality and
severely restricted in their economic and legal rights, but the decree
acknowledged for the first time the validity of Jewish marriages.

Catholicism was also challenged by powerful intellectual forces,
for a significant portion of the *philosophes* identified with the
Enlightenment were sharply critical of the established religion, which
they saw as a bastion of superstition and clerical power that held the
forces of reason and progress in check. It is likely that only a few
accepted the radical materialism and atheism of Baron Holbach, but
the free circulation and lively discussion of such ideas in Paris salons
just before the Revolution placed Catholicism in a defensive posture
among those who played a central role in shaping public opinion.

Finally, in the 1780s small circles of French men and women
concentrated in Paris and Lyon began experimenting with ways to
communicate with the dead in private ceremonies unrelated to the
Catholic sacramental system. Inspired by the experiments in hypno-
tism of Viennese physician Franz Anton Mesmer (1734–1815), who
established himself in Paris in 1778, they discovered that certain
people, generally women, were able to communicate with the world
of spirits when put into a state of suspended animation. During their
trances these women gave medical advice, provided information
about the state of dead friends and relatives, and predicted the future
of individuals and of France. In Lyon the Abbé Jean-Antoine de
Castellas, dean of Saint John's cathedral, headed a group called 'La
Concorde' that closely followed the reports of Jeanne Rochette, a
working-class girl whose trances were carefully transcribed by her
bourgeois and aristocratic adepts between 1785 and 1787. Rochette
described the dead as inhabiting a world that resembled but did
not mirror perfectly the Catholic model, for while there were levels
of punishment based on earthly sins, no one was destined to suffer
an eternity in hell. The ideas of Rochette and her fellow visionaries

circulated privately in the 1780s, appealing to dissidents unhappy with the rigours of Catholic doctrine, and with the spiritual monopoly claimed by a male clergy. In the freer atmosphere of the nineteenth century similar ideas developed into Spiritualism, a religion which obtained a public hearing and a following that allowed it to compete openly with Catholicism.

Both the sustained influence and the potential fragility of Catholicism were manifest in the early days of the Revolution, when the Church was at the centre of the reform efforts undertaken by the National Assembly. Catholic services marked both the opening ceremonies of the Estates-General in 1789, and the Feast of the Federation on 14 July 1790, when Bishop Talleyrand presided at a mass for as many as 400,000 on the 'altar of the fatherland' located on the Champ de Mars to commemorate the taking of the Bastille. The use of Catholic ritual to sanctify the Revolution parallels the crucial role that the Church played in the events of 1789 and 1790. The transformation of the Estates-General into a National Assembly, for example, owed a great deal to the decision by representatives of the clergy to join their colleagues from the third estate. The Church was also instrumental in dealing with the financial crisis when the Constituent Assembly nationalized church property (approximately 10 per cent of French land), to be sold as a way of amortizing the state debt. In the course of these deliberations in 1789 a majority of the Assembly became increasingly confident in its sovereign authority, and of its obligation to impose internal reform on the Church, eliminating all that was deemed useless and irrational. Thus in February 1790 the Assembly decreed that perpetual vows would no longer be recognized, and it authorized monks and nuns to leave their congregations. Even this measure did not alienate most of the clerical representatives in the Assembly, primarily secular priests who served in parishes and who shared the laity's resentment of monastic wealth and privilege. Still, it is remarkable that such sweeping reforms were enacted without substantial opposition from inside the Church.

However, the Civil Constitution of the Clergy passed by the Constituent Assembly in July 1790, which radically altered the structure of the Catholic Church, initiated a crisis that would divide the nation and lead to long years of civil strife. The Civil Constitution's most lasting contribution was the rationalization of the religious map; as a result of this measure French dioceses still reflect the administrative unit of the department, also created by the Revolution. Much more controversial was the introduction of the electoral principle for naming both bishops and parish clergy, an innovation that struck at the heart of traditional authority in the Church. The Civil Constitution was opposed by most of the clergy in the Assembly and signed by the king only under severe pressure, and against his own judgement.

The attempt to enforce the Civil Constitution provoked widespread political conflict and violence, which later contributed substantially to the Terror. In November 1790, fearful about the potential disloyalty of the clergy, the Assembly took the momentous step of requiring an oath in which the clergy would declare their loyalty to the new system. Through the work of Timothy Tackett we know that in January 1791 half of the clergy took the oath, while the other half refused, a sign of the deep division inside the Church over the course of the Revolution. But the crisis over the oath extended much further. Political leaders such as Mirabeau used the debate to make angry speeches in the Assembly which cast division between orthodox Christianity and the Revolution in the starkest terms. According to Mirabeau clerical opposition was leading the people to a choice between Christianity and liberty, with the inevitable result that they would choose freedom. 'The people will abjure Christianity; they will curse their pastors; they will recognize and adore God as the creator of nature and liberty, while everything that reminds them of the God of the Gospel will be odious to them . . .'

The crisis over the oath involved communities as well as clergy. In areas such as western France, where most clergy proved refractory, large crowds gathered to prevent officials from administering it. But pressure was also exerted in the opposite sense, especially in Paris, where a crowd packed the church of Saint-Sulpice on the day of the oath-taking ceremony. When the *curé* refused they stormed the altar shouting 'the oath or the lamppost'. Mapping the degree of acceptance or rejection of the oath reveals a France divided by its attitude towards the Catholicism that had been the official religion for over a millennium. Non-juring clergy predominated in western France, especially the Breton peninsula, in the north, in the east, in the Massif Central and in the south-west. Oath-takers represented the majority in the Paris region, and in bands extending south-west towards Bordeaux, and south-east, down the Rhone valley, towards Lyon. The patterns that emerged in 1791 proved enduring, and closely resemble those showing religious observance in the centuries that followed.

Although it was not the only issue, the debate over the Civil Constitution played a crucial role in dividing France over the progress of the Revolution, a process that culminated in the collapse of the monarchy. Louis XVI's deep attachment to Catholicism was an important factor in his growing alienation from the Revolution, an attachment that also helped him face death with courage and hope in his ultimate salvation. By 1793 militant supporters of the Revolution were convinced that they were confronted with a powerful and conspiratorial opposition of devout Catholics manipulated by a fanatical clergy. Faced with this, and with the additional threat of foreign invasion, an all-out assault was mounted against Christianity, a campaign that was most intense in the winter of 1793 and the spring of 1794, a period coinciding with the Reign of Terror.

The attack on Christianity provides some of the most dramatic moments in the history of the Revolution. Historians have tackled the complexity of these events by distinguishing between negative and positive dechristianization. The first was characterized by the closing of churches, the removal of bells and sacred vessels, the abdication of the clergy, and iconoclastic attacks on statues, shrines, churches and cemeteries. Positive dechristianization covers the varied attempts to provide a religious substitute for Catholicism: festivals in honour of Reason and the Supreme Being; cults of great men designed to honour those from the past who had advanced the cause of reason and liberty; a cult of martyrs who died for the Revolution, such as Jean-Paul Marat; and a new calendar to efface the old rhythm of feast days honouring saints and Sunday worship.

Devout Catholics did not remain passive in the face of dechristianization. In western France, the 1793 rebellion known as the Vendée was fuelled by numerous factors, including a resentment against taxes and military conscription decreed from Paris. But intense devotion to the clergy, who overwhelmingly rejected the oath, and to the Catholic sacramental system, were important motives that drove this infamous civil war. Although most intense in the Vendée, resistance to dechristianization was general, as demonstrated in the coolness towards the revolutionary cults, the tendency to ignore the new calendar, and in a residual devotion to Catholic rituals. The Thermidorean reaction brought an end to the Terror, but

Catholicism was still officially proscribed, and many parishes had no regular ministers or services throughout the 1790s.

The Napoleonic treaty with the Roman Catholic Church of 1801 resolved some of the major difficulties emerging from the Revolution. The Church accepted, for example, the redrawing of ecclesiastical boundaries and the loss of property in exchange for state support, and also agreed to a system in which the French government nominated bishops. Yet Catholicism was not declared the official religion of France, merely referred to as the 'religion of the majority'. In the Organic Articles that Napoleon imposed as an addendum to the Concordat in 1802 the state asserted crucial rights over the Church and its clergy, who were not permitted to meet nor receive communications from Rome without state approval. The Concordat established the government as a neutral agent with the task of encouraging religious peace. Even in those periods when the state and the Catholic Church cooperated, the bureaucrats who administered the Ministry for Ecclesiastical Affairs worked to temper the language and behaviour of the clergy, pressing bishops to remove priests whose politics were too outspoken, or whose sermons caused dissension in the parish community.

The opening years of the nineteenth century saw another major development which was to have profound consequences for religious life in nineteenth-century France. The publication of Chateaubriand's *The Genius of Christianity* in 1802 marks a major turning point in the status of religion among French intellectuals. The writings of *philosophes* such as Voltaire sanctioned a sceptical frame of mind which mocked the pretensions of any religion to assert dogmatic truths. Both official ritual and popular practice were ridiculed as vain superstitions that deceived believers into thinking that their behaviour could somehow produce supernatural effects. Voltaire's scepticism did not disappear in the nineteenth century, when cheap editions kept his ideas in circulation, but Chateaubriand offered an intellectually fashionable challenge to the premiss that religion needed to be measured by a rationalistic standard. For Chateaubriand, and for the Romantic school in general, critiques based on logic-chopping missed the point, for religion worked primarily as an emotional and aesthetic force. Whether writing about Gothic churches or peasant shrines, Chateaubriand managed to convey a sense of awe and respect which he placed at the centre of religious experience. Louis de Bonald and Joseph de Maistre also argued forcefully against the rationalism of the Enlightenment, which they held responsible for the Revolution, and saw Catholicism as central to the reconstruction of the social order. They were primarily political theorists, and their work had little impact on the spiritual life of the French people, but Chateaubriand's florid descriptions of Catholic sites and practices resonated throughout the century, in the work of preachers and popular writers.

Religious life in France as it emerged from the revolutionary and Napoleonic era had been profoundly altered, most evident in terms of institutional change. It is much harder to grasp the ways in which popular religious belief and feeling changed over the course of this quarter-century. We know that the authority of the Church was weaker, that many people had little or no formal religious education as a result of the revolutionary disruption, that alternative religious systems appeared, and that many lay people became accustomed to making choices about what to believe, or what not to believe, that would have been difficult to imagine before the Revolution. This fluidity and pluralism were relative, of course, for the Concordat was correct in asserting that Catholicism remained the religion of the majority. If we adopt Peter Berger's metaphor of religion as a sacred canopy, we might say that the storms of the Revolution did substantial damage, but that the structure, now somewhat leaky and tattered, managed to stay up. Substantial numbers took advantage of the pluralistic possibilities available to them. The result of such choices could result in religious uncertainty, and for some in unbelief and indifference, but religious choice also encouraged experimentation and the creation of new religious forms both inside and outside Catholicism.

The Catholic Church in the nineteenth century

Church–state relations were governed by the Concordat from 1801 until 1905. Like the Conseil d'État and the legal codes, this Napoleonic tool provided institutional stability for a nation that experienced three political revolutions and dramatic social change over the course of the nineteenth century. The Concordat provided for administrative continuity in the official management of religious affairs, but it did not remove Catholicism from the political stage. During the Bourbon Restoration (1814–30) a close alliance between throne and altar was accompanied by a contentious campaign of rechristianization based on aggressive preaching by missionary priests. The Church paid a price for its ties to the Bourbons during the July Revolution, when crowds attacked the episcopal palace in Paris and the monumental crosses raised by the missionaries to mark the return of Catholicism. The Church adopted a much more cautious relationship with the Orleanists, and by 1848 many Catholic leaders, including Louis Veuillot, editor of the popular newspaper, *L'Univers*, and the Comte de Montalembert, had learned to use the language of liberty to defend a call for Catholic secondary schools. This campaign, led by laymen, was not universally welcomed by the upper clergy, but it accorded well with the political and social reform movement of the 1840s. Indeed, it prepared the way for a brief honeymoon between Catholics and Republicans following the February Revolution of 1848, which led many to hope that the parties divided in the 1790s had finally been reconciled. Instead, fears about socialism, and the Church's support of Pope Pius IX against the Roman Republic that was briefly established in Italy in 1848, led Catholics into an alliance with Louis-Napoleon both as president and emperor. This relationship soured in the 1860s, when Napoleon III supported Italian unification at the expense of the Papal States. Defeat in the Franco-Prussian War and the revolution of 1870 brought to power a regime that, until 1873, seemed likely to restore the Comte de Chambord, the Bourbon pretender who was also a devout Catholic, and who had the support of the Church leadership. The subsequent collapse of the Bourbon candidacy opened the way for republicans such as Léon Gambetta and Jules Ferry to carry on a campaign against the Catholic Church that produced a wave of secularizing legislation in the 1880s.

This summary does not do justice to the complexity of the issues involved, or the depth of feeling among Catholics and their opponents. It is important to note also that Protestants and Jews did not share the anti-republican bias characteristic of many Catholics, and were among the most enthusiastic supporters of the Third Republic during the 1870s. Despite the political conflicts over religion that dominate many historical accounts, Catholicism remained throughout this period, as it had in 1801, 'the religion of the majority'. The basis for this claim is the attachment of the vast majority of the French people to the Catholic sacraments that sanctified the key moments of their lives. They sought baptism to mark their births, and demanded religious services to celebrate their marriages and deaths. For the Catholic clergy of the nineteenth century such adherence, while appreciated, was deemed insufficient. From their perspective, Catholics were also expected to attend mass each Sunday, and to confess and receive communion at least once each year, during the Easter season.

When these more demanding criteria are applied France looks much less faithful to Catholicism, with differences shaped by region, gender, and social class. Although statistical evidence is better for the latter part of the century, it is telling that even in Paris, which provoked deep anxiety among the clergy as a centre of disbelief, over 90 per cent of the population continued to be baptized during the Second Empire. In the same period, however, only 14 per cent of those living in the diocese of Paris took Easter Communion. Similar contrasts can be found in some rural areas, such as the Beauce region of the diocese of Orléans, where only 14 per cent made their Easter duty, while 76 per cent received the Last Sacraments. The low number of *pascalisants* might suggest that certain areas were undergoing a process of 'dechristianization', but such a claim requires us to accept the views of the clergy about who counts as a Catholic, and needs to be balanced by the impressive evidence of continued attachment to the sacramental rites.

The clergy were certainly frightened by the growth of cities and the social demands made by women and the poor, which they saw as threatening to destroy a rural society of pious peasants. The Abbé François Courtade, for example, suggested in 1871 that 'The people of Paris are without faith and without God. The notion and the feeling for the divine seem to have entirely withdrawn from them.' Historians who have studied the matter generally see some relationship between social change and Catholic practice, but avoid the alarmist reaction of Courtade and his colleagues. Urban dwellers might be less inclined to practice Catholicism regularly, but in the 'dechristianized' Limousin the citizens of Limoges were more loyal than their rural counterparts. In Paris practice was not uniformly low, and was more regular in middle-class and aristocratic neighbourhoods than in working-class *quartiers*, where church construction lagged behind population growth and the clergy were scarcer. Finally, women of all social classes and regions were more inclined to attend mass than men. Sweeping generalizations about Catholic practice in nineteenth-century France need, therefore, to be regarded with a dose of scepticism. Claims that France was 'dechristianized' tend to be based on clerical standards, and are insufficiently sensitive to the variations in practice across regions, classes, and gender.

There can be no doubt that the clergy were a central force in religious life in France. The loss of a generation of clergy during the revolutionary era had produced a personnel crisis, and throughout the Restoration bishops struggled to staff their rectories and schools with qualified incumbents. By 1830, however, the tide had turned, and clerical recruitment was remarkably healthy for most of the century, with a decline commencing only with the policy of 'laicization' carried out by the Third Republic in the 1880s.

French clergy 1815–1878

	1815	1830	1848	1878
Diocesan clergy	36,000	40,600	47,000	56,000
Regular clergy (male)		10,000		30,000
Regular clergy (female)	15,000	30,000	66,000	135,000

The numbers suggest a numerous cadre of Catholic leaders, but they are meaningless unless we keep in mind the ways in which these men and women interacted with the Catholic population. As much as they might complain about some of their parishioners, parish priests ministered at some point to almost every person in France, particularly at key transitional moments in their lives. They also intersected with their parishioners when they taught catechism, visited the sick, distributed charity, and officiated at Sunday mass. This set of tasks suggests a kind of ideal, the 'bon curé' attentive to the spiritual and material needs of his flock, an important model for both clergy and laity in the nineteenth century. Robert Gildea calls attention in his essay to the importance of the clergy as mediators between the parish and the wider world, defenders of local culture against a centralizing state. Clerical mediation, however, occurred on a vertical as well as a horizontal plane, as priests sought to invoke and placate supernatural as well as social forces.

All of these tasks could create disharmony as well as concord, for the French archives are full of complaints from parishioners about priests who smacked children, who failed to give the right catechism answer, and thundered against the immorality of dancing, an obsession with many clergy. In particularly dramatic cases a priest might deny a religious burial to someone who had refused to accept the Last Sacraments on his or her deathbed. Especially in the first half of the century, such refusals could provoke a small-scale rebellion, with parishioners organizing their own procession, and sometimes going so far as to break into the church for a service led by the local mayor. And finally, there were a few occasions when the local priest would violate his vow of chastity. Scandals over such moral lapses were relatively rare: Philippe Boutry's intensive study of the diocese of Belley, in the south-east, turned up only six cases for the period 1815–80. But Boutry notes the constant rumours about clerical misbehaviour, which helped feed the anticlerical literature on this topic that developed rapidly after 1860.

The pastoral success of Jean-Marie-Baptiste Vianney, whose parish in the village of Ars, near Lyon, became a model for the clergy, suggests the impact a devoted parish priest could have on his community. Arriving in a town relatively indifferent to the Church in 1818, by the time of his death in 1859 Ars had become a model of Catholic parish life, with virtually universal practice among both men and women, dancing forbidden, and the priest honoured as a saintly, ascetic, and charitable minister. Pilgrims began coming to Ars to confess to Vianney in large numbers, and the village was already drawing between 60,000 and 80,000 people a year at the time of his death. Ars remains a major shrine today, and Vianney, canonized in 1925, has become the patron saint of parish priests for the Roman Catholic Church.

Vianney's remarkable success is a telling example of the aspirations and possibilities of the diocesan clergy, and of their relationship with their parishes. More typical, perhaps, was the career of Edouard Pierchon, of the village of Haveluy, near Lille. Like Vianney, Pierchon served a single parish for most of his life, ministering to his community of less than 1,000 inhabitants from 1834 to 1894 (in this they were both somewhat unusual, for most diocesan clergy served a number of parishes in their career). In a manuscript history of his village written in the early 1850s Pierchon describes his successful raising of a new bell, a typical event in nineteenth-century villages that established the Catholic Church as the centre for local identity. Pierchon also describes the construction of a 'Calvary', a shrine decorated with a large crucifix that drew pilgrims from the surrounding region, suggesting another characteristic development of nineteenth-century Catholicism.

Pierchon was especially preoccupied with a protracted dispute he had with the tax-collector, Jean-François Parent, over the issue of Catholic schools. Although Pierchon succeeded in establishing private Catholic schools for both girls and boys, Parent convinced the municipal council to build a public school in 1851, setting up a long-running and vicious competition for students. Pierchon's history of Haveluy shows him deeply involved with his parishioners, ministering to them in both ordinary and extraordinary times, as when the cholera epidemic arrived in 1849. He is palpably concerned with their salvation, and thoroughly convinced that this can be gained only by punctilious orthodox practice, which carried with it an implicit but insistent call for deference to clerical authority. Pierchon's manuscript suggests the hard work and moral rectitude of the nineteenth-century French clergy, but it also conveys the arrogance and intrusiveness that could annoy and in some cases alienate parishioners. And it shows that even in a devout and rural region, a sustained commitment to the Catholic sacraments could be accompanied by resistance to the standards and leadership of the orthodox clergy.

The establishment of Catholic elementary schools in Haveluy calls attention to the importance of male and female religious orders in the schools of nineteenth-century France. Three out of four Catholic nuns worked as teachers, and dominated girls' education throughout our period. Male religious orders were relatively less significant, contributing 15 per cent of teachers to the public schools and 20 per cent to the private sector. Even if they were not taught by nuns or brothers, however, French schoolchildren (apart from the small minority of Protestants and Jews who attended their own private schools) underwent Catholic indoctrination. The Guizot law of 1833 that mandated the creation of primary schools in France put priests on the local school-boards and decreed that moral and religious instruction be an essential part of the curriculum. The Falloux law of 1850 confirmed this principle, and a ministerial regulation from 1851 called for the teaching of prayers, the recitation of the catechism, and history lessons covering the Old and New Testaments. Of course, the example of Haveluy suggests that the attempt to impose Catholicism through the schools could be resisted. French schools served as vehicles of religious education, a place where boys and girls learned to pray at the same time as they learned to read and write, but the desire to separate Catholicism from public education grew throughout this period, producing a movement that would finally succeed in passing laws to secularize education in the 1880s.

The sacraments and the schools provided crucial occasions for the Catholic clergy to try to exercise their influence over the French population, with results that can be regarded as a mixed success. There was intervention in other areas, such as the distribution of charity and the provision of health care, this last dominated by nursing orders such as the Daughters of Charity. Clerical activism is a crucial element in assessing the state of Catholicism in France, and historians have recently been particularly sensitive to the importance of careers available to women inside the Church. The relative weight of female clergy shifted dramatically during our period, for in 1790 only one out of three of the clergy were women, a figure that rose to almost two in three by 1880. For ambitious women who sought careers outside marriage, the Catholic Church offered the only real alternative throughout this period, providing them with public roles and substantial authority. As Bonnie Smith demonstrated in her work on the department of the Nord, married middle-class women also found a social outlet in church organizations, which provided essential social services to the poor in this rapidly developing industrial zone.

The cult of saints and shrines

Over the past generation historians have begun to pay much more attention to ordinary Catholics whose beliefs and practices constitute essential evidence for the state of religion in France. Catholicism as experienced by the laity was heavily influenced by the clergy, but it was not wholly defined by them. In fact the clergy in the nineteenth century sometimes appeared to be responding to popular pressure, channelling religious forces they could not quite control. At the centre of this popular Catholicism was the cult of the saints, and in particular the shrines that honoured them and offered benefits to their devotees.

The invocation of saintly assistance has deep roots in Christian history, descending from a pagan past that merged with Christianity as the new religion spread out from its Mediterranean base. Official Catholic doctrine sanctioned the cult of saints, but insisted that the holy dead who were asked to help cure a sick child or produce rain for a dry field could not act on their own, but only through their ability to intercede with God. In practice, however, this distinction was difficult to maintain, and lay people frequently addressed the saints as independent and powerful agents. Although the clergy acted at times to suppress cults that they feared were superstitious, and sought to control shrines and pilgrimages, on the whole they acted to encourage these practices in the nineteenth century, reversing the more sceptical and repressive policy inherited from the eighteenth century. The clergy had more sympathy with these popular religious forms in part because they were now recruited more from peasant and artisan classes sympathetic to such practices. Saints and shrines were also favoured by the Romantic intellectual climate, a counter to the rationalism that had fomented the Revolution. For a Church frightened by the social forces observed in modern cities, rural shrines testified to the supernatural commitments among ordinary French people, and provided a means to mobilize its supporters with processions and pilgrimages that could draw tens of thousands. As Robert Gildea has suggested, these ceremonies, multiplied thousands of times in the course of the century, generated a strong sense of local and regional identity and, by the latter part of the century, they were capable of bringing huge crowds together in national pilgrimages as well.

Although the Catholic Church sought to profit from the cult of saints and shrines, the appeal of these practices was based primarily on their ability to address the full range of problems that people faced as they moved through life. Sicknesses of all varieties, fertility problems, desire for educational success, a good number in the draft lottery, collective disasters such as drought or dearth, and defeat in war, all of these and more could be addressed through a bewildering array of prayers, devotions, and shrines that offered individuals and communities material and spiritual assistance. Some saints had specialities that were familiar to all Catholics, so that Saint Anthony was known to help people find lost objects, Saint Clair would be invoked for problems with eyes, and so on. While saints could be approached simply by prayer, it was believed especially efficacious to call on their help at shrines. Pilgrims had a vast number of such sites to choose from, ranging from a humble statue placed in the niche of a tree to magnificent shrine churches such as the cathedral of Chartres, or Notre-Dame de Rocamadour. Among the most vibrant evidence for the cult of the saints are the ex-voto gifts left in thanksgiving by pilgrims whose prayers had been answered. In Provence scenes painted by local artists of miraculous acts continued to be commissioned throughout the nineteenth century. Shrines, like village churches, were also sites where communities gathered to express their solidarity. In Brittany collective pilgrimages known as *pardons* would gather villages and in some cases several communities at isolated chapels where prayers would be combined with feasting and games.

Of all the saints venerated by the French in the nineteenth century, Mary was the most prominent. Devotion to Mary was based on shrines inherited from the medieval era and the Counter-Reformation, but was fuelled as well by a remarkable series of apparitions that produced some of the most famous religious sites in the modern world. The first of these took place in Paris in 1830, where Mary revealed herself to Catherine Labouré, a Sister of Charity, in the form of a medal that included the words: 'O Mary conceived without sin, pray for us who have recourse to thee.' The cult dedicated to this apparition took off in 1832 when the medal became a popular talisman used to ward off disease and to heal people from the cholera epidemic which devastated Paris in that year. In 1846 Mary appeared again, this time at La Salette, in an isolated part of the French Alps, to two young shepherds, Maximin Giraud and Mélanie Calvat. Mary blamed the potato blight that was causing severe food shortages on the sins of the local people, particularly their cursing and their refusal to attend Sunday mass. The most famous shrine in France, Our Lady of Lourdes, is based on a series of apparitions to Bernadette Soubirous, in the Pyrenees, in 1858. Following the directions of Mary, Bernadette discovered a fountain that was credited with thousands of cures, and which remains at the centre of the Lourdes pilgrimage, the most popular in France, and famous throughout the Catholic world. Finally, in 1870, at Pontmain, near an area where French and German troops were heavily engaged in battle, several young children saw an apparition that reassured them and their community that they would be spared invasion. All of these apparitions were eventually approved by the Church, and became the basis for magazines, confraternal organizations, and pilgrimages sponsored by an approving clergy who sought to integrate the cults into their orthodox agenda.

The support for Mary, a universal saint, may sometimes have been at the expense of local cults, making Marian devotions a central element in the progress of ultramontanism. At Lourdes, for example, the cult won approval in part because of Mary's announcement to Bernadette that she was the 'Immaculate Conception'. Mary's intervention thereby confirmed a papal decree of 1854, and implicitly supported the doctrine of papal infallibility, which was declared at the First Vatican Council of 1870. But for all its ties to institutional Catholicism, Marian piety remained a fundamentally popular movement. Those who saw Mary were generally women and children, and generally poor, and the appeal of the Marian devotions would seem to rest on their ability to convince the original visionaries and their communities that health and protection were available from an attentive and caring mother watching over them in heaven. The privileged position accorded women and children in the cult of Mary suggests its role as a kind of counter-culture, a place where divine attention and supernatural rewards were given to the humble and the weak instead of the worldly and powerful. In another sense, however, the cult of Mary can be seen as reinforcing the commonly held values of the day. The cult of domesticity that developed in the nineteenth century, with its emphasis on the nurturing and moralizing role of the wife and mother, fits smoothly into the wave of Marian devotion, which provided a key model for the values that women were expected to embody.

The cult of the dead

Saints were invoked for their ability to help people with their problems in this world, but they were also messengers from beyond the grave, demonstrating the continuing ties that bind the living and the dead. As Philippe Ariès argued in *The Hour of Our Death*, death was a central element in nineteenth-century French culture, generating beliefs and rituals that were in many ways innovative, and which have had an enduring impact ever since. Catholicism, once again, played a crucial but not exclusive role in shaping French beliefs about death and the afterlife. The French clergy drilled into their catechism classes and their sermon audiences the basic doctrine that all people possessed an immortal soul that could be saved only through intercession of the Catholic Church and its sacraments. Eternal heavenly bliss awaited those who listened; an eternity of torture awaited those who refused. Large graphic illustrations to hammer the point home were still being used by missionaries in Brittany into the twentieth century.

Hellfire preaching seems to have been especially popular among missionaries, such as the Redemptorists, who were charged with reviving the faith of the French people during the Restoration. These hard truths were gradually and increasingly mixed with other more consoling messages over the course of the nineteenth century, inspired by the spread of the theology of Alphonse de Liguori. Purgatory, a 'third place' where people could hope to spend a set amount of time being purified prior to their entry into heaven, had been a focal point in the teaching of the Counter-Reformation Church, but its importance as an alternative to the stark realities of hell grew in the nineteenth century. Having masses said for the intention of the dead, praying to Christ and the saints, and engaging in charitable work and penitential practices were among the ways the living could help suffering souls in Purgatory pass more quickly into heaven. The enormous number of indulgences for the dead, propagated by the ubiquitous holy cards, and the vast network of church-sponsored confraternities, all of which could boast a prayer or a practice that could shorten the period of suffering, fed a vast market among the living for products and rituals designed to help the dead.

The cemetery provided a site for honouring the dead that reveals both the vigour of Catholicism and the emerging power of alternative religious sensibilities. In 1804 a law regulating cemeteries attempted to sort out the problems inherited from the Revolution, when they had been declared state property. The law confirmed that cemeteries were communal property, charged mayors with ensuring that the dead were buried with decency and respect, and decreed that crowded churchyards in towns and villages should be closed in favour of new sites situated out of town. The Parisian cemetery of Père

Lachaise, opened in 1804, designed with curving pathways lined with trees, represented a new model of a cemetery where the dead could be visited in a romantic landscape, rather than in a crowded yard bordering a church. But the law also acknowledged the rights of the organized religions (Catholicism, Protestantism, and Judaism) to bury their dead in ground consecrated according to their particular rites. The co-management of cemeteries by public and religious officials was the source of numerous conflicts over the course of the century. Catholic clergy would periodically object to burying someone who died without the Last Sacraments, and try to have them placed in dishonoured corners alongside suicides and stillborn children. Mayors would frequently defend the rights of the citizens to what was felt to be their rightful place in the communal cemetery, alongside family and friends. Conflicts over the cemeteries were resolved only in 1881, when the Third Republic passed legislation that granted cities unequivocal control over their burial grounds.

The secularization of the cemetery in 1881 might be read as the culminating point of a century-long process of dechristianization, fuelled by battles between the clergy and parishioners, but we need to be cautious in making such judgements. Throughout this period, and into the final part of the century as well, the vast majority of the French population continued to insist on decorating their graves with a cross. In both small villages and in major metropolises, people flocked to the cemetery on 1 November (All Saints' Day), and 2 November (All Souls' Day), Catholic holidays marked by prayers and processions to remember and assist the dead. Seen in this context, the objections against those clergy who tried to restrict access to Catholic burial seem to have been less an attack on Christianity than an argument for more tolerant treatment of the dead, and a more generous assessment about who merited salvation.

In thinking about their dead the French not only resisted some of the rigours of Catholic doctrine and practice. They also experimented with new practices that exercised broad appeal, most notably the spiritualist *séances* in which circles of men and women would join hands and, with the help of a medium, carry on conversations with both the famous dead, and departed family members and friends. Originating in private circles during the 1780s, in the early nineteenth century 'somnambulism' went public, with theatrical performances in which hypnotists would put their *somnambules* into a trance, and then seek their advice on curing the sick who sought their help. By the 1840s some of the hypnotists, such as Louis-Alphonse Cahagnet, were combining requests for medical advice with theological questions about death and the afterlife. What emerged was a universe in which souls experienced a long process of expiation and purification through a series of reincarnations in other worlds. Spiritualism thus linked a rejection of an eternal hell, and a conviction that all will be saved, with a vision of the afterlife that was compatible with the fashionable ideas of progress and science.

The diffuse set of ideas and practices of spiritualism were given form in the work of Hippolyte Rivail (1804–69), to whom the spirits gave the name Alan Kardec. Working with a number of mediums, a term that he brought into common usage, in the 1850s Kardec synthesized the messages of the spirit world into *Le Livre des esprits*, which went through at least thirty-five editions between 1856 and 1889. Kardec also published a journal, the *Revue spirite*, and travelled indefatigably as an evangelist of the new religion. Kardec's version of spiritualism not only brought dead relatives and friends into direct contact with the living. The spirits also described a universe in which equality was a supreme value and gender a contingent characteristic. According to the spirits who spoke to Kardec's mediums, individual progress towards perfection could depend on the actions that men and women took to advance social reforms in this world. Spiritualist support for reform was not just empty rhetoric. Pierre-Gaetan Leymarie, for example, who succeeded Kardec as the editor of the *Revue spirite*, was deeply committed to educational reform, and collaborated closely with Jean Macé, the founder of the influential Ligue de l'Enseignment, whose Paris offices were located in Leymarie's home.

It is hard to know how many of the French people were persuaded by spiritualism, but its appeal was broad and significant, ranging in the 1850s from working-class circles, to the Republican exiles surrounding Victor Hugo on Jersey, to the family of Napoleon III. The Catholic Church issued a number of condemnations, and claimed that spirit manifestations were in fact the work of demons. But many individuals seemed to have no difficulty in mixing a dose of spiritualism into their religious lives, rendering it an important part of the French religious repertoire of the nineteenth century.

Religion and radical reform

The linkage of social reform to spiritualism was not exceptional, and in fact most of the individuals and organizations that advocated change did so partly on the basis of religious inspiration. The first half of the nineteenth century has been called an age of prophets, exemplified by the work of utopian socialists such as Étienne Cabet, Charles Fourier, Pierre Buchez, and Louis Blanc, all of whom insisted that their ideas about equality were inspired by 'true Christianity', as opposed to the teachings of the Church, which distorted the message of Jesus. The Comte de Saint-Simon (1760–1825), who envisioned an industrial society led by a technocratic élite, concluded a prolific publishing career with a work entitled *Nouveau Christianisme* (1825), in which he identified brotherly love as the essential doctrine of Christianity and accused the organized churches of heresy. Following Saint-Simon's death some of his followers, led by Barthélemy Prosper Enfantin (1769–1864), organized themselves into a full-blown religious cult that criticized private property, condemned Christian asceticism in favour of 'the rehabilitation of the flesh', and advocated the emancipation of women. At their headquarters in Ménilmontant near Paris the Saint-Simonians for a time in the early 1830s were the centre of a religious counter-culture that incorporated music and art into liturgical celebrations to express their heterodox ideas. After its suppression by the government, former members Philippe Buchez and Jean Reynaud continued to work religious themes into their social criticism, which led Buchez to Christian Socialism and Reynaud to spiritualism. Both of these figures were also political activists, with Buchez being named President of the National Assembly of the Second Republic in 1848, and Reynaud serving in the Ministry of Education.

Masonic lodges, active throughout the century, and societies of freethinkers, which emerged after 1848, saw traditional religion as an impediment to progress and condemned Catholicism for its focus on the next world rather than the here-below. As Philip Nord and Jacqueline Lalouette have pointed out, masons and freethinkers were profoundly touched by their earlier contact with utopian ideas, and their reform agendas were grounded in a belief that men carried within them a divine spark that could be the basis both for a relationship with a transcendent God, and for social progress in this world. The outright denial of God and an afterlife was resisted by frightened members of the middle class because it seemed to offer a recipe for social anarchy. Atheism nonetheless became fashionable among some male élites in the second half of the century, as can be seen in the decision of the general assembly of the major masonic society to suppress an obligatory belief in the 'Grand Architect of the Universe' in 1877. The religion of positivism invented by Auguste Comte (1798–1857) in the latter years of his life suggests, however, that even some of those who denied a personal God and the immortality of the soul felt the need to express their hope for human progress based on science and reason in elaborate rituals and a cult in honour of great men.

Jean-François Parent, the tax collector from the village of Haveluy, whom we met earlier during his confrontation with the local *curé*, provides a practical example of this combination of religious conviction with anticlericalism. Parent consistently rejected the Abbé Pierchon's attempts to castigate him as lacking religion, and insisted that he was in fact more authentically religious than his parish priest. Like more sophisticated theorists of rational religion, Parent understood the essence of religion to be a moral code oriented to life in this world rather than a theological system designed to produce salvation in the next. Orthodox Catholics tried to insist that such beliefs were inherently irreligious, but their anticlerical opponents were just as determined to deny the clergy the right to define what qualified as religious.

French civil religion

One reason for the state's devotion to the Concordat, and for its prosecution of groups such as the Saint-Simonians, was its desire to control religious expression in France, which as recently as the Revolution had produced bloody civil turmoil. Throughout the century government officials combined this policy of surveillance with attempts to create a version of Rousseau's 'religion of the citizen', civil rituals intended to sacralize the political regime by linking people together around a set of basic beliefs. The nature and character of these rituals varied from regime to regime, and were themselves frequently a source of controversy rather than harmony. It would take the blood and terror of the First World War to forge a civil religion that was generally accepted, but this achievement was based in part on the experiments of the nineteenth century, through which we can see the origins of a cult of the French nation.

Bourbons, Orleanists, Bonapartists, and Republicans all struggled to imagine France as a site of glory based on its historic achievements and providential tasks, a mythic ideal of social and religious harmony. The Bourbon monarchy's public rituals were closely identified with Catholicism, as the regime recalled France's historic position as 'the eldest daughter of the Church'. The most dramatic example of the Bourbon attempt to recreate a monarchy based on divine right occurred in 1825, when Charles X was consecrated at Reims. Like his forebears, Charles was anointed with oils that were reputedly brought directly from heaven by angels, and like them he engaged in the 'royal touch', a ritual in which he laid his hands on those with scrofula, claiming the miraculous power to heal them.

As gratifying as such rituals may have been to Catholic traditionalists, they excluded all of those who remained attached to the values of the Revolution and the glory of the Napoleonic era. The Orleanists understood the need for a more inclusive civil religion, to judge by the rituals that surrounded the transfer of the Emperor's remains from Saint Helena to the Invalides in Paris in 1840. While focusing primarily on national glory the rituals that surrounded Napoleon's last journey to Paris successfully integrated the clergy without granting the Church a dominating role. The three-month voyage concluded with a solemn procession that passed under the Arc de Triomphe and down the Champs-Élysées before ending with a mass by Archbishop Affre at the Invalides. The final emplacement in an elaborate crypt took place in 1861, where Napoleon still lies as a central figure of French civil religion.

The transfer of Napoleon's remains was framed by a liturgy that reconciled Catholicism with the French state and its history, and did so without reference to the Bourbon monarchy. Following the February Revolution of 1848 ceremonies that seemed to reconcile Catholicism with Republicanism were common, a reflection of the hopes of Catholic leaders that the new regime would grant the Church freedom to open its own secondary schools. On 4 March a state funeral honouring those who died in the February rioting processed from the church of the Madeleine to the Place de la Bastille, where the dead were buried in the crypt of the column raised to celebrate the Revolution of July 1830. The route of the procession, coupled with the prominence of the Catholic clergy at the services, managed to link the Catholic Church with the Revolutions of 1789 and 1830, as well as the more recent events of 1848.

The blessing of the liberty trees raised in villages throughout France in 1848 testifies to a broad acceptance of the Republic by the clergy, and to their willingness to experiment with liturgical forms that sanctified a regime that was dedicated to the principles of liberty, equality, and fraternity. But such rituals could sometimes evoke antagonism as well as solidarity, as in the heated exchange between the Abbé Pierchon and his old opponent Parent, at Haveluy. Pierchon agreed to bless the tree in the presence of the entire village, at a ceremony on 9 April 1848, but before the blessing he insisted on a brief speech, explaining that liberty must not degenerate into licence. From the opposite side of the trench where the tree was planted, Parent interrupted Pierchon: 'If you want to preach at us for two hours go back to the church and preach as much as you want. We asked you here to bless our liberty tree, do you want to bless it or not?'

Such events suggest the difficulties that accompanied the slow emergence of a French civil religion. The death of Archbishop Affre on the Paris barricades during the June Days of 1848 frightened Catholics, and helped push them towards a Napoleonic regime that would guarantee protection for established religion and the social order. First as President and then as Emperor, Louis-Napoleon cultivated Catholic support by defending Pius IX and the papal territories against the attacks of Italian nationalists. Given such support it is not surprising that the Catholic clergy were willing to invest the Napoleonic regime with appropriate religious ceremonies. These included the singing of the traditional prayer for the ruler, the 'Te Deum', at an elaborate ceremony three weeks after the *coup d'état* of December 1851, and the integration of the Catholic mass into the national holiday instituted on 15 August, the birthday of Napoleon I. In his study of the rituals of the Second Empire Matthew Truesdale emphasizes the importance of such references to Napoleon I and concludes that 'it was not divine authority that sacralized the regime in these ceremonies, it was history'. It might be fairer, however, to see Napoleon III as attempting to combine the two, which became inextricably tied together as France moved towards a civil religion that divinized its history as an organic development, ordained by Providence for the good of the French people and the whole world.

Republicans were also conscious of the need for symbolic representation and ritual celebration, as was already clear during the French Revolution. The figure of a woman had been used at that time to represent the new regime, and a giant female appeared again in the funeral procession on 4 March 1848 to honour those who died in the February Revolution. During the Second Empire this figure assumed a name, Marianne, who continued to serve as an emblem for a republican religion. In his *Lettre à Marianne* of 1856 the republican writer Félix Pyat used formulae borrowed from the Hail Mary, perhaps the most popular Catholic prayer, and from Catholic litanies to the Virgin, to honour the Republican goddess:

Hail Marianne, full of strength, the people are with thee. Blessed is the fruit of thy womb, the Republic! Holy Marianne, Mother of Right, have mercy upon us! Deliver us!
Virgin of Liberty, deliver us from kings and popes!
Virgin of Equality, deliver us from aristocrats!
Virgin of Fraternity, deliver us from soldiers!
Virgin of Justice, deliver us from judges!

Pyat's prayer mimicked the form of Catholic prayer, but had little in common with the people who pleaded for miracles at Lourdes. Events in the 1870s would confirm the distance between Catholics and Republicans, producing a cultural conflict that was simultaneously religious and political.

The culture wars of the Third Republic

The sudden collapse of the Second Empire in September 1870, the humiliating defeat at the hands of the Prussian invaders, and the bloody suppression of the Paris Commune in May 1871 constituted a political catastrophe of such monumental proportions that it seemed destined to end in an apocalyptic climax. For Catholics, the troubles that threatened to destroy the nation were a result of individual moral failings encouraged by collective decisions to restrict the power of the Church, the only institution capable of teaching charity and restraint and thereby guaranteeing social order. The fate of Archbishop Darboy of Paris, murdered along with several other clergymen at the height of the civil war in May 1871, suggested that the worst days of the Revolution had returned. The decision in 1870 to pull French troops out of Italy, where they had protected the Pope in his papal enclave, made military sense to French generals concerned with the Prussian onslaught. To French Catholics this was an abandonment of the French mission to protect the Pope, and a clear source of the divine disapproval that led to military defeat.

Apocalyptic thinking offers promises for rapid redemption as well as punishment for sin. In the early 1870s the conservative majority in the National Assembly was supported by a wave of mass pilgrimages to Lourdes and other sites that contributed to a mood among Catholics that better days were ahead, if only France would return to the Church. This wave of devotional fervour, however, became closely linked not only with royalism, but with international adventurism, for some Catholic leaders hoped that a restored Henry V would lead a French campaign to restore the papal territories to the Pope. The decision of the National Assembly to build a church dedicated to the Sacred Heart on Montmartre, in Paris, illustrates the close links that tied Catholic devotions to a royalist political programme in the 1870s. The cult originated in a series of seventeenth-century visions in which Jesus called on Louis XIV to dedicate France to his Sacred Heart. For some devotees the failure to do so had initiated a long trail of disasters that had since plagued France and the Bourbons. The church of Sacré-Cœur was subsequently built and still stands, a testimony to the religious mood of despair and hope that was characteristic of the early 1870s.

The Catholic revival of the 1870s suggested to Republicans that the Catholic Church, revitalized in the course of the nineteenth century, was seeking a return to the Old Regime. In response, politicians led by Léon Gambetta gathered crowds of thousands to hear that 'clericalism is the real enemy'. In taking on Catholicism Republicans raised statues and busts of Marianne in public spaces that had formerly been filled with kings or emperors, a female symbol of the Republic that offered the French an alternative to the Virgin of Lourdes. Republicans also organized 'civil funerals', burials ostentatiously conducted without the presence of the Catholic clergy, as a way of demonstrating their independence, rituals that drew as many as 100,000 to honour the Protestant historian Edgar Quinet. Through ceremonies like these anticlericals were creating a cult of the great man who died for his political principles, and whose memory can inspire the living. This theme, initially evoked during the French Revolution, would be enshrined in the Pantheon, whose history neatly encapsulates the struggles between Catholicism and the French civil religion. Originally built in Paris as the church of Sainte-Geneviève, this site was taken over by the revolutionary regime, returned to the Church by Napoleon I, and then seized definitively by the republican state in 1885.

Conclusion

The culture war that began in the 1870s would continue for decades, and echoes of it, though muted, can still be heard today. In the 1880s Republicans voted for reforms that created an elementary school system with secular, obligatory, and free education as the centrepiece of a laicized state. Catholic politicians fought long and hard, with substantial public support, in their losing battle to defend the prerogatives of the Church. Catholics continued to have difficulty accepting the distinction advanced by Gambetta and his colleagues between 'clericalism' and 'religion', with the latter understood as a world of private spiritual experience walled off from the state. The fact that the Republic was willing to organize holidays, such as 14 July 1880, when the nation celebrated the first modern Bastille Day, suggested that public ceremonies would be used to inculcate beliefs that might violate the religious sensibilities of some citizens. But despite the fears of Catholics, and the hopes of some anticlerical extremists, the Third Republic did not repeat the mistakes of the First and try to destroy the Church. The republican mainstream was willing and in fact committed to a regime that granted individuals and families the right to choose to be Catholics, Protestants, Jews, Spiritualists, Freemasons, freethinkers, or nothing at all. Yet like their predecessors the

Republicans also hoped to create a 'civil religion' that would embrace all of the French people under a new sacred canopy raised in honour of the nation, its historical glory, and future promise.

4

Class and Gender

Elinor Accampo

The order to which this book is dedicated is a species of dignity, or honourable quality, which pertains to a number of persons in the same manner and under the same name . . . [B]esides the rank it gives them, it also brings a particular aptitude and capacity to attain either offices or *seigneuries* . . . In French it is particularly called Estate, as being the dignity and the quality which is the most stable and most inseparable from a man . . . As for its definition, order may be defined as *dignity with aptitude for public power.*

Charles Loyseau, *A Treatise on Orders*

Introduction

First published in 1610, Charles Loyseau's justification for the Estates System in France remained an authoritative force until the Revolution of 1789 overturned the Old Regime. The author carefully explained that for society to have order, it had to *be ordered* into the three estates of the clergy, the nobility, and the rest of society. In principle, only members of the first two estates could exercise public power or hold public office because only they had dignity in their persons, acquired from both blood and service, as well as from the absence of servitude and 'commonness'. Loyseau wrote that nobility derived from dignity, and that 'ennoblement purges the blood and the posterity of the ennobled'. Inherent to their dignity was the freedom from any need to perform activities for 'sordid profit', that is from having to sell their labour. To engage in such activity would result in forfeiture of one's privileged status. The third estate, according to Loyseau, did not in fact constitute an 'order' at all, for its members worked for profit. Those 'who gained their living only by the labour of their arms' rather than by the labour of their minds held the lowest place on the scale; Loyseau considered them 'the most vile of the common people'. It was this absence of dignity among members of the third estate that justified their exclusion from public power. No mention was made of what place women held within this system; but in Loyseau's scheme their state of dependence precluded any possibility for dignity.

Loyseau's justification for the three estates only imperfectly reflected Old Regime society, for many bourgeois men had been able to use the fruits of their labour to purchase public office and become ennobled. By the 1780s the contradictions between the theory of social order and its practical manifestations had come to breaking point. Moreover, a large number of 'commoners' believed they had the right to exercise public power, and indeed did so through their public criticism of the regime. But in 1789, revolutionary legislation swept away the world of corporate order, abandoning, in principle, blood and birth as a source of 'order' in society. Henceforth, dignity and the 'aptitude for public power' associated with it would be acquired through civil society rather than qualities 'inseparable from a man' born into an 'estate'. The language of human rights helped instil the desire for personal dignity, which through the nineteenth century manifested itself as the struggle to obtain political power on the part of those who continued to be excluded from citizenship. The developments unleashed by the political and economic revolutions of this period—enfranchisement, capitalism, urbanization, rising literacy, geographical mobility, a greatly expanded subjective experience of private life, and new forms of desire—all gave rise to a more pronounced sense of subjective personhood. These new forms of individualism competed with the formation of collective consciousness based on class, religion, and language, provoked new definitions of masculinity and femininity, and gave new meaning to sexuality and its relationship to gender.

This chapter is about the way French people experienced social class and gender identity—and their intersection—from 1788 to 1880. The application of 'class' and 'gender' as categories of analysis presents a daunting task, as both concepts have recently undergone considerable scrutiny and contestation about their meaning and usefulness. The classic, Marxist conception of class derives from one's relation to the means of production. But Marx's definition extended beyond that economic relationship, by insisting that class occurs only when individuals are conscious of it, and engage in a common battle against another class. The word 'class' as a designation of social division came into use from 1770 to 1840, gradually replacing the words 'order', 'rank', and 'estate', indicating an increasing awareness that one's social position resulted from productive activity rather than from birth alone. Of bourgeois origin, it reflected the inadequacy of Old Regime classification by orders, and indeed a new set of values. Turning Loyseau's logic on its head, the language used conferred a measure of dignity upon work, for the very term 'working class' implied usefulness and productivity in opposition to both the unemployed and the 'idle' nobility. But the use of 'lower', 'middle', and 'upper' also reveals the persistence of hierarchy and the inferiority of the working poor, and terms such as 'proletariat' and 'dangerous classes' reflected bourgeois fears. Jacques Rancière and other historians have argued that the outlook of the bourgeoisie toward the working classes not only justified the power of the former, but nourished a conscious response to these perceptions among workers. Whatever its origins, the 'dignity of labour' became an essential component of working-class discourse and worker identity, and a basis for demanding public power.

More recently, the 'linguistic turn' in history has privileged cultural over economic factors in the formation of individual and class identities. In this perspective, economic conditions alone did not determine modes of life; they were also deeply influenced by religious beliefs, rituals, community bonds, ethnicity, gender identity, sexual practices, and other cultural factors. Culture creates 'webs of significance' that shape the individual's understanding of his or her subjective experience. Industrial capitalism not only created new modes of production and social divisions, but new forms of consumption as well which, in turn, created new desires and hopes that also shaped individual and collective identity. The identification of powerful cultural factors shaping individual identity has led many historians to be wary of focusing too heavily on class consciousness.

Though the definition of social class has become more problematic in recent years, historians still connect it to a determining external referent, the capitalist economy. Unlike class, gender has been conceptualized independently of any constant referent such as biological sex. Instead, it is conceived as a product of changing social and cultural forces. Historians include class, occupation, race, ethnicity, and religion among the factors interacting with individuals to produce notions of 'womanhood' and 'manhood'. Throughout the nineteenth century the vicissitudes in French politics also defined gender: republicanism deemed public virtue and rationality as essentials of manhood, while motherhood remained the one 'essential' element of womanhood. Though motherhood became the most common justification for denying women citizenship over the course of the nineteenth century, it also became a basis for laying claim to female dignity and thus (somewhat paradoxically) for demanding public power.

Though gender and class as categories of analysis cannot do full justice to the subjective experiences of men and women who lived in France during this century of political and economic revolution, we can make little sense of their history without them. As this chapter will show, these categories allow us to pose questions about historical experience even though the answers often demonstrate how fluid and unfixed these categories can be.

Class and gender in the revolutionary era

For most people in the eighteenth century, life consisted of a struggle for survival against poor harvests, disease, war, and the monetary demands of landowners and the state. In the 1780s, the first estate, the clergy, constituted about 0.4 per cent of the French population of some 28 million, and owned roughly 10 per cent of the land, from which they enjoyed an enormous income supplemented by tithes and other fees. About 1.6 per cent of the population belonged to the second estate, the nobility of the sword and the robe, who owned some 25 per cent of the land and were largely exempt from direct taxes. While their economic status varied enormously, they enjoyed extensive income-producing privileges as landlords or officeholders. The remainder of the population belonged to the third estate, whose social and economic status varied considerably. At the top of this order ranked a powerful bourgeoisie whose wealth derived from banking, commerce, and the professions. Below them were other 'middling' sorts—less successful professionals, merchants, and retailers; still lower on the scale stood shopkeepers and artisans, ranging from apprentices through masters, followed by unskilled urban labourers and peasants. Peasants, who comprised roughly 80 per cent of the French population, owned some 30 per cent of the land, and their economic status varied according to the size and productivity of their holdings, and the severity of their feudal burdens. Beggars, vagabonds, prostitutes, and criminals occupied the bottom of this social order, and might have made up as much as 10 to 20 per cent of the urban population.

Gender played a vital role in the way this social system functioned. Survival, even among the wealthy, depended on a tight regulation of marriage, family life, and the division of work. Among noble families, for example, marriage functioned to form alliances so that landholdings could be perpetuated through blood kin and provide the basis for political alliances, clientage, and patronage. If in this class women's prime responsibility was to reproduce, they did not themselves bear the burdens of child-rearing or work of any other sort. Instead, they devoted their lives to pleasure. The pursuit of pleasure constituted, indeed, an important element of artistocratic identity for both women and men, which often included sexual libertinism. As illustrated in Choderlos de Laclos's *Les Liaisons dangereuses*, aristocratic women could wield considerable social power through their sexuality. Many of them also enjoyed prestige and influence by hosting salons attended by *philosophes* and other members of the intellectual élite.

Less privileged women performed an enormous variety of labour in both countryside and city. Rural men primarily worked in the fields, while women tended animals, participated in harvests, made cheese, prepared food and clothing, and in addition engaged in all stages of textile production, integrating these tasks with child-rearing. Family survival depended on marriages that could reproduce enough children to provide labour, but not more than the land could support. In the towns, women often worked with their husbands in a craft or trade, giving their babies over to wet-nurses so that their work would not be interrupted by the need to breastfeed. They assisted their husbands in producing, packaging, delivering, and selling goods. Some women pursued work in trades different from that of their husbands, such as in the production of veils, gloves and lace, which sometimes took place in all-female workshops. Urban women even participated in an array of occupations normally associated with men, such as masonry and small metal production. Among these women as well, productive tasks coexisted with running a household. Male occupations were organized into a corporations or guilds, which regulated the quality of work and contributed to the formation of a work-related identity. Few corporations permitted female membership, further limiting their access to skill and economic independence. Women in some trades formed their own associations, but these were neither as numerous nor as powerful as men's corporations.

By abolishing the Estates System, and dissolving guilds and corporations through the Allarde and Le Chapelier Laws of 1791, legislators of the constitutional monarchy sought to create a civic society based on the private individual's capacity to speak in the name of the public good. Yet in the perceptions of the Constituent Assembly, that capacity was determined by wealth, age, and gender. The first constitution granted the vote to roughly 4.3 million men who were over 25 years of age and who paid the equivalent of three days' unskilled labour in taxes—about 60 per cent of the adult male population. But their political voice was an indirect one, for they could only vote for members of electoral colleges who paid taxes equivalent to the value of ten days of labour. Some 50,000 second-degree electors then voted for deputies to the Legislative Assembly, eligibility for which required considerably more wealth. These voting restrictions contradicted the principles of equality set forth in the Declaration of the Rights of Man and Citizen. By establishing wealth as the most important criterion for active citizenship, and at the same time destroying the corporate order, the Assembly provided the foundations of a class-based society.

The new definition of citizenship also altered the political balance of power between men and women. Women certainly held a status inferior to men under the Old Regime, but both men and women experienced relationships of inequality as peasants, within workshops, or in relation to superior estates and the royal court. Certain sorts of women—those of the court, *salonnières*, or actresses, for example—exerted considerable public power. But the principle that all men were equal categorically excluded women as 'individuals' who could speak for the public good. The logic for this exclusion can be found in the writings of Jean-Jacques Rousseau, whose thinking not only had an enormous impact on the course of the French

Revolution, but whose ideas about gender remained current through the nineteenth century. Rousseau held that according to natural law, men and women were complementary, and that by nature women were modest, submissive, and self-sacrificing. Only within a conjugal union could women be chaste and virtuous, and nurture a positive influence on children and men. To men belonged the calling of public life and citizenship, where they could exercise virtue by working for the public good. But if women entered public life, the dark side of their nature emerged. Outside the domestic hearth, women cor- rupted men through their sexual power. They 'naturally' behaved immodestly, seducing men and diverting them from the virtue required for public life.

This ideology of 'separate spheres' for men and women, divided respectively between public and private, did not emerge in a void. Several historians have argued that a sense of the 'sacredness' of private life emerged over the course of the eighteenth century, and that the Revolution created a new language of political culture that translated it into the modern 'gender system' in which men could only govern themselves virtuously in the public sphere if women were eliminated from it. Such distinct separation of spheres had not been necessary in the Old Regime because the exercise of public power depended upon dignity conferred through birth. In the new regime, by contrast, government and civic society depended upon virtuous and dignified behaviour in public life. Women, children, and the poor could be neither virtuous nor dignified, for they were incapable of placing the public good above private needs.

From 1789 to 1792, women, *sans-culottes*, and other members of disenfranchised groups became 'active citizens' by demonstrating in the streets, participating in political clubs, and voicing their opinions in legislative halls. To the original agenda of political and financial reform they added demands for social justice by calling for price controls on food and other items necessary for survival. From August to October 1789, for example, hundreds of women from the central markets of Paris participated in daily marches protesting about the scarcity of bread and the king's failure to ratify the Declaration of the Rights of Man and Citizen. At the same time, 2,000–3,000 women took over the hall where the National Assembly met, inverting gender roles by intimidating deputies with armed force and by voting on legislation concerned with the distribution of grain.

Although most militant women did not make overtly 'feminist' demands, the Revolution did spawn a consciousness among some that human rights were 'universal', and encouraged demands for civil equality in marriage, divorce, property rights, and education. Olympe de Gouges's *Declaration of the Rights of Women* (1791) offered a poignant critique of female exclusion from the Declaration of the Rights of Man. She stated that 'woman is born free and remains equal to man in rights' and therefore should partake in all 'public dignities, offices and employments.' Although none of the national assemblies ever seriously considered legislation that would grant women such 'dignities', the very claims made on behalf of women's rights permitted a more deliberate definition of gender spheres. Members of the Society of Revolutionary Republican Women, formed in May 1793, sought to arm themselves in order to combat 'internal enemies' of the Republic, and actively participated in the elimination of moderates from the National Convention in the insurrection of 31 May to 2 June 1793. This direct and uninvited political action proved too much for the Jacobin leadership; the Convention not only banned the Society, but prohibited all women's clubs, virtually legislating women out of public life.

Most telling in the rhetoric of Jacobin legislators was the way they located gender difference in the body: 'Nature herself indicated the preference' for men taking on public duties because of their physical strength, and their capacity for difficult work 'whether in armies or in the senate'. Anaxagoras Chaumette stated it most pointedly when he claimed that women were making themselves into men, and queried, 'Since when is it permitted to give up one's sex? Is it to men that nature confided domestic cares? Has she given us breasts to breastfeed?' Sex had replaced blood as the most 'natural' source of difference. The revolutionary crisis had produced fears about the loss of sexual differentiation. The principle that human rights were 'universal' threatened to erode gender boundaries—boundaries that accrued more fundamental significance as an organizing principle of social order precisely because the estates-based 'order' of the Old Regime had disappeared. The reinscription of sex difference became a new source of order in the ancient meaning of the term, and the basis for social cohesion.

Jean-Jacques Rousseau and his revolutionary disciples created the foundation for what recent historians have termed 'republican motherhood', which offered a new role for women fundamental to the emergence of a liberal political culture. Women responded positively to this new ideal, for it endowed motherhood, and thus womanhood, with a new sense of dignity and purpose. In this manner, the Revolution significantly contributed to the rise in the importance of motherhood as an institution and the new ideology of motherhood generated iconic representations of women nurturing not only their own babies with their breasts, but the French Republic as well. The female Republican symbol, later baptized as Marianne, was represented with prominent nude breasts, and numerous celebrations focused on women's sustaining power.

The Napoleonic regime and its impact

In a number of ways the Napoleonic government carried to completion the gender and class-related developments of the Revolution. Throughout the 1790s, most men and women were preoccupied with everyday matters of material existence and often survival itself in the face of war, civil war, poor harvests, and high prices. The former third estate initially benefited from the abolition of tithes, feudal dues, tolls, and the injustices of the tax-farming system. The old élites of the Church and aristocracy either emigrated, accepted their diminished prerogatives, or became victims of revolutionary terror. The urban bourgeoisie acquired property, political influence, and the advantage of 'careers open to talent'. Although his regime was authoritarian and hierarchical, Napoleon provided the illusion of full citizenship by granting near-universal male suffrage, and filling his expanding bureaucracy with educated bourgeois. Recovery and expansion in some industrial sectors also fostered the growth and economic power of the middle classes, and the Napoleonic Code created a legal system that greatly favoured private property and its accumulation. Peasants expanded their land ownership to over 40 per cent, though wealthy farmers held one-third of these lands. The urban workers, on the other hand, fared no better than they had during the 1790s. The Le Chapelier Law of 1791, whose prohibitions remained in force until 1864, rendered workers' strikes and associations in defence of their economic interests difficult at best.

The Napoleonic regime consolidated the new bases for gender differentiation articulated in the 1790s. The new law code reflected the perceived threat that unregulated female sexuality posed to the family. Property had to be protected from the 'independence, fickleness, and frivolity of women'. To ensure that husbands had legal authority over wives, the infamous article 213 stated, 'A husband owes protection to his wife, a wife obedience to her husband.' Though spouses were supposed to be mutually faithful, a wife's infidelity posed far more danger than that of her husband, because any illegitimate child would destroy his honour and undermine his patrimony. Thus penalties for adultery were, according to this logic, justifiably unequal: a woman could be imprisoned in a house of correction for a term as long as two years, while a man would only be fined up to 2,000 francs. A husband, too, could literally get away with murder if he discovered his wife in the act of adultery. A wife did not have such recourse, and could only sue for divorce if her husband brought his mistress into the family home. Gender inequality also extended to single women who bore children. The code protected a man, married or single, from any requirement to support an illegitimate child, or even from being identified as the father. In addition to articles regulating female sexuality, the Napoleonic Code prohibited women from making legal contracts, participating in lawsuits, or even serving as witnesses in court and to civil acts such as births, deaths and marriages. They needed permission from their husbands to engage in business, even that of selling produce at markets. These legal restrictions obviously limited women's options, particularly denying them any opportunity for economic independence.

The articles in the Code regulating relations between family members stemmed from the notion that the father, a citizen in his own right and capable of self-rule, would at once exercise complete (and presumably benevolent) authority within his own family and represent the family in his clearly defined relationship to the state. Pre-nuptial agreements among the wealthier classes and lack of enforcement among the poor mitigated its power to some extent. Nonetheless, the moral spirit behind the Code qualified the way French women and men experienced class and gender relations throughout the nineteenth century.

Gender, class formation, and early industrialization

The French nineteenth century has commonly been referred to as the 'bourgeois century', but precisely how and when—or even whether—this class asserted its economic, political, and moral hegemony remains controversial. The bourgeoisie is defined as a class whose wealth derives from the capitalistic activities of trade, finance, and manufacturing. Yet France industrialized slowly and unevenly, and the political and economic power of landed wealth persisted. The bourgeoisie had no consciousness of itself as a class by 1815; they had difficulty establishing their own distinctive culture because the aristocracy continued to serve as models for manners, ideology, conspicuous consumption, and political leadership. During the Restoration they began to distinguish themselves rhetorically from the aristocracy as they competed for political power, thus identifying themselves with civil and political liberties, and the values of the market place. Only after 1830 did they succeed in developing their own distinct identity, but they did not win political power as a class. In 1846, 45 per cent of the July Monarchy's parliamentary deputies were nobles, either from the Old Regime or the Napoleonic Empire. But such analysis of political power becomes meaningless in the face of an 'osmosis' that occurred between industry, finance, land, and the bureaucracy. The family of Casimir Périer is a good illustration of the fluidity of class definitions: originally lawyers and landowners, this family increased its landownership during the Revolution, and then invested in soap, glass, and coal, making it impossible to distinguish any single source of its wealth.

Even if its economic origins are blurred, the bourgeoisie did develop a distinct moral identity in the first half of the century. I would suggest that, more than in any other social class, gender distinctions became as important to that identity as the accumulation and expenditure of wealth. Robert Nye has shown that bourgeois men forged a newly distinct male identity around codes of honour appropriated from the old nobility. These codes consisted of a set of values and manners, some of which had roots in the feudal past, while others developed from disciplinary needs peculiar to the bourgeoisie as they became preoccupied with sex and the control of reproduction. Like Foucault, Nye argues that sex played a role for the bourgeoisie that blood had for the nobility. Proper sexual choices assured one's legacy. 'Manly' sexual characteristics became, over the course of the century, more precisely defined by doctors, scientists, and jurists. 'Deviant' behaviour—bachelorhood, homosexuality, non-reproductive sexuality, and unwillingness to work and to support a family—not only became pathologized, but intertwined with the cultural construction of male and female sexual and gender identities. In this context gender identity also became an increasingly important location for one's personal sense of dignity.

As Catherine Hall has noted in the history of private life during this period, 'A man's dignity lay in his occupation; a woman's gentility was destroyed if she had one.' But wherein lay a woman's dignity? As the nineteenth-century world of market capitalism and political rights stressed individualism for men, the opposite occurred for women. The paradox for them resided in the fact that respectable bourgeois women could only have dignity to the degree that they identified with motherhood and with their families; but that very self-identification rendered impossible the sense of individual independence so essential to the definition of civic dignity. Middle-class women nonetheless created space in which they could lay claim to other forms of esteem. In her classic study of the department of the Nord, Bonnie Smith demonstrated the powerful and pervasive influence of female domestic culture among the bourgeoisie. However, rather than complementing one another as Rousseau imagined, private and public spheres constituted entirely separate, parallel worlds. As women devoted themselves more exclusively to domesticity and motherhood, men left the home to work and to socialize with other men, or so the standard argument runs. As men pursued the 'modern' values of science and individualism, women devoted themselves increasingly to the biological and cultural demands of motherhood, and turned toward religion for solace.

A sartorial revolution reflected and reinforced these bourgeois gender distinctions. Between 1830 and 1914, the female body became more covered and constricted than ever before. Clad in taffeta and tight corsets, women advertised their family's social and economic status. With the important exception of the dandy, men's garments lost the flair and colour they once had, and became the shapeless black or grey three-piece suit appropriate for their life of toil rather than for the pursuit of libertine pleasure. The blandness of men's clothing shifted attention from the status indicated by their outward appearance to their interior character, which was reflected in consumerism of a different sort. From the 1830s bourgeois men increasingly defined themselves as individuals and as citizens through the practice of collecting prized objects of art and geological or biological specimens. This activity contrasted sharply with female consumerism which, rather than showcasing individual taste, emphasized physical fragility and self-identification with the family.

It is crucial to bear in mind, however, that the ideology of separate spheres and the morality behind it, like the dark three-piece suits of upper-class men, diverts the gaze from a reality that was often very different. In fact, women never actually left the city streets, while others, both married and single, entered public life as writers, actresses or political activists, escaping the codes of the new 'gender system'. Drawing on the examples of such lives, fiction also allowed women far more individualism than did cultural codes. One of the most common literary characters was the *lorette*, a woman who appeared in public dressed as a man. Sexual practices crossed boundaries as well. As Lenard Berlanstein has shown in his study of women in the theatre, aristocratic and bourgeois men shared an erotic culture central to their masculine identity that was based on competitive (thus public) womanizing and sexual prowess—despite the post-revolutionary 'sacredness' of family life and domesticity. One need only recall Flaubert's *Sentimental Education*, whose main character—drawn largely on the author's personal experience—witnessed the debauchery of both the old élite and the new bourgeois man. The philandering and cheating entrepreneur who loved his 'perfect' wife and preserved the façade of domesticity within his home, also practised the libertine behaviour associated with the old aristocracy.

Popular fiction produced during the July Monarchy frequently portrayed cross-dressing, hermaphrodism, and same-sex love, as exemplified in various works by Henri de Latouche, Honoré de Balzac, and Théophile Gautier. Actual same-sex relationships did seem to be regarded with tolerance in the July Monarchy. But what most disturbed the medical world was the fact that such relations often occurred between upper-class and lower-class men, thus confusing or reversing class hierarchies. Working-class servants in bourgeois homes provide further examples of boundary-crossing in class, gender, and privacy, for they became witness to family secrets, and often fell victim to rape or seduction by male household members. Many of them ultimately had little choice but to join the ever-growing ranks of prostitutes patronized by the very same men who in their appearance embraced the new morality of separate spheres. Though such relationships existed in the Old Regime as well, they assumed a different meaning in the nineteenth century in the context of bourgeois morality: they at once provided an opportunity for liberation from rigid moral values, and an occasion for severe reprobation, especially for women, given the restrictions of the Napoleonic Code. Despite such contraventions, the bourgeoisie exerted enormous influence with its prolific moralistic discourse, through which the experience of gender and class often came to be understood and regulated.

Aristocrats and peasants: persistence of tradition, or break with the past?

According to a Marxist conception of class formation, the nobility and peasants should have declined in numbers and influence over the course of the nineteenth century as France slowly industrialized. In fact both persisted, but they were transformed as well, particularly because nobles did not survive the Revolution of 1789 unscathed. Many suffered from the loss of seigneurial rights and, certainly among émigrés, from the loss of land. As a whole, the aristocracy lost about 20 per cent of the land they had held in the Old Regime. But their experiences varied widely; in regions where the nobility remained on their estates and kept a low profile, they suffered fewer losses. Especially for the older generation of returned émigrés, the horrors of 1789 appeared as God's punishment for their sins. In the effort to reinstate social hierarchy, and shore up their own prestige, aristocrats newly embraced the values of Church and King. Inexorably, perhaps, the aristocracy and the monarchy inclined—at least in their self-representations—towards the bourgeois domestic values that had emerged after 1789.

Memories of the Revolution also influenced the relationship that notables (locally powerful aristocrats and bourgeois) enjoyed with peasants, particularly as the latter experienced economic change. Nobles who could afford to do so continued to exert influence over 'their' peasants, with whom they often formed important anti-modern, anti-capitalist, and pro-clerical political linkages during the first half of the nineteenth century. A system of clientage, the ecclesiastical hierarchy and the revival of Catholicism, contributed to this process. Alexis de Tocqueville's account of peasants in his village going to the nearest town to vote in the election of April 1848 aptly illustrates the weight of tradition. Having returned to his estate from Paris in order to participate, Tocqueville perceived the local people to be 'more respectful than ever', and 'positively affectionate'. As a democratic gesture Tocqueville walked in alphabetical order with the 170 electors (the entire, adult-male population) to perform this 'solemn duty'. When they arrived at the top of the hill overlooking the land from which he inherited his noble title, the group halted, and Tocqueville cautioned the peasants to march as a united body until they all voted, so as to avoid those in town who might wish to deceive them with offers of food or shelter from the rain. Tocqueville concluded that almost all voted for the same candidate who was, of course, himself. He implicitly suggested in this account that peasants lacked the independence to master their own citizenship and civic duty.

Yet Tocqueville would not have enjoyed such deference in other parts of rural France. Even where the landed élite persisted in dominating economically, they did not always do so in cultural or political terms. Rural communities became increasingly dependent on towns as markets for their produce and for the supply of consumer goods and services and, by the 1840s, peasants in many areas became less isolated than previously. Among the services available was money-lending, which ultimately victimized impoverished peasants and created intense hostility on their part towards the local bourgeoisie. The very weight of traditional community values—particularly common memories and lingering antagonisms from the Revolution, like threats to common lands, fuelled opposition to local notables. In areas such as the Ariège, in the Pyrenees these unresolved issues assumed political form and sometimes resulted in violence.

The lives of French peasants varied so much according to

geographical location, economic activity, and relationships with the
élite that it is impossible to generalize about them. Most historians
concur that in the first half of the century the majority of peasants
retained a traditional consciousness rooted in a culture shared with
artisans and even notables. Their common linguistic and educational universe centred on ritualized behaviour, festivals, local
patois, codes of politeness, and proverbs. Female sociability—such
as gossip, criticism, and ostracism, in workplace, market or
church—created informal social controls. Particularly important in
this regard was the *veillée*, in which twenty or thirty women and
men gathered together in the evening, in a home or barn, to sew,
repair tools, sing, tell stories, play games, and court potential marriage partners. Although in times of prosperity men increasingly
went to cafés and clubs where they socialized without women,
sociability in the countryside was more sexually integrated than
among urban workers and the bourgeoisie. Separation of private
and public had little meaning in this milieu. The family remained
the basic unit of production and exchange, with marriage an important aspect. Perhaps what peasants held most in common was the
objective of owning land, which represented their source of dignity
in the community. The necessity of acquiring and maintaining
land continued to inhibit the penetration of urban, middle-class
values.

Workers and the Revolution of 1848

Although French capitalism had the appearance of being 'retarded' in
relation to other modernizing economies, it did bring distinctive
transformations in class structure and class consciousness among
workers. Rather than large-scale factories, small and medium-sized
industrial enterprises began emerging around the 1830s, while older
forms of craft production persisted. Cities grew relatively slowly, and
the segregation between home and work characteristic of industrialization was never so complete in France as it became elsewhere. Types
of workers thus ranged from peasants who supplemented their
income with domestic industry, usually in textiles, to highly skilled
craftsmen in towns and cities who concentrated on luxury items.

Industrial workers, especially in metal production, tended to congregate in towns dominated by a single, large-scale enterprise. Large cities such as Paris, Lyon, and Marseille housed workers of all kinds. Demography also played an important role in the formation of social class and gender roles. While Great Britain's population grew by 350 per cent during the nineteenth century, that of France increased by little more than 30 per cent, from roughly 29 million people in 1801 to 39 million in 1901. Low fertility rates in France produced a persistent labour shortage, resulting in a much higher proportion of women entering the workforce than in other industrializing countries. By 1866, women constituted at least 30 per cent of the industrial labour force, employed mostly in the textile and clothing industries.

Class consciousness in the nineteenth century developed first among artisans engaged in traditional forms of production, rather than in the industrial working class. The slow pace of industrialization partly explains the precociousness of worker consciousness, for its artisan base produced what William Sewell has called a 'corporate idiom' within which the language for militancy emerged. The Revolution of 1789 left a linguistic legacy that shaped artisans' self-conception as workers and as citizens. By 1848, they demanded not only guarantees of the right to work, but also the ability to use their skills to control the means of production—that their work, in short, should confer dignity. This vision encapsulated their conception of liberty and citizenship.

The workers in the area around Saint-Étienne and Lyon exemplify the extraordinary diversity of strategies by which they and their families survived, or failed to survive, in the face of economic transformation. Silk production, which was prevalent in this region, offers a good example of a family-based artisanal industry. Though it did not mechanize, capitalism forced it to restructure. Strong corporate traditions dating to the Old Regime tightly controlled the quality of production, prices, and wages. But as in the case of other crafts, wholesalers increasingly took over the commerce of raw materials and finished products, setting their own standards for prices and quality.

Silk production varied widely, depending on the type of loom used and the final product, ranging from simple looms producing low-quality silk cloth, operated by women weavers in the countryside, to large and complex mechanisms in cities such as Saint-Étienne operated by highly skilled male weavers who produced fancy ribbons. In the first half of the nineteenth century, most urban silk-weavers were men working in their own homes, often employing journeymen. But they also worked very closely with wives who would weave or perform important auxiliary tasks such as winding bobbins, obtaining raw materials from wholesalers, delivering finished products to them, and negotiating prices of materials and labour. Children also participated in the simpler tasks. If the labour of wives and daughters was not needed in the home, they entered workshops that prepared silk for production.

During a century when political rights derived from property, artisans viewed their skills as such, and therefore as a form of patrimony. They expected to pass their skills on to their children as they grew to adulthood. Rather than becoming divided through inheritance as land did, skills were consolidated and fostered strong functional bonds and solidarity. In textile industries daughters and sons of weavers inherited skills, and chose spouses in the same profession. Family and gender roles reinforced occupational identity and determined strategies for preserving that identity in the face of adversity. But preserving the male weaver's artisan identity often came at the expense of his wife and female children who became proletarianized, thus effectively splitting class identity within his own family. For example, in the region around Cholet (Maine-et-Loire) hand-weavers of linen managed to preserve their craft for a century after linen production had become mechanized. They refused to enter into the new factory industries because their identity as men and as fathers derived from their ability to exert control over the production process and to own the means of production. Instead, as their wages declined, they sent their wives and children into unskilled work in shoe and garment production. Wives' and daughters' wages outside the family workshop preserved the fiction of the father-weaver's independence, even as his own wages declined and he became increasingly dependent on merchants for supplies and access to markets.

Thus working-class men and women often occupied different habitats within the world of production—which helps explain why the term 'worker' always refers to a man, unless preceded by the qualification 'woman'—in turn raising the question of whether men and women could even be considered members of the same social class. Working-class women, moreover, had to combine their productive activities with managing households and raising children. Despite the crucial importance of female contributions to working-class families, their wage labour and unpaid household work did not constitute 'property' in the sense that men's work did; less skilled, often interrupted by childbearing, women's work could not provide economic independence.

Craft organizations further reinforced male workers' occupational identity to the exclusion of women. Although the Allarde and Le Chapelier Laws of 1791 made such organizations illegal, craftsmen's associations persisted among a number of trades, particularly in building and small metallurgy, but also among some skilled textile workers, shoemakers, leather-workers, barrel-makers, bakers, hatters, printers, masons, and others. The most common association, the *compagnonnage*, was a brotherhood of journeymen that upheld rituals and traditions dating from the mid-seventeenth century. They made collective efforts to control entry into their trades, and to establish work, product quality, and wage standards. Within these communities workers conceived of themselves as perfecting a mechanical art, a notion starkly contradicting Loyseau's judgement that manual labour could never confer dignity. Mutual aid, elaborate ritual, and extensive socialization characterized these brotherhoods, creating fierce loyalty among the members and ensuring status in local communities. Such associations also created the solidarity necessary for opposing masters and merchants.

It would be a mistake for historians to locate worker identity in their labour alone, or to romanticize the relationship artisans had with their crafts. Although in government reports many artisans spoke of their products with a language of love and pride, in memoirs and autobiographies others described their work lives as dehumanizing drudgery. Worker consciousness did not emerge solely from craft identity. The culture of post-revolutionary society created a desire for full citizenship, for the vote, as well as for the right to have dignity and respect through the consumption of material and cultural products, particularly the right to wear decent clothes and to obtain an education. Such desires grew out of the social-democratic and republican political traditions that originated with the revolutionary crisis of 1789–94, persisted in memory, and were revived in the first half of the nineteenth century.

Artisans such as the glassmakers of Rive-de-Gier and Carmaux, porcelain-workers at Limoges, and silk-workers in Lyon formed and led the labour movement. By 1830 workers' corporations were well established in cities all over France. It must also be noted, however, that corporate values among artisans also impeded working-class consciousness because they fostered vicious rivalries between crafts, and strikes of journeymen against masters within the same craft. Their lack of solidarity was revealed dramatically in the July Revolution of 1830, which ousted the Bourbon monarchy, when for the most part only skilled artisans in Paris made up the crowds that fought royal troops. But the worker insurrections in Lyon in 1831 and 1834 marked the first point at which workers expressed 'class consciousness' in the sense that they began to broaden their identity and conception of 'association' beyond their own trades. Their motto, 'Live Working or Die Fighting', terrified the ruling classes not just in France, but throughout Europe.

Though these outbreaks failed, the lessons were not lost on newly conscious workers, whose activities were driven underground until the 1840s when issues of work organization re-emerged in a new intellectual context. In 1839 and 1840, three influential socialist tracts appeared: Étienne Cabet's *Voyage in Icaria*, Louis Blanc's *The Organization of Labour*, and Pierre-Joseph Proudhon's *What is Property?* These and other publications caused urban workers throughout France to discuss ideas about reorganizing labour on the basis of collective ownership and cooperation. During the 1840s more cohesive views developed about the creativity of labour and its relationship to the state. Workers argued that the latter should emanate from trades organized into corporations that would work together to make a harmonious society. This vision, however, was in itself exclusionary, for it applied only to those in skilled trades, and did not include unskilled industrial workers or women.

As Claire Goldberg Moses has shown, women were more vocal during these years than previously, and feminism re-emerged among some of the groups that came to be known as 'utopian' socialists. Followers of the Comte de Saint-Simon were the first among French socialists to concern themselves with female emancipation. In addition to advocating worker control over the means of production, Saint-Simon's followers organized a 'religion' with an androgynous God, 'Father and Mother', under the leadership of Prosper Enfantin.

Enfantin's originality lay in the fact that he privileged emotion—one of the traits that disqualified women from citizenship in 1793—over reason, believing that only 'love' could provide the necessary bond for a peaceful society. This feminism sought to replace the radical individualism and greed of capitalism with peaceful association. The doctrine might be understood as a further elaboration of the 'gender system' that emerged from the Revolution of 1789, in which women in domestic private life were considered a source of social cohesion and stability. In this utopian socialist framework the same female qualities were valued in the public context of association rather than the private context of the family.

The women attracted to Saint-Simonianism were of both middle- and working-class origin; initially, they concerned themselves more with the emancipation of workers than with the condition of women. They all referred to themselves as 'proletarian' and claimed 'the people' were beginning to understand their own dignity. But the experience of subordination within a movement that advocated egalitarianism made these self-proclaimed 'proletarians' into feminists as well, who believed that women of all classes were oppressed and that their own emancipation would result in the emancipation of the worker. These and other feminist groups organized against the Napoleonic Code, and made explicit demands that mothers have rights over their own children equal to that of fathers, in addition to demands for rights to work, to vote, to sit on juries, to attend universities, and to practise law and medicine. The lives and ideas of these feminists, among whom Flora Tristan was the most renowned, suggest that the utopian socialist movement broke down class and gender boundaries and conceived of progress in terms of those whose rights had been most systematically repressed since the Revolution.

Industrial workers, threatened craftsmen, and indebted small peasants all joined in an anti-capitalist revolt in the Revolution of 1848. The 'corporate idiom' prevailed in skilled workers' articulation of demands for the right to work and for a republic based on representation through corporations. However, the Provisional Government, dominated by middle-class moderates, refused to implement this vision and their method of dealing with the huge number of unemployed eventuated in class warfare. The surtax of 45 per cent to alleviate unemployment drove a wedge between rural France and Paris, further fuelling class tensions. The bloody battle of the 'June

Days' in response to abolition of unemployment assistance destroyed all dreams of fraternity between the working classes and the bourgeoisie, and for a republic that was both democratic and social; class warfare justified the bourgeois perception that urban workers were 'dangerous'.

Demands for political and social rights in 1848 involved women in revolutionary activity just as they had in the Revolution of 1789. Yet this time feminist clubs and newspapers proliferated in unprecedented fashion, and the movement as a whole became the most advanced in the western world. Most feminists, however, were not concerned with their autonomy from men and children, or with their rights as individuals. They instead focused on motherhood as the very reason for greater access to education and the right to participate in civil and political life. They used a paradoxical language asking for rights 'to sacrifice [themselves] to all of humanity', internalizing self-sacrifice as a 'natural' female quality, just as Rousseau and his disciples had done. Like feminists in the early 1790s and 1840s, they argued that this 'private' role had a supremely important public function, suggesting a fluidity in the boundaries between private and public. Indeed, as Karen Offen has shown, the concept of mother-educator not only became a source of dignity for women, but was also used by subsequent French feminists to justify a 'quasi-political' purpose in life despite their formal exclusion from politics. As in 1793, so after the June Days of 1848, the National Assembly prohibited women from further participation in political associations. The coup of 1851 resulted in the severe repression of socialism and feminism, which silenced both movements for most of the Second Empire.

Economic growth, population decline, and the problem of female labour after 1850

The new Bonapartist regime sought to end class conflict through economic expansion and the illusion of political representation. Universal manhood suffrage was restored for the election of the parliament, but elections were tightly controlled and rigged in favour of the élites. The economic boom of the 1850s allowed the regime's strategy of class reconciliation to work for a time, but it also produced further social and cultural change, both in rapidly growing cities and the countryside.

From 1852 to 1880, the urban population grew by 44 per cent, while the overall population grew by only 5 per cent, from 35.8 to 37.7 million. Migration had profound effects on both countryside and city. Improved communications, transportation, market integration, and the development of factory production caused a decline in rural industry in the 1850s and 1860s, making it more difficult for the rural population to rely on a combination of agriculture and domestic industry. Inhabitants of the countryside followed work opportunities into towns and cities, and their departure undermined community cohesion and identity. Young people were either forced by necessity to leave their families, or chose to do so in order to pursue better opportunities. In many regions rural populations also became less dependent on the moral and material support of the clergy, especially as clubs, cafés, and cabarets replaced the church as centres of sociability and entertainment. The *veillée*, a key preserve of oral tradition, also gradually disappeared for the same reasons. Mechanization in agriculture caused a decline in traditional festivities, and thus a deterioration of communal solidarity. The family lost cohesion as well. Sons and daughters, whose migration to towns and cities was facilitated by expanded and cheaper train travel, adopted the more cosmopolitan values of individualism both in the pursuit of occupations and in their choice of marriage partners. They also brought these values back to the countryside. Peasant mimicry of urban fashion, such as their mail-order purchases from the Printemps department store in Paris, symbolized the demise of tradition as well as a transformation in their own sense of subjective desire. Women performed less farm labour, and their activities became more limited to household chores and child-rearing. These changes occurred gradually and unevenly in rural France, but they generally lowered the status of women's work and made gender roles more 'bourgeois' in their differentiation.

Industrial expansion during the Second Empire shifted the balance of labour from artisan craft production to a new proletariat of the factory, iron-forge, and mine. The industrialization of textile production in particular made the 'woman worker' into a much more visible phenomenon: by 1866 women constituted 34.2 per cent of the labour force engaged in manufacturing, and by 1886, this proportion rose to 38.2 per cent. Female labour was a source of debate across the political spectrum, among socialist critics of capitalism as well as conservative social reformers. The latter argued that economic independence (an essential ingredient for citizenship among men) caused disorder and decay in women. Women's wages remained half those of men, and hardly provided for subsistence, let alone independence. But few observers found any injustice in such wage differentials, for political economists reasoned, circuitously, that only men's wages assured the reproduction of the labour force, and neither women's productive nor reproductive labour had, in their view, any 'value-creating status'. Employers calculated men's wages on the basis of individual subsistence, so that if a worker had a family, he was usually compelled to rely on the supplementary labour of his wife and children. Women's wages were calculated on the assumption that they supplemented a family economy rather than providing individual subsistence. Thus men could embody individual liberty through their work, while women, regardless of their work, would remain dependent.

Political economists and social reformers regarded unmarried women workers as a source of moral disorder precisely because their wage-labour was not intended to allow for self-sufficiency, and they feared these women would fall into prostitution for greater economic gain. Thus, just as patriarchy and capitalism intersected within individual families to produce class and gender identities, so they determined the way in which political economists understood the economy and formulated policy. Not only did this mentality prohibit a truly free market for labour, it also sought to ensure 'social cohesion' by denying women the ability to survive independently of families, though not all women had families upon whom they could rely.

Across the political spectrum, in Judith Coffin's words, 'women wage-earners appeared as exploited bodies rather than as underpaid producers or disenfranchized citizens'. The alarming drop in France's crude birth rate (from 28.1 to 20.2 births per 1,000 inhabitants during the nineteenth century) fuelled consternation over female labour in the medical community, whose scientific and political influence had grown considerably. Physicians viewed women's work as incompatible with both motherhood and femininity itself. Reflecting broader literary trends, medical and political discourse also suggested that the use of machines unleashed female sexuality and led to moral decay. Health professionals became increasingly concerned not just with low birth rates, but with high rates of infant mortality, and blamed working women for both. These concerns led to a debate throughout the 1860s about maternal responsibilities, culminating in efforts to eliminate wet-nursing, and in the conviction that women's bodies belonged to their children, not to themselves.

What is remarkable about the literature of the second half of the century—whether in social theory, newspaper articles, novels or plays—is that writers across the political spectrum, from conservatives such as Hippolyte Taine to radicals such as Pierre-Joseph Proudhon, all shared the perception of a crisis in femininity. Emblematic of this theme in fiction, Émile Zola's *Nana* (1880) capped a thirty-year trend in the literary representation of such concerns. Modelled on the true story of the actress Blanche d'Antigny, Nana seduced, betrayed, humiliated, and exploited important men of the upper classes with her irresistible sexuality. For Zola and his readers, she symbolized all that was corrupt in the Second Empire. Not only did she transgress 'true womanhood', but she crossed class boundaries as well. Indeed, the need to police gender also required the policing of class boundaries.

A renewed belief in Rousseau's precepts and the 'ideology of domesticity' offered a remedy for working-class misery and social disorder, which to some degree penetrated the working-class mentality. The ideas of Pierre-Joseph Proudhon epitomized this position and helped promote anti-feminism within the working-class Left. Proudhon's stance on women's roles grew out of his particular version of socialism, which was based on small, independent producers who worked in family workshops. Despite the centrality of family in his vision, Proudhon believed that men and women were so different from one another that they shared no real 'society' between them. Like social reformers of the most conservative hue, he reasoned that impoverished, unstable working-class homes in industrialized towns succumbed to debauchery. His infamous statement that women were either housewives or harlots reflected his own ideological commitment to 'separate spheres', and his belief in women's particular susceptibility to prostitution. He declared (with obvious error) that men did not have the same propensity. He opposed female emancipation because it would weaken the household and home workshop and undermine marriage. Even though Proudhon's notions differed from the bourgeois conception of private and public spheres because it focused on the household organized around work, it paralleled the earlier post-1789 ideologies in considering a homebound, submissive and subordinate role for woman as not only 'natural', but necessary for social cohesion.

Whether workers agreed with Proudhon or not, for the most part they failed to incorporate women into the working-class movement, or argue for their rights, as the utopian socialists had in the 1830s and 1840s. The ideal of a housewife, who could devote herself to making a home and rearing children, emerged within working-class discourse instead. Despite the general rise in standards of living during the Second Empire, most working-class families could not achieve this ideal, particularly in highly industrialized cities such as Lille, where the mortality rate among children under the age of 5 reached 40 per cent. Working-class songs from this city criticized wives who did not work in the mills, blamed them for producing too many children, and castigated them for being too devout and deferential to the clergy.

The early Third Republic and the crisis in gender identity

The Franco-Prussian War and the Paris Commune left behind a deepened sense of national degeneration that compelled politicians, physicians, and 'experts' of all kinds to scrutinize more closely the apparent 'impotence' and 'barrenness' of the French population. These concerns also prompted debate in the Worker Congresses of 1876 and 1879, suggesting that this bourgeois, professional discourse had become part of the way workers understood their own collective experience. At the Congress of 1876, more than one worker expressed the sentiment that, 'the cause [for depopulation in France] is . . . the excessive work our period demands of women, which makes for a poor constitution and renders them incapable of raising and suckling their children.' One socialist echoed the medical view by stating:

The feminine organism is subjected to a certain indisposition owing to her nature, from puberty until menopause. Between the two bodily revolutions, there are periodical illnesses or sufferings that the woman supports more or less easily according to her well-being, hardships and privations that influence her character and render it weak and violent ... that which renders woman improper for industrial work is precisely that which renders her proper for maternity.

Even these delegates thus viewed women workers as 'exploited bodies' who undermined the working class, rather than as human beings worthy of greater recognition for the work they performed, and the rights that their work should grant them. They gave no consideration to the manner in which 'hardships and privations' rendered the male character 'weak and violent'.

The standard interpretation of the early Third Republic is that the rapid defeat by the Prussians and the loss of Alsace-Lorraine between 1870 and 1871, as well as the persistently low birth rate, served to create a profound crisis of confidence in France, which many historians have interpreted as a 'crisis of masculinity'. Reformers and legislators (many of whom were also physicians) considered the defeat and low birth rates to be a sign of 'impotence', the 'degeneration' of the French 'race', and the 'decadence' of French culture. While other western European countries also began to experience lower birth rates in the last third of the nineteenth century, France was distinguished by its sluggish population growth. This raised concerns over women's reluctance to bear children, the apparent 'individualism' that prevented them from doing so, and the figurative if not real 'impotence' of men. The revival of feminism in the late 1860s and the rise of the independent, and often permanently single, 'New Woman' further deepened the alarm about a crisis in gender identity.

The economic expansion and industrialization of the 1850s and 1860s had a lasting impact on class and gender consciousness that had become noticeable by 1880. The mass production of consumer goods, the creation of department stores, the staging of international exhibitions from the 1850s onwards, and the new opportunities for leisure and entertainment, all became focal points of desire, imagination, and 'dream worlds'. Indeed, the emergence of a mass consumer society helped to undermine the consciousness of class difference, and produced new ways for individuals, especially women, to express themselves in the public sphere. The large-scale production of household goods, as well as those items of interior decoration and clothing that mimicked upper-class finery, provided a general appearance of wealth. One social commentator, who analysed the democratization of luxury over the course of two centuries, asked in 1900: 'What does inequality of income matter when it no longer gives rise to inequality in actual enjoyments?' How and what one consumed increasingly became part of one's identity and a source of dignity.

Despite an enduring discourse that pitted the 'Real Woman' against the 'New Woman', and the persistence of the ideology of domesticity, the firm establishment of a republican regime by 1880 resulted in a more open 'public sphere'. The notion that the sexes represented polar opposites began to break down, as did the public/ private dichotomy. This in turn fostered a new tolerance for women as individuals with their own destinies outside the home. Lenard Berlanstein has recently argued that material progress, free-market choices, and mass consumption resulted in the 'open secret' of a 'mass evasion of the ideal of domestic virtue'.

Conclusion

While 'class' and 'gender' as categories of analysis imply differences between people, this chapter has suggested that men and women (though by no means all men and women) across social classes had at least one thing in common throughout the nineteenth century: the pursuit of legitimacy in the public sphere through a claim on human dignity. The working classes—artisans, skilled and unskilled workers—sought dignity through their labour, which also required public recognition of their worth based on what they did, rather than wealth they acquired. Dignity in labour meant control over labour, hence the importance of cooperative experiments and mutual aid societies among artisans. Among peasants, owning one's own farm conferred the highest respect and dignity. This concept does not, in fact, differ all that much from Loyseau's, even though he called work of the hands 'mercenary'. Having control over the use of one's body made profit 'honourable'. Obstacles to these ends, of course, fostered class consciousness and class conflict. The democratization of citizenship undermined what had previously determined workers' consciousness of themselves as a class apart, as did mass consumption.

Although workers maintained an identity of militant opposition through labour organizations after 1880, most of them became integrated into the new Republican order.

But what of women? Their exclusion from the right to vote, the right to hold office, and the right to be witness in a court of law, is a clear indication that they did not achieve the sort of 'dignity' that conferred public power during the period under consideration. Especially after 1789, the 'natural' differences between the sexes became a source of rank, status, and order. Each revolution in France witnessed a blurring of gender and class boundaries, and in the wake of each, a need to reinstate them. Women's work became an issue in every revolution as well, providing the occasion to articulate how it differed from men's work. Fear of population decline, the medical perception that industrial labour ravaged women's bodies, and labour legislation restricting women's work, all placed greater emphasis on women as mothers. Increasingly over the course of the nineteenth century, motherhood became the only 'legitimate' occupation for women. It is not surprising then, that motherhood became so central to French feminism, whose advocates argued that it conferred dignity because it had a public function, and therefore made women worthy of public power. But by its very nature, motherhood could not dignify women as individuals because the socio-medical politics of the Third Republic conceived of women's bodies as belonging to their children (born or unborn), not to the 'body politic'.

Was France unique in its experience of class and gender? We must bear in mind that the language of difference with regard to these categories gave rise to ideologies that might have informed people's understanding of their own experience, but which did not always reflect the reality of that experience. Nonetheless, from 1788 to 1880 the cycle of 'revolution and reaction' compelled those who had political, economic, and cultural power to redefine gender and class distinctions in the wake of social upheaval. In this respect France differed from other modernizing nations. Although the artisanal vision contained within the 'corporate idiom' never became established, workers did succeed in asserting their dignity, and social class ceased being the basis of exclusion from citizenship. Worker militancy certainly persisted, but it attracted fewer adherents than in other countries. By 1880 the political and economic structures that would undermine the practice of separate spheres were largely in place, but the memories of repeated revolutions, defeat in war, and the persistent sense of demographic crisis, all lent more importance to gender difference than in other countries.

5

Town and country

Peter McPhee

Introduction

The northernmost province of Old Regime France was Cambrésis, part of the French kingdom only since 1677. Near the cathedral town of Cambrai was Montigny, a rural community of about 600 people in 1789. During the eighteenth century, large owners and tenants succeeded in monopolizing its land, increasingly specializing in corn, while poorer peasants instead found spinning and weaving linen the answer to poverty. They were part of a flourishing if vulnerable rural industry based on merchants 'putting out' spinning and weaving to rural households. In the Cambrésis, suggests its historian Liana Viardi, 'one could even argue that it is in the eighteenth-century countryside that one encounters entrepreneurship in its purest, most unregulated, form'.

The example of economic change in Montigny highlights a weakness of the diffusion or 'trickling down' model, which remains dominant in writing on the history of relations between town and country. The model assumes, first, that the countryside was peopled by tradition-bound, homogeneous 'peasants' and, secondly, that processes of economic, social, and political change began with towns and their educated inhabitants enlightening the rural masses. This urban-centred model is so pervasive because of the bureaucratic structures which created the records historians work with when they study rural societies. These bureaucracies were organized hierarchically in an urban network descending from Paris to regional capitals and villages; implicit in their procedures was a hierarchical model of the dissemination and collecting of information. Public officials generated an enormous body of material recording those elements of rural life they deemed important: censuses, land surveys, agricultural statistics, and reports on public order. Little of this material relates to how rural people made sense of their world, and even less is in their own words. This remains the central methodological problem in writing about relations between town and country.

Town and country under the Old Regime

Perhaps 28 million people inhabited France in 1788. Using a measure of an urban community as having 2,000 people, perhaps two persons in ten lived in an urban centre. The great majority inhabited 40,000 rural communities or parishes with an average of about 600 residents. These parishes were the smallest units of an administrative hierarchy which claimed sovereignty over the king's territory. The institutional structures of public life—in administration, customs, and measures, the law, taxation, and the Church—everywhere bore the imprint of privilege and historical accretion across seven centuries of territorial expansion by the monarchy. The Corbières region of Languedoc, for example, was a geographically well-defined area whose 129 parishes all spoke Occitan, with the exception of three Catalan villages on its southern border. Yet the region was divided for administrative, ecclesiastical, judicial, and tax purposes between Carcassonne, Narbonne, Limoux, and Perpignan. These boundaries were not consistent: for example, neighbouring villages administered from Perpignan were in different dioceses. There were ten different volumes for which the term *setier* was used (normally about 85 litres), and no fewer than fifty different measures of area: the *sétérée* ranged from just 0.16 hectares on the lowlands to 0.51 in highland areas.

The monarchy had sought to impose linguistic uniformity by requiring priests and those in the liberal professions to use French. However, France in the 1780s was a society in which people's main allegiance was to their particular province or *pays*. In daily life most subjects of Louis XVI spoke their own language or dialect, and lived within distinctive cultures. Several million people in Languedoc spoke variants of Occitan; Flemish was spoken in the north-east; German in Lorraine. There were minorities of Basques, Catalans, and Celts. Cultural unity across France lay essentially in formal adherence to Christianity, especially Catholicism. The Church also played a social role as the centre of information and access to outside news. As the most literate person in small communities and as the person who read government decrees as well as sermons at mass, the priest was everywhere a key intermediary with the outside world. Moreover, in regions of dispersed dwellings, such as parts of the West and much of the Massif Central, Sunday mass was the time when the parish felt its communal identity.

Regional cultures and minority languages and dialects were underpinned by economic structures which sought to meet the needs of the household within a regional or micro-regional market. The rural economy was essentially a peasant economy: that is, household-based agrarian production had a primarily subsistence orientation, a complex, polycultural system which sought to produce as much as possible of a household's consumption needs. Paradoxical as it may seem, rural France was also the centre of most manufacturing. The textile industry in particular was largely based on women's part-time work in Normandy, the Velay, and Picardy. Rural industry of this type was linked to regional specialities centred on provincial towns, such as sheepskin gloves in Millau, ribbons in Saint-Étienne, lace in Le Puy, and silk in Lyon. A rural world in which households engaged in a highly complex occupational strategy to secure their own subsistence could inevitably expect only low yields for grain crops grown in unsuitable or exhausted soil. Consequently most rural communities had restricted 'surpluses' which could be marketed to substantial towns; far more important were nearby small towns or *bourgs*, centres of micro-regions whose weekly, monthly or annual market-fairs were as much an occasion for the collective rituals of local cultures as for the exchange of produce.

Rural communities consumed so much of what they produced that towns and cities faced both chronic problems of food supply and a limited rural demand for their goods and services. However, although only 20 per cent of French people lived in urban communities, in a European context France was remarkable for the number and size of its towns. Apart from Paris, with between 550,000 and 700,000 inhabitants, there were seven cities with more than 50,000 people (Lyon, Marseille, Bordeaux, Nantes, Lille, Rouen, and Toulouse), and another seventy with 10,000–40,000. These cities and towns all had large-scale manufacturing and were involved in an international trading network, but most—including Paris—were dominated by artisan-type craftwork for the needs of the urban population itself and the immediate hinterland, and by a range of administrative, judicial, ecclesiastical, and policing functions; they were provincial capitals. Only one person in forty lived in Paris, and communication between the government at Versailles and the rest of its territory was usually slow and uncertain.

The solution to the paradox of how an essentially peasant society could sustain so many substantial towns and cities lies in the functions these provincial centres fulfilled in the eighteenth century. In an important sense, inland towns were parasitic on the countryside, for the bulk of the seigneurial dues, rents, tithes, and fees collected by the first two estates of the realm were spent in urban centres. To return to the example with which this chapter began, the cathedral chapter of Cambrai drew its wealth from properties in villages like Montigny, where it owned 46 per cent of the total area in 1754. It was also the seigneur of the village, though this was a region where the feudal regime weighed lightly. In Angers, in western France, the clergy (1.5 per cent of the population) owned some 75 per cent of urban property; clerks, carpenters, cooks, and cleaners depended on them, as did the lawyers who ran the Church's fifty-three legal courts for the prosecution of rural defaulters on tithes and rents on its vast estates. In the countryside around Angers, the Benedictine abbey of Ronceray owned five manors, twelve barns and wine-presses, six mills, forty-six farms, and six houses, bringing an annual revenue of 27,000 livres into the town.

However, the most important link between town and country was the supply of foodstuffs. In times of dearth, tension mounted over rival claims to the grains and wheat that constituted the staple diet of working people. Town and country were linked in many other ways, for example, by the practice of wet-nursing. About half of the 20,000 babies born in Paris each year were sent to wet-nurses in Normandy, Picardy and the Champagne; one-third would die before their mothers saw them again. A human trade of another kind involved scores of thousands of men from highland areas with a long 'dead season' in winter who migrated to towns seasonally, or for years at a time, to look for work.

The series of revolts which erupted in the spring and summer of 1789 therefore occurred in a society characterized by the primacy of regional identities within a territory over which the absolute monarchy had a limited hold. Nevertheless, the invitation to rural people to participate in the formulation of *cahiers de doléances* and elections to the Estates-General was enthusiastically welcomed. In the small parishes of rural Normandy, for instance, some 85 per cent of those eligible to vote did so. Then, once the monarchy proved incapable of managing the reform process, the summer and autumn of 1789 was the occasion for the collapse of centuries of royal state-making. The taking of the Bastille was only the most spectacular instance of the popular conquest of local power. In many rural areas, fear of aristocratic revenge added to the hope of change to make the hungry countryside a tinderbox. Fear escalated into a 'Grande Peur' ignited by imagined sightings of 'brigands' destroying ripening crops. Bush fires of panic, racing from village to village, engulfed most of the countryside. Once the feared noble forces failed to materialize, village militias instead turned their weapons on the system itself, compelling seigneurs or their agents to hand over feudal registers to be burned on the village square.

The French Revolution

From 1789 to 1791, revolutionaries reshaped every aspect of institutional and public life according to principles of rationality, uniformity, and humanity. The bedrock of this sweeping, energetic programme of reform was a new, uniform administrative system. The 40,000 new communes, usually the same as the old parishes, served as the base for a nested hierarchy of cantons, districts, and eighty-three departments. The departments were designed to facilitate the accessibility of administration (each capital was to be no more than a day's ride from any commune) and were to be administered in precisely the same way, with an identical structure of responsibilities, personnel and powers. The creation of this new map of France was the work of urban élites with a distinctive vision of spatial organization and institutional hierarchy. It was designed to give reality to two of their key words: to 'regenerate' the nation while cementing its 'unity'. The departments also represented an important, pre-emptive victory of the new state over the resurgent provincial identities expressed since

1787. Their very names, drawn from rivers, mountains, and other natural features, undercut claims to other provincial and ethnic loyalties: the Basque country would be the 'Basses-Pyrénées', not the 'Pays Basque'.

Diocesan boundaries now coincided with departmental limits. All French citizens, whatever their social background and residence, were to be judged according to a single uniform legal code, and taxed by the same obligatory proportional taxes on wealth, especially landed property. The uniformity of administrative structures was reflected, later, in the imposition of a national, decimal system of weights, measures, and currency. These evident benefits to business and commerce were accentuated by the abolition of tolls and internal customs: there was to be free trade within a national market.

The revolutionary project of creating a citizenry which would express its sovereignty through the uniform institutional structures of a regenerated nation faced its greatest challenge after the declaration of war on Austria and Prussia in 1792. By mid-1793, the Republic proclaimed the previous September was at war with most of Europe, with foreign troops on its soil in the south-west, south-east and north-east. A year later the military challenge had been met, by an extraordinary mobilization of the nation's resources and repression of opponents: the Terror. Essential to this mobilization was the creation by the Jacobin government of a rural–urban alliance by a mixture of intimidation, force, and policies aimed at popular grievances: seigneurial dues were finally abolished, and price and wage controls were introduced.

However, the military success of the Terror came at an enormous cost in human life, and most victims of the Terror were peasants, not aristocrats. In western France in particular, rejection of the Revolution and its demands in 1793 was to escalate into a civil war—known, like the region itself, as 'the Vendée'—which resulted in perhaps as many as 200,000 deaths on both sides. The immediate cause of rebellion was a national levy of 300,000 conscripts in March 1793. The underlying causes of the rebellion, however, lay in the rejection by western rural communities of a Revolution which they had come to see as godless, bourgeois, and urban. The departments south of the Loire where violence flared were in a region of *bocage* (scattered farms separated by high hedgerows), poor communications with the outside world, and a mix of subsistence farming and cattle-raising, with textile production based in small village centres (*bourgs*). The exactions of seigneurs and the state before 1789 had been comparatively light. A numerous, locally recruited, well-remunerated and active clergy played a pivotal social role in this region of dispersed habitat.

In this region, the Revolution's local government law created a puzzling separation of municipality and vestry by excluding many men and all women used to discussing parish matters after mass. State taxes were now heavier and collected more rigorously by local bourgeois who also monopolized new offices and municipal councils, and bought up church lands in 1791. Priests rejected the Revolution's imposition of an urban, civic concept of priesthood and the zealous enforcement of reforms to the Church by bourgeois officials in Angers, long characterized by their hostility to clerical wealth and values. Esteemed local clergy were further encouraged in their stand by community disappointment with the Revolution. The conscription decree focused peasant hatreds, for the bourgeois officials who enforced it were exempt from the ballot. Whereas the republican 'blues' were mainly bourgeois, artisans, and shopkeepers, the rebels represented a cross-section of rural society. The cleavage between town and country was expressed in rebel songs threatening that 'You'll perish in your towns, cursed *patauds* (bourgeois patriots), Just like caterpillars, Your feet in the air'.

The local terrain suited guerilla-type ambushes and retreat, and exacerbated a vicious cycle of killing and reprisals by both sides convinced of the treachery of the other. For the republican troops, the rebels were superstitious and cruel, manipulated in their ignorance by malevolent priests and nobles. For the rebels, the extent of the reprisals—which some historians incorrectly describe as 'genocide'—reinforced an image of Paris which was to be widely held in many rural areas for the next century. Reports of the bloodshed at the Bastille in July 1789 and the 'September massacres' of 1792, in which perhaps 1,200 prisoners were summarily killed on the streets of Paris, horrified rural people. Paris, the capital of enlightenment and government, was also imagined as the capital of blood.

While the Republic ultimately crushed the rebellion in the Vendée, successive regimes were to face extraordinary resistance to their demands for conscripts, especially once wars of revolutionary defence became wars of territorial expansion in 1794. In September 1798, the

Directory introduced an annual conscription of single men aged 20–25 years (the Jourdan Law), sharply intensifying resentment of military service. It both increased the numbers of healthy young men removed from the household to fight on foreign, often distant, soil and also introduced a system of 'replacements' whereby wealthy conscripts could buy a substitute from among poor or unemployed young men who had missed the ballot. Again, those regions where the hold of the royal state before 1789 had been weakest, or which had been incorporated more recently into the state (such as parts of the West, Massif Central and the Pyrenees), particularly resented the exactions of a more intrusive state. In areas far from Paris, draft evasion and desertion became endemic, often with the tacit approval of most of the community. The Napoleonic Empire encountered similar limitations to the control it claimed over the countryside. From 1808 onwards, resistance to the levies of young men and taxes again became endemic: by 1810, there were some 160,000 deserters from the armies, often in bands who worked, stole and intimidated officials with the complicity of the local community. The imperial regime pursued the deserters and draft evaders relentlessly and punitively; however, its lack of success pointed to the crumbling support for the regime and the limits to acceptance of the state's demands in many areas of the countryside.

The impact of the Revolution

Nevertheless, those peasants who owned their own land were direct and substantial beneficiaries of the Revolution. As a result of land sales, the total of peasant holdings increased from perhaps one-third to two-fifths of the area of France, and they were no longer subject to the tithe or seigneurial exactions. The incidence of such exactions had varied enormously, but a total weight of 20–25 per cent of the produce of peasant proprietors (not to mention the costs of seigneurial monopolies and other irregular payments) was common outside the west of France. Producers now retained an extra portion of their output which was often directly consumed by a better-fed population. In the isolated village of Pont-de-Montvert (Lozère), where chestnuts had been a staple food, only one man in seven was 1.6

metres tall in 1792; by 1830 this was the average height. The retention of a greater share of produce also increased the safety margin for middling and larger peasant landholders and made the risks of market specialization more acceptable. In the countryside around Bayeux in Normandy, for example, the heavy, damp soils were quickly converted to cattle-raising once the Church ceased exacting a fixed tithe in grain.

The example of Bayeux points to a most important dimension of the impact of the Revolution: a watershed in rural–urban relations. In many ways the provincial centres of Old Regime institutions had been parasitic on the countryside: cathedral chapters, religious orders, and nobles had extracted 'surplus' from peasants which was expended in provincial towns through the direct employment of domestic servants, the indirect maintenance of skilled trades, especially in luxury goods, and the provision of charity. By 1830 the population of Bayeux had declined by 15 per cent, leaving administrators, those involved in the rich cattle and dairy industries, and farm suppliers, but fewer artisans. As a direct result of the Revolution, the countryside liberated itself from urban seigneurial and episcopal control, leaving marketing and administration as the remaining links.

The reforms and wars of the revolutionary period had disparate effects on rural economies. In the southern department of the Aude, for example, the ending of seigneurial and church exactions, coupled with the collapse of the textile industry, encouraged peasants to turn to wine as a cash crop. During the thirty years after 1789, the estimates provided by mayors for the area under vines in the department showed an increase of 75 per cent, from 29,000 to 51,000 hectares. The volume of wine produced may well have trebled to 900,000 hecto-litres at the same time. On the other hand, at the northern extremity of the country, in Montigny and its region of Cambrésis, the period saw the collapse of the distinctive rural textile economy. The free trade treaty with England in 1786 had been a body blow to the textile industry; now the revolutionary and imperial wars of 1792–1815, which swept back and forth across the region, would destroy the market for linen. When the vast church lands were sold as national property after 1790, the merchant-weavers rushed to buy them as a refuge from a collapsing industry. Consequently, by 1815 the country-side was again as rural as it had been a century earlier, and a reconstructed textile industry was later centred in towns.

The Revolution and Empire everywhere had a profound impact on collective identity, on the *francisation* or 'Frenchification' of the citizens of a new society. This jump in collective consciousness was in part due to participation in elections and referenda within a national context; while turnout was generally below 30 per cent, elections created a radical shift in assumptions about the political arena. So did the revolutionary change in the focus of legitimacy, from divinely ordained monarch to nation, however narrowly defined. Electoral participation was often as high in small rural communities as in towns. Moreover, during the years of revolutionary and imperial wars, millions of young rural conscripts were mixed within a French national military bureaucracy, and exposed to the language of France, *patrie*, and nation. Social élites among linguistic minorities now accepted the necessity, even the virtue, of facility in French. However, this new 'double identity' was limited to an acceptance of national institutions and a French political discourse: there is little evidence that popular cultures and minority languages were thereby eroded. French remained the daily language of a minority and rural France a land of great cultural and linguistic diversity.

For the first time, the state was invested with the resonance of being the institutional form of a more emotional entity, 'the nation'; it also became more powerful and intrusive. Just three months after seizing power, Napoleon issued a new administrative decree on 16 February 1800 (28 Pluviôse VIII) which effectively reduced local government to a rubber stamp: henceforth councils were to restrict themselves to the management of communal finances and resources within rigid limits of control. The mayors and deputy-mayors of towns with more than 5,000 people were to be directly appointed by Napoleon himself, while others were to be named by the prefect in charge of the department. The prefect was the most powerful local face of the regime in every department, directing political and civil police and able to draw upon the Minister of War's gendarmerie, some 30,000 strong by 1811.

The primary nexus in public life was now that between the individual and the state. Before 1789, the major form of redistribution of wealth or surplus extraction had been the payment of 'tribute' of various types to the state, the Church, and seigneurs. By 1815 the claims of the privileged orders were irredeemably lost; now wealth was appropriated from its rural producers by the state and through relations of production (through rent, markets and labour). The state alone could levy tribute of taxes, men and obedience, indicating its pre-eminence as an agent of social control. Accordingly, the new state had a more pressing need for reliable, precise information about human and physical resources and political attitudes. After 1800 in particular, a uniform, hierarchical apparatus of administration provided the vehicle through which an internal army of civil engineers, military officers, statisticians, and bureaucrats described, measured and counted. The dominance of the nation-state in the collection of taxes and information and in the policing of its citizens was reflected in the number of its officers: from fewer than a thousand employees in the 1780s, the central bureaucracy in Paris swelled to 25,000 by 1810.

The new bureaucracy's population censuses, economic surveys, topographical descriptions and land registers are prized by historians, but they also furnish an insight into the attitudes of senior officials who decided what they needed to know and how to categorize it. For example, the land registers or *cadastres* commenced in 1807 were predicated on the assumptions of mathematical exactitude and private property: every metre of the country was to be owned by an individual, a commune, or the state, and its tax liability assessed according to its productive value. A land of enormous diversity in resource use and culture became thereby a socially constructed map of individuals and private property uniformly measured, taxed and valued. The attitudes of the Napoleonic élite also expressed a *mentalité* which assumed a hierarchy of capacity, civilization, and race, inside as well as outside France. In 1800, prefectoral responses to a ministerial enquiry into France's regional nature and resources resorted to a dualistic imagery, privileging Paris over the provinces, plains over mountains, town over country, bourgeois over peasant, north (except Brittany) over south, French over patois, and men over women. Such distinctions were imputed to climatic factors as well as to occupation or gender: the typical southerner was 'as variable as his climate; he is uncouth, brutal, lively, passionate, lazy or taciturn'.

Changes in urban and rural France, 1815–1848

The population of France grew 16 per cent (from 30.5 to 35.4 million) in the years 1821–46. The population of rural communities, those with fewer than 2,000 inhabitants, increased significantly, from 23.4 to 26.9 million between 1811 and 1841 (constituting about four-fifths of the total). Moreover, most centres of up to 10,000 people were also 'rural', for, while some small towns were essentially industrial, most were directly dependent on the rural economy. About one-tenth of the national population lived in these country towns. The urban population as a whole grew quickly, by 0.7 per cent annually from 1811 to 1831, then by 1 per cent per annum over the next twenty years. Urban France was as diverse as the countryside around it. There were stable, long-established administrative and trading centres (Bordeaux, Nantes), old cities where new industries unleashed a rapid spurt of social change and population increase (Limoges, Saint-Étienne), declining towns whose administrative or economic importance had withered away during the Revolution and Empire (Beaucaire, Autun), and new, mono-industrial factory cities (Decazeville, Le Creusot, Roubaix, Montceau-les-Mines). Every town and city remained tied to its hinterland by a nexus of administrative, military, and economic functions and through its workforce: in 1820, some 17 per cent of Perpignan's 12,500 inhabitants were agricultural labourers and market-gardeners. In makeshift suburbs (*faubourgs*), on the semi-rural edges of expanding cities such as Lyon and Reims, congregated increasing numbers of rural migrants who aroused in élites a morbid fear of 'marginals', seen as semi-urban and semi-civilized. On the 'margins of city life', in John Merriman's phrase, were the liminal spaces between town and country, peopled by 'marginal' groups.

The first half of the nineteenth century was remarkable for the extent of geographical mobility between town and country. The inability of most households to acquire or rent enough land to sustain their members, even with textile work, lay behind the mobility of much of the rural population. Up to 500,000 people left their home department each year (many more moved about within their own department) to work elsewhere in order to supplement the household budget. Most of these seasonal migrants went to other rural areas at harvest-time, but there were long-standing and increasing links with particular cities: 10,000 Savoyards went to factories in Lyon, while 25,000–35,000 Creusois walked for weeks to Paris to work in the building trades. Such departures, which were usually seasonal but could be for years at a time, were part of an ancient economic cycle of temporary migrations which had never been as extensive as in the first half of the nineteenth century and involved one in five rural families. A different type of movement continued to link the increasing number of urban women seeking wet-nurses for their infants in the rural hinterlands of Paris, Lyon, and Marseille. Meanwhile, from 1816 to 1831, 12,700 prostitutes were registered in Paris, two-thirds of them young provincial migrants. This rural mobility and increasing contact with 'corrupting' urban centres added urgency to the Church's crusade to recapture its social authority by rechristianizing the countryside through missions, religious education, and clerical rejuvenation.

In most parts of France, however, the Revolution had undermined the patterns of deference which the Restoration monarchy sought to recreate. The monarchy's own policies also antagonized many rural people. For example, a new National Forest Code in 1827 restricted the entry of livestock to wooded areas. At the same time, owners of private forests were closing off access, in defiance of ancient customary rights to forest resources, as wood became an increasingly valuable commodity in the expanding charcoal-fuelled metallurgical industry. Between May 1829 and March 1831 bands of peasants in the Ariège department of the central Pyrenees intimidated forest guards and charcoal-burners and attacked the property of forest and forge-owners. The rioters were all men but—commonly wearing women's headscarves and their long woollen shirts outside their trousers, belted like dresses—they presented themselves as 'demoiselles', perhaps as a disguise which would prevent recognition. News of the Revolution of July 1830 in Paris transformed the nature of these mountain protests. Larger groups of peasants now dropped their disguises: tax offices were raided and forges destroyed as rioters openly confronted local power-holders and the state rather than their employees. In the process, the peasantry made this revolution their own. The battle cry of the parliamentary opposition in Paris was

'Liberty!' (in terms of political and civil freedoms); the peasants of the Ariège took up the cry and adapted it to their own cause of free access to the forests. The new government made concessions to the protesters in 1831, though without surrendering its claim to control forest resources.

The constitutional monarchy of Louis-Philippe established in 1830 was the most stable regime France had known since 1789, in large measure because of its internal repression of dissent and maintenance of external peace. Together these policies facilitated the embedding of national structures in rural France; it was in these years, for example, that the first effective controls were placed on smuggling, hitherto endemic along the thinly policed mountain frontiers and coasts. The regime also introduced two pieces of legislation which were to have a profound effect on rural life and the relation between urban and rural politics and culture. First, from 1831 municipal councils were once again to be elected rather than appointed, as they had been under the Empire and Restoration, and in communities of fewer than 1,000 people the wealthiest 10 per cent of the population (up to 40 per cent of adult males) were able to vote. After thirty years of state tutelage politics made a legal reappearance in every village. Almost 3 million adult males were eligible to vote for municipal councils, fifteen times the number in national elections.

Secondly, in 1833, laws proposed by François Guizot required communes to provide a primary school for boys. By mid-century there were still 2,690 communes (about one in fourteen) without schools, but the number of primary students had increased from fewer than 2 million in 1832 to 3.5 million (62 per cent of whom were boys) in 1847. Most of those schools were rural in every way: children attended school for four or five years after turning six, but only in the winter months when their farm labour was not essential. While there were in many areas deep-seated economic and cultural obstacles to schooling, especially for girls, the increased emphasis being placed on facility in written French would have important consequences for minority cultures. In general, these cultures were oral: relatively few people were literate in their own daily language. French was not only the language of the bureaucracy and of social élites, but young rural people in particular were now increasingly exposed to French as the language of the written word, indeed as somehow signifying 'progress' itself.

The political economy of the July Monarchy (1830–48) created a political climate and infrastructure for accelerated agricultural change. But, whatever the importance of large-scale capitalist enterprise, the most significant aspect of agrarian change after 1830 was that it was due to more intensive and specialized agriculture on smallholdings in specific areas. Much of this produce was sold at local market-fairs: some 6,000 small towns and *bourgs* held regular days of marketing for the exchange of produce, as much a socio-cultural occasion as a market. Other marketing networks were more extensive, for the buying and selling of commodities within a regional, national, or even international market: transport from the Burgundian Côte-d'Or by cart and canal carried over 200,000 hectolitres of wine the 300 kilometres to Paris each year.

In the first half of the century, France's largest industry, clothing and textiles, remained mainly rural and decentralized. Over 40,000 rural workers were engaged in the woollen industry of Champagne, and there were 25,000 textile workers in silk, cotton, and linen in a 50-kilometre radius around Saint-Quentin (Aisne). Above all, rural industry involved part-time work by women. There were 40,000 lace-makers in the Calvados and 145,000 textile-workers in the Seine-Inférieure (in the village of Auffay studied by Gay Gullickson, two-thirds of women earned money in this way). Such work was closely integrated into the rhythms of the agricultural year: these women also spent three or four months working on the land. In contrast, most southern industry was artisanal and centred in small towns: in the *bourgs* around Brignoles (Var), for example, there were perfumeries, soap and paper works, and tanneries (fifteen in Barjols alone). In the upland areas south of Brignoles, there were hundreds of cork-makers and workers in small lignite mines and forges.

For many inhabitants of cities, the countryside was a monochrome land of 'peasants', despite the complexities of social status and occupation which in fact characterized every rural community. Rural communities often sustained a remarkable range of occupations. The village of Gabian, north of Béziers in the department of the Hérault, had fewer than 1,000 inhabitants, but in the 1840s its winegrowing economy supported an innkeeper, a barber, two butchers, two bakers, two saddlers, two café-keepers, a road-mender, a hat-maker, a cart-builder, six boot-makers, three boiler-makers, a surveyor, several teachers, six stonemasons, two merchants, three blacksmiths, four carpenters, a notary, a health officer, a tax-collector, four plasterers, a second-hand clothes seller, a locksmith, three tailors, a weaver, a shearer, and two wine-barrel makers.

The mid-century crisis, 1846–1852

The July Monarchy was the first regime in French history to consistently follow a policy of non-intervention in the workings of the rural market-place, and in turn was seen as a heartless regime dominated by urban financiers. The failure of the grain and potato harvests in 1846 led to waves of food rioting across much of northern France during the following winter. However, once the July Monarchy was succeeded by the Second Republic in February 1848, rural people were to manifest striking new forms of political behaviour. First, whereas during the 1790s the levels of electoral participation had rarely risen above 30 per cent, in town or country, the first elections by direct, universal manhood suffrage in April 1848 attracted an 84 per cent turnout. Secondly, in the legislative elections of May 1849, in an atmosphere of political polarization and continuing socio-economic tension in many regions, rural voters responded to party lists of departmental candidates. The results were to reveal regional political tendencies that would characterize French political life until the 1980s. Conservative candidates of the 'party of Order' won about 53 per cent of the votes nationwide, *démocrates-socialistes* or 'reds' 35 per cent, and 'moderate' republicans 12 per cent. There were three great areas of success for the party of Order: in the north-east and Normandy, Brittany, and the West. The Left, on the other hand, polled heavily in areas on the Mediterranean littoral, the south-east, and in parts of central France.

The regional variations reveal the importance of urban–rural relations and of memory, particularly of the years of Revolution and Empire. The political geography of mid-century France is best explained in terms of the economic and social structures of a community or region and the historically conditioned perceptions its people had of the world in which they lived. Regions which voted for the Party of Order often produced cattle and grain for urban markets: voters had few contacts with urban populations and were united in their mistrust of towns personified by unscrupulous merchants. In many subsistence areas, too, the programme of the Left seemed of little relevance, and notables and priests were able to use their control of information to paint the 'reds' as enemies of the Church, the family, and honest toil. The acquiescence of the economically vulnerable in the continued pre-eminence of local élites was reinforced in areas where there was a historic mistrust of republicanism dating back to the religious battles of the French Revolution, nourished by the vigorous campaigns of a renascent Church after 1800.

In contrast, the rural heartlands of the Left were characterized by multifaceted economic activity and links with towns in the production of foodstuffs, artisanal manufactures and raw materials (such as wine, tools, silk, animal skins, and cork). Such products required a range of urban–rural contact and work processes, united producers with urban consumers in opposition to indirect taxes on foodstuffs, and facilitated popular contestation of the power of local élites. These, too, were often areas where there had been a significant base of popular support for the French Revolution's abolition of seigneurialism and reform of the Church. It was in rural areas such as these, too, that the *coup d'état* of Louis-Napoleon in December 1851 met angry resistance. While some form of protest occurred in fifty-six departments, armed resistance was concentrated in thirteen departments in the centre, the south-west, the Mediterranean littoral and the southeast. Perhaps 70,000 people, from 775 communes, actually took up arms in the largest rural insurrection since the 1790s. Some 27,000 of them, mainly rural and small-town people, would be tried and sentenced.

Change in town and country, 1850–1880

Despair at the hopes for social change in the countryside after 1851 quickened the rate of departure of the poorest sections of rural society. By the mid-nineteenth century the population of rural France had reached its historic peak (27 million) and the cultivated land surface its maximum. The rural population had already begun to decline across about 40 per cent of the country; after 1851, this decline became an exodus which was never to be reversed. In the years 1851 to

1856, the population of rural France declined by 579,000, then by 70,000 annually. By 1866 sixty-five departments had experienced an excess of emigration over natural increase. Those who left were overwhelmingly farm-labourers, wholly or partly dependent on wagework: between 1862 and 1882 alone, the numbers of full-time labourers and farm servants declined by over 257,000, while the total of labourers who also owned a tiny plot fell by over 407,000.

In contrast, these decades were a time of unprecedented growth and importance for large towns: the total urban population grew by 44 per cent to over 13 million between 1851 and 1881, while the three biggest cities, Paris, Lyon, and Marseille, more than trebled in size. However, not only was French urban growth gradual within the context of northern Europe, but the spectacular surge in cities like Paris, Roubaix and Saint-Étienne was atypical; indeed, the experience of ancient southern textile centres such as Lodève was rather one of decline. Urban France in 1880, as in 1780, was still predominantly a slowly changing world of country towns and regional centres. Half of the urban population lived in towns of fewer than 10,000 people. These were essentially agro-towns with artisanal small industry, which serviced the rural hinterland as administrative, marketing, and cultural centres. Certainly, however, the rapid extension of rail networks was transforming marketing structures: by 1870 Paris was drawing its foodstuffs from as far afield as 250 kilometres, compared with just 50 under the July Monarchy.

In many parts of the countryside, the Second Empire (1852–70) was a period of stability and prosperity and remained genuinely popular. In the north of the Dordogne, for example, long-standing hatred of nobles, anticlericalism, and mistrust of urban radicals had combined with unprecedented prosperity to generate a fervent Bonapartism. News of reverses in the Franco-Prussian war, in the summer of 1870, reached the drought-afflicted countryside at the same time as the anxious villagers around Hautefaye were attending a market and celebrating Napoleon's saint's-day, on 15 August. A young nobleman accused of shouting 'Long live the Republic!' was deemed a 'Prussian', systematically beaten for two hours by a crowd of up to 800 chanting 'Long live Napoleon!', and then burned to death. However, in other areas news of the Emperor's capture and the proclamation of the Republic on 4 September was the signal for enthusiastic proclamations by rural municipal councils, and Bonapartists were purged from local councils. Yet, despite such support for the new Republic, and a ready acceptance of the Emperor's fall almost everywhere, the national elections of February 1871 were a disaster for the republicans. They only won about 150 of the 650 seats in the National Assembly, the overwhelming majority being royalists of various hues.

The term 'rural' carried a sharp pejorative edge around 1870: the appalling murder at Hautefaye in August 1870 and the conservative Assembly elected in February 1871 confirmed urban, bourgeois republicans in their belief that the countryside was primitive and reactionary. During the century after 1780, the categories 'urban' and 'rural' were constructs dominated by such presuppositions. Peasants—a term used interchangeably with 'rural'—were for most urban people a distinct mass about whom contradictory cultural certainties were expressed. They were assumed to be naive, credulous and superstitious and yet cunning and suspicious; they personified the passive, toiling, long-suffering backbone of the rural virtues, but were susceptible in their ignorance to unreasoning violence, as at Hautefaye. In return, Paris, and to a lesser extent Lyon, were seen by countryfolk to be insatiable in their thirst for the nation's riches and in their taste for insurrection.

The rural response to the crisis of 1871 was in fact far more complex than a simple reflection of conservative, peasant, provincial France. The victory of royalist notables in February was partly due to the speed of the elections; in the space of the single week allowed for campaigning, it was inevitably well-known notables who were best placed. Thereafter, at a local level and particularly in the south, the years from 1871 to 1877 were a time of protracted conflict over the nature of the new regime, between the forces of social order and republicans of various types. This lengthy political process which took place between 1868 and 1877 paralleled those transitions that occurred from 1828 to 1834 and 1846 to 1852. However, on this occasion the outcome was radically different. In the legislative elections of 20 February 1876, for the first time, the majority of Frenchmen clearly chose a republican regime as the best guarantee of civil liberties and social progress. Whereas in 1849 the *démocrates-socialistes* had won more than 50 per cent of the vote in just sixteen departments, now republicans polled a majority in fifty-one. The west of the Massif Central, the east and the south remained their heartlands, but republicans had even made successful inroads into parts of the north-east and the west where fewer than 20 per cent had voted for the left in 1849. On the other hand, parties of the Right continued to dominate Brittany, Normandy, the west and south-west, and Bonapartist candidates continued to do well in some regions.

The response of MacMahon's government of 'moral Order' was to counter-attack by dissolving the Assembly and unleashing a punitive purge of local officials and associations. However, in new elections on 14 October 1877, the republican victory of the previous year was repeated: this was a significant turning point in French political history. In some regions, certainly such as the Vendée, the Republic was long mistrusted for its secularism, and its consolidation served to revivify negative memories dating from the 1790s. Yet the understanding of popular sovereignty as meaning periodic electoral participation had now become embedded in mass political culture. The percentage of adult males who voted in national elections during the Second Republic ranged from 68 to 84, under the Second Empire from 63 to 82, and under the Third Republic from 69 to 85. The victory of electoral democracy was not unchallenged: three times during the past century, in 1799, 1815, and 1851, the seizure of power 'from above' had resolved political instability and social fears. These events left a potent legacy in French public life: the lure of the strong man supported by the army.

Changes to political culture by 1880 were part of a wider process in the formation of the French nation-state. In the decades after 1789 the 'nation' became the symbolic legitimation of the state's coercive powers. This legitimation also drew on the attachment of hundreds of thousands of rural people to whom the state offered employment, depending on social background, as administrators, teachers, gendarmes, road and rail workers. For example, army officers were disproportionately drawn from departments close to the frontiers: three of Napoleon's generals were born in the south-western village of Lagrasse (Aude). Never before had the state had such an uncontested hold on the lives and loyalties of French people. By 1880 it was widely perceived as the administrative and political essence of an older, deeper universal entity claiming an almost timeless reality. This perception was moulded by decades of involvement in the educational, political, institutional, and commercial structures of a territory which, since 1789, had elided national identity and citizenship. The celebration of Bastille Day as an annual festival after 1880 symbolized this national culture at the same time as celebrating the triumph of the Republic.

By this time many of the acute social tensions and sources of misery which underpinned the violent struggles of the Second Republic had been dissipated. The exodus of the poorest sections of the rural community and the transition to market-oriented specialization had defused the explosive class conflicts of mid-century. The majority of rural people were committed to the Republic but, except in certain areas of the south, this was a republicanism of small farmers, people proud of their economic independence and social dignity, for whom a democratic regime offered guarantees of gradual self-improvement and protection against a return of the time of the notables or the arrival of working-class collectivism. By 1880, the countryside appeared to urban élites as a rustic haven from the menace of working-class communities rather than, as in 1851, the primary source of threats to power and property. At the same time, as Alain Corbin has suggested, there was even a shift in bourgeois perceptions of agreeable smells. A more prosperous countryside, which was seen as the stable basis of both imperial and republican regimes and which was now easily accessible by train, seemed less the home of the unpleasant odour of manure-heap and sweat and instead a flowered, simple haven of nature. It was in these decades that the urban middle classes developed a predilection for vases and lithographs bearing images of bucolic rural scenes.

The modernization of rural France?

The slight easing of pressure on soil resources with the exodus of the rural poor is one reason why the decades between 1852 and 1880 have been described by Maurice Agulhon as 'the peak of rural civilization'. Never before had so many country folk lived in relative security, and even prosperity for many, nor had such easy access to education, travel and outside ideas. Never again would rural France be such a diverse human and natural environment in terms of its languages, cultures, fauna and flora, and patterns of production. At first glance, too, France might seem to have remained a nation of smallholding peasants, tenant farmers, and labourers: farms smaller than 20 hectares covered perhaps one-third of the countryside in 1789 and about half in 1884, while the number of people living in rural communities, perhaps 22.5 million in the 1780s, was 24.6 million a century later. Historians have seen such apparent continuity as evidence of the limited impact of the French Revolution and of the 'backward' nature of the French economy in the nineteenth century. However, such statistics hide a multitude of changes, both striking and subtle, which varied across the country in their timing, nature, and impact but were nonetheless felt everywhere. Ultimately, these changes would slowly erode the cultural and economic distinctiveness and diversity of the countryside.

Historians have often sought to identify the turning point in the process by which rural people became more involved in agricultural specialization and national markets, more open to urban culture, and more accepting of the institutions and demands of the state. Some have seen the years of the French Revolution as decisive, others the decades between 1830 and 1850; at the other extreme, the decades after 1880 are described as having turned 'peasants into Frenchmen', while even the 1950s have been seen as the moment of 'rural revolution' in France. Given the diversity of rural France, such a search for a watershed between 'traditional' and 'modern' is bound to be illusory. An alternative model would instead describe change as occurring everywhere in rural France but varying in timing, nature, and intensity according to region, class, and gender.

The most important transformation in rural society was that by which peasant polyculture became specialized small farming. Market specialization, evident only in the hinterland of large cities in the eighteenth century, was facilitated by the Revolution, which removed the exactions of seigneurs and Church, put up church and émigré property for sale, and created the institutional environment for a national market. Small farming coexisted with large-scale, capitalist farming in particular areas, and became more specialized by region across the century. By 1880, most rural people were 'peasants' (*paysans*) only in their attachment to their *pays* and no longer in terms of the way they produced. The centuries-old network of markets and fairs—which had cultural as well as economic functions—survived and indeed expanded, but the articles for sale were changing and production for the national market often bypassed them altogether. Such changes were paralleled by the disappearance from the countryside of the textile and metallurgical industries, which became concentrated in urban centres, and the more frequent purchase of urban manufactures, many of them previously produced within rural communities themselves: the grocer and dressmaker replaced the charcoal-burner and weaver. These changes to complex polycultural routines would slowly erode the regional cultures with which they were interdependent, at the same time as schooling and retailing were exposing rural people more consistently to Parisian values. Such cultural transformations were, however, gradual and incomplete: distinctive rural cultures and languages survived as disparate ways of seeing the world.

A gradual but fundamental economic transformation in urban–rural relations occurred with the urbanization and mechanization of industry. In the industrial towns around Saint-Étienne, the labour of temporary migrants who retained close links with their villages was replaced from the 1860s by a permanent working-class labour force. In nearby villages such as Marlhes, domestic textile work declined as the industry became mechanized in cities; instead, farmers concentrated on supplying Saint-Étienne with meat, milk, and cheese. In the Isère, rural industry endured, but the male weavers who had worked at home for Lyon silk manufacturers were increasingly replaced by women working in local factories.

Agricultural specialization and rural exodus hastened the abandonment of ancient agrarian routines and, with them, the celebrations and rituals associated with the seasonal routines of agricultural and religious life. Where specialization in labour-intensive production generated population growth, rural people were not only in more frequent contact with outside influences, but were also living with migrants from elsewhere. With the rural exodus and the collapse of rural industry the countryside was losing the occupational and economic complexity which was at the heart of distinctive regional activities. Specialization made villages more prosperous, but also more vulnerable: in the southern village of Gabian, where 600 hectares (two-fifths of the total land area) had been planted with vines, the arrival of the phylloxera louse in 1879 reduced the vineyards to just 3 hectares within three years.

The essential characteristic of urban–rural relations—that it was a constant two-way process of contact and adaptation—is evident in two other important cultural changes which occurred in the nineteenth-century countryside. First, beginning in the early years of the century and reaching a peak after 1860, urban and rural women took their own initiatives to continue to reconstruct a Church shattered by the Revolution. In the religious orders founded or reestablished early in the century, bourgeois and artisan women from towns had predominated among recruits, but in newer orders, such as that of Saint-Gildas in Amiens, rural women made up two-thirds of novices. Of course, the response of rural women to this 'feminine Catholicism' varied: in 1883, 97.4 per cent of all women were attending Easter mass in the diocese of Rennes; in that of Orléans, just 25.4 per cent of adult women did so.

Secondly, in the three decades after 1850 there was an acceleration in the social acceptance of education that had been evident since the turn of the century: more children were sent to school and they attended more regularly. Between 1850 and 1877, while the national population was virtually stable, the number of school pupils increased from 3.3 to 4.7 million (including an increase from 1.5 to 2.3 million girls); of those enrolled, four-fifths rather than two-thirds attended all year. The state's teachers were an increasing presence in rural France: 111,000 in 1877 compared with 76,000 in the 1840s. By now, virtually all children were receiving primary schooling and perhaps two-thirds of them were functionally literate. In 1881 85 per cent of men and 77 per cent of women were at least able to sign their marriage certificate: a century earlier the figures were 47 and 27 per cent.

From 1867 onwards communes of more than 500 people were required to have girls as well as boys schools, and in 1881–3 the Ferry laws institutionalized free, compulsory, and secular education for boys and girls. However, the impulse for mass education came as much from rural people as from the ambitions of educators and governments. In Pont-de-Montvert (Lozère), the municipal council successfully petitioned in 1880 for funds for schools in four hamlets with populations of 120, 66, 46 and 20 inhabitants. Schoolteaching also became a favoured avenue of social mobility for motivated young rural people: for example, of the 567 teachers trained in the department of the Vosges between 1862 and 1892, 61 per cent were from agricultural backgrounds. Rural youths constituted just 12 per cent of the few boys who went on to secondary school, but many of them subsequently entered business or the public service.

The Guizot laws of 1833 had placed emphasis on basic skills of literacy and numeracy within a Christian, moralizing framework; there was little formal attention paid to history and geography before secondary school. Now, under the Third Republic, there was a deliberate endeavour to inculcate values of patriotism and republican unity, with regional diversity used as a way of celebrating France's natural richness. Even if a majority of people still commonly used another language, or a dialect of French, there was by 1880 a near-universal acceptance of the value of primary education in French. Teachers and children shared a mental map which situated them within a French historical, linguistic, and geographical mental universe. For example, the municipal council of Gabian, in Occitan-speaking Languedoc, voted funds in 1876 to purchase 'absolutely essential' French-language classroom materials (including maps of the Hérault, France, Europe, and the world) and 'desirable' materials (maps of Asia, Africa, the Americas, and 'collections of pictures for teaching history and natural history'). In *Le Tour de la France par deux enfants* by G. Bruno (the pseudonym of Augustine Fouillée), which was reprinted 209 times between 1877 and 1891, children all over France were presented with an image of their nation as a land of natural beauty and social harmony, an ideal society of peasants and artisans.

While regional forms of collective and personal rituals endured, since the 1840s a new male space, the café or *cabaret*, had challenged the family gathering or *veillée*. In general, women were excluded from this new space where men assumed that they were making the important decisions with their peers; here, too, French newspapers were available and French was spoken, depending on the subject and the audience. The polarity of the café (male, non-familial, irreligious, open to French oral and written culture, often left-wing) and the *veillée* (familial, closed, perpetuating a non-French oral, often religious tradition, praised by the Church) went beyond leisure to symbolize important contrasts of politics, religion, and gender. In these years a massive increase occurred in the production, distribution and consumption of books and newspapers, interdependent with the changing techniques and imperatives of a capitalist economy, and with mass literacy. These changes also underpinned an important shift in the social history of reading, for the popular practice of collective reading in cafés, working-men's clubs, and at *veillées* gradually gave way to individual, private reading, to a different relationship between reader and text. In the process, a literary, urban, and bourgeois national culture gradually diluted the diversity of regional, oral, and working-class cultures.

The decades after mid-century thus represented an important acceleration of *francisation* 'from below', whereby members of minority cultures came to accept, consciously or not, the increasing relevance of French culture as well as national institutions. This acceptance of the nation, already apparent during the French Revolution, was accelerated by the repeated experience of electoral participation across the century. In the process, access to French language and culture came to be valued by many members of ethnic minorities as tantamount to access to 'progress' itself.

Of course, the victory of urban influences was never complete or uncontested. For example, folk tales about death present in regional cultures—misleadingly described as 'superstitions' by many clergy and historians—took for granted the potency of local saints and of rituals as cures for disease, and constantly challenged the claims of clergy and doctors about why, how and to what end people died. Doctors, trained in Paris, Montpellier, and Strasbourg, were a rare sight in many regions: there were more than 8,000 people for each doctor in parts of Brittany and the Alps. By 1880 doctors had still not won a social victory over their rural rivals, the secular and religious healers who proliferated in the countryside. These familiar healers were not only far cheaper, but were more tolerant of poverty and patient self-diagnosis, and offered a more wide-ranging explanation of ill-health. In fact, higher calorific intake was the main reason why rural death rates continued to decline and remained well below those of urban areas: 20.8 per thousand between 1879 and 1883, compared with 25.2 in towns.

Some historians of the family have argued that, after 1850, bourgeois practices of birth control, notions of romantic love and acceptance of the concept of childhood began to 'trickle down' to the rural masses, so that the rural family became 'modernized'. Such arguments are both ethnocentric in their privileging of the urban and modern and incorrect in detail. Forms of contraception had always been practised in those rural communities where smaller families had been economically necessary, and certainly well before feminists and social reformers began to explicitly challenge church teachings in the

1880s. Proceeding from the complementarity of men and women's work, Martine Segalen has argued that the pre-capitalist family was not patriarchal, and that there had always been love and respect between men, women and children. Nor did rural people need to learn about 'affective' relationships from their social betters. Then, as now, relations varied—as in every social group—from the loving to the violent, but peasant women's economic and cultural importance may have bolstered their status within the family.

Conclusion

Segalen argues that the importance of women's productive work was undermined only with the mechanization of farming after the First World War. However, the seeds of this change were sown much earlier, in the transition from peasant polyculture to specialized small farming. In the 1780s France was an agrarian, pre-capitalist society in which most of the population, the location of most industry and the sources of power and most wealth were rural. Control of land and its producers was the source of the extraction of surplus product by the nobility, clergy, some bourgeois, and the state. Over the following century, in part due to the forces unleashed by the Revolution, an interconnected series of gradual transformations were to alter this society irreversibly, if by no means completely. By 1880 France was essentially a capitalist society in which market-oriented agriculture and a disproportionately growing urban industrial economy were the source of the extraction of surplus value, by economic élites and the state, from the labour of urban and rural wage-labourers and the self-employed.

During the hundred years from 1780 to 1880, France's towns and cities had also gone through a series of qualitative changes in their function, size and relationship with the countryside. In the late-eighteenth century, a maximum of 20 per cent of the population lived in communities of more than 2,000 people, while perhaps 8 per cent inhabited the seventy-five genuine towns of 10,000 or more. However, most towns and cities were parasitic on the countryside, drawing men and taxes for the state, along with rents, seigneurial dues, and tithes which noble and clerical élites largely expended within the towns themselves. The retailing and craft industries of these provincial towns, and even Paris, focused essentially on the needs of the urban population, including luxury goods for wealthy nobles, clerics, and bourgeois. In 1880, by contrast, the urban population of France was 35 per cent of the total; between 1811 and 1881, the population living in towns had increased from 4.2 to 9.8 million. The corollary of these changes, together with greater specialization in the countryside, was that by 1880 urban entrepreneurs had largely conquered 'the home market for capital', as Karl Marx put it. Never before had such a large proportion of the population been dependent on selling its labour or produce in order to purchase the necessities of life.

However, the history of relations between town and country in the century after 1780 should not be understood simply as the conquest of the countryside by the city. Urban–rural relations were always multifaceted and dynamic, and the migrants who left for the city took with them values which contributed to the distinctive culture of the urban communities they joined. Indeed, John Merriman, on the basis of his study of Limoges, has wondered who was conquering whom. Here the ancient neighbourhoods of the *château* and the *cité* were swamped by new working-class suburbs as the city grew from 22,000 in 1806 to 64,000 in 1881. The migrants who flooded into the porcelain factories of Limoges were rural people who created the distinctive working-class culture of 'the red city'. Understanding French history as the triumph of the centralized nation-state, as the victory of urban values and a capitalist economy, neglects the extent to which these processes were incomplete and contested. The history of relations between town and country is much better understood as a process of negotiation and adaptation.

6

Province and nation

Robert Gildea

Introduction

The French nation was forged in the crucible of the French Revolution. It is commonly seen as a civic nation, defined subjectively by political will, rather than as a nation defined objectively by ethnicity, language, or religion. One of the tasks of this chapter will be to examine how valid this distinction is, or to what extent there were linguistic, ethnic, or indeed religious dimensions to French identity. The French nation is also generally considered to be unified and unimpeded by regional diversity. It will be argued here that province and *pays* were as important as objects of loyalty in the nineteenth century as the nation. Lastly, the nation will be examined in its relationship with the outside world through the concept of the *patrie* and patriotism, manifested in the specific form of revolutionary patriotism, the liberating and civilizing mission and the cult of *grandeur*.

Nation or king?

In *What is the Third Estate?*, a pamphlet which in many ways set the agenda for the French Revolution, the Abbé Sieyès defined the nation as 'a body of associates living under a common law and represented by the same legislature'. It was not divided between privileged and unprivileged or between estates or corporations, each with different rights, but composed of citizens with equal rights and duties under the law. That law, moreover, was not imposed arbitrarily by a superior authority, but made by representatives of a people deemed to be sovereign. The word was made flesh on 17 June 1789 when the chamber of the third estate approved Sieyès's motion that since it was made up of representatives elected by 96 per cent of the French nation, it should supersede the Estates-General, call itself the National Assembly, and act as the 'one and indivisible representation' of the nation.

The question that Sieyès did not answer was the relationship of the king to the nation. At the Fête de la Fédération, on 14 July 1790, 14,000 National Guardsmen assembled from all over France on the Champ de Mars in Paris took the oath proclaimed by their commander, Lafayette: 'We swear to remain forever faithful to the Nation, Law and King, to defend with all our strength the constitution decreed by the National Assembly and accepted by the king ... to stay united to all Frenchmen by the indissoluble ties of fraternity.' The constitution finally accepted by the king in September 1791 laid down that the nation was sovereign, but exercised its powers by delegation, and that 'its representatives are the legislative body and the king'. The alliance between king and nation was nevertheless unstable: the king accepted the constitution only with reluctance and was drawn to those, mostly nobles and often army officers, who rejected the new social contract, emigrated beyond the frontiers, and were fighting the Revolution with the help of foreign powers. When the Legislative Assembly declared war on those powers, the position of the king became untenable and, on 10 August 1792, the Paris crowd deposed the king and the nation reinvented itself as a republic. As for what should be done with the deposed king, Robespierre told the Convention on 3 December 1792 that Louis had violated the social contract, that he was 'a traitor to the French nation' and that 'Louis must die so that the *patrie* can live'. In January 1793 Louis XVI was duly executed.

The issue now arose whether the French nation, as a community of free and equal brothers (women being excluded from citizenship) could adequately exercise sovereign power alone. The experience of civil war, the Terror, and anarchy suggested to many Frenchmen that it could not. Whole regions of France, like the Vendée, which as a counter-revolutionary zone spread far beyond the confines of the department, took up arms for God and King. Louis XVIII, as king-in-waiting, issued a declaration from Verona in 1795 promising that if he were restored he would not take his revenge but be 'only the tender and indulgent father who, satisfied by the repentance of his children, suspends justice in order to lavish on them the treasures of his clemency'. A return to this father/children model of a monarchical polity was judged premature, and in 1804 a compromise was agreed by which one of the revolutionary fraternity—Napoleon Bonaparte—crowned himself emperor in imitation of Charlemagne. Yet he was regarded as a representative of the French nation, ratified by plebiscite and calling himself 'Emperor of the French'.

This compromise solution was itself unstable, as Napoleon veered between divine-right pretensions, referring to 'my subjects' at the high point of the Empire, and threatening to become the 'king of a jacquerie', or peasant uprising, during the Hundred Days in 1815. The reunion of king and people was realized in a parliamentary monarchy under the Charter granted by Louis XVIII and expressed symbolically by the return of the equestrian statue of the well-loved Henri IV to the Pont-Neuf, dragged to its plinth by the enthusiastic people of Paris. The coronation of Charles X, however, epitomized less the union of king and people than the firm subordination of one to the other. Held in 1825 at Reims, like that of his brother Louis XVI fifty years before, it was modelled on the consecration of Clovis in 496. Charles promised to obey the constitution that Louis XVIII had *granted* to his people, to give justice to his subjects, and to 'protect this fair France that I am pleased to govern'.

In liberal circles during the Restoration there was a feeling that the French nation had been dissolved and that sovereignty had reverted to the person of the king. In order to reassert the nation as the legitimate focus of sovereignty and the bourgeoisie as the constituent element of the nation, liberal politicians—who were also historians and journalists—sought to refashion the credentials of the bourgeoisie and to deflate the pretensions of absolute monarchy. Augustin Thierry, in his *Letters on the History of France* that began to appear in 1820, argued that the union of king and a proud, revolutionary nation had not been a flash in the pan in 1789 but had a long and honourable pedigree. He stated that towns had not been *given* their liberties by the grace of kings but that those liberties had been conquered as a result of insurrections against king and lords in the eleventh century. The urban bourgeoisie had won the right to be represented in the Estates-General from the fourteenth century, forged the French state in alliance with the king and in 1789 had founded the French nation.

François Guizot, in his *History of Civilization in France* (1829–32), went so far as to argue that the bourgeoisie, or third estate, was more fully developed in France than in any other country, and had not only undertaken French Revolution but (since that had known grim moments) was 'the most active and determined element of French civilization'. Other young liberal historians, Thiers and Mignet, sought to overcome the bad press suffered by the French Revolution since the Terror by highlighting the marriage of king and nation in the constitutional monarchy of 1789–92, secured by the bourgeoisie in the teeth of both the reactionary aristocracy and the 'vile multitude'. In January 1830 they founded a paper called *Le National* and master-minded the transition to a nation which through its representatives had the power to create a modern, contractual monarchy on its own terms. The new pretender, Louis–Philippe, was not crowned but, having promised to govern only in the interests of the French people, was duly acclaimed by the representatives of the nation 'king of the French'.

The search for a durable solution to the problem of representing the French nation goes a long way to explaining continued political instability between 1830 and 1880. Three models were attempted: that of a constitutional monarchy, harking back to 1789; a revival of the Empire; and two more experiments with the Republic. The criterion for success was a polity which detracted least from the pretensions of a sovereign nation to manage its own affairs; reasons for failure can be found largely in the historical burdens carried by all those polities.

Although the July Monarchy was designed to reconcile king and nation, each side was unwilling to allow significant limitations on its own power. Moreover, once the king's head had been removed, it was extremely difficult for the monarchy to recover an aura that could overcome criticism. The nation recovered its republican form in 1848 and tried to shed its association with the Jacobin dictatorship and Terror of 1793. But in acquiring the image of clemency and fraternity it allowed its opponents a free reign to undermine it from within. Louis-Napoleon Bonaparte, elected President of the Republic by universal suffrage in December 1848, made every effort to provide strong leadership for the nation while continuing to respect its sovereignty. Even when he resurrected the Empire he did it on the basis of feeling the pulse of the people during his provincial tours and putting it to a formal plebiscite. Though there was talk of a coronation, the precedent of 1804 was studiously ignored. Only the birthday of Napoleon I on 15 August, celebrated as the Fête Impériale, was revived in 1852 to 'unite everybody in a common sentiment of national glory'. The imperial mode of representing the nation has been forcefully attacked, not least to secure republican legitimacy, but it was arguably the polity that suited the French people best. The Republic was reintroduced almost by accident, after the military defeat of the Second Empire, and it took ten years and the support of partisans of the July Monarchy before the Third Republic was firmly established as parliamentary regime, deliberately keeping the president weak. Celebration of the 14th of July, which had been officially banned since 1805, was resumed as the festival of the republican nation in 1880, and Sieyès would doubtless have been happy with a polity which finally gave power to the parliamentary representatives of the nation, mediating between government and people.

Nation, province, and *pays*

When the Nation came together in 1789 it had to find a way not only of representing itself politically but of running itself administratively. On the night of 4 August 1789 towns, cities, and provinces surrendered their privileges in matters of taxation and self-administration. They opened the way to an administrative reorganization of France that permitted a degree of centralization of which enlightened ministers of the *Ancien Régime* had only dreamed.

It should be emphasized that 4 August was no wave of the magic wand. Forces opposed to centralization were just as strong as those in favour of it, if not more so. The kingdom of France had been put together like a mosaic, piece by piece. Provincial privileges had been retained even if they had been incorporated as a result of conquest, and many outlying provinces nourished memories of independence or benign rule by a foreign power. For most French people the 'nation' was not that defined by the Abbé Sieyès, but a much smaller community, essentially a province, but commonly called (for example) the Breton, Provençal, Artesian, or Béarnais nation. The introduction in 1787 of provincial assemblies, to assist tax-raising, into some central parts of France which had not previously possessed them—in the Bourbonnais, Berry, and

Haute–Guyenne—instilled a provincial sentiment where none had existed before.

The 'noble revolt' against tax reforms and attacks on privilege in 1788, which forced the government to call the Estates-General, witnessed a revival of provincial estates in outlying *pays d'états* such as Provence and Franche–Comté. Annexed to the French crown in 1481 and 1678 respectively, the powers of these provinces had gradually been eroded by administrative centralization. Although the three orders in these provinces/nations sent representatives to the Estates-General in 1789 they also drafted *cahiers* calling for the respect of their local customs and privileges and were not prepared to concede that the king or Estates-General could overrule them. The estates of Béarn, which had been incorporated into the French monarchy somewhat against their will in 1620, in fact refused to send deputies to the Estates-General at all, 'given that the sovereignty of Béarn forms a separate state, having its own constitution, guaranteed by the reigning sovereign'. The nobility of Artois (incorporated in 1659), who did elect deputies to the Estates-General, nevertheless claimed 'that the province of Artois, in constitutional matters, is absolutely foreign to and independent of the Estates-General. It is up to the Artesian nation to pronounce on this point.' Alsace had only been a part of France since 1648 and Baron Jean de Turckheim, deputy of the third estate of Strasbourg, thought that the night of 4 August was a bad dream from which he would wake up. He reported that the deputies from Strasbourg had been sorely embarrassed by this wave of self-denial, and that any abandonment of privilege must be subject to ratification by the city.

Events nevertheless moved fast and the original reasons for the calling of the Estates-General were overtaken by its transformation into a National Assembly which claimed constituent powers and set about building a single nation, sweeping away municipal and provincial privileges. Baron de Turckheim was the only Alsatian deputy to resign. Baron de Dietrich, another deputy from Alsace and later mayor of Strasbourg, told the *échevins* (elders) of the city in December 1789 that they should not protest to the king or claim that their deputies had exceeded their old mandates. He argued that their deputies were mandated as 'representatives of the nation' and that 'you have, by your mandates, yourselves undermined the foundation of your privileges; you have surrendered to the nation the destruction or preservation of your privileges'. Enthusiasts for the new nation had the wind in their sails and popular legend holds that it was in Dietrich's salon that the young captain Rouget de l'Isle first sang what became the French national anthem, the 'Marseillaise', in 1792.

The administrative division of France into departments was conceived as a means to finish off provincial privileges and break down provincial loyalties. In September 1789 Sieyès and his colleague, Thouret, deputy of the third estate for Rouen, introduced a radical plan for a geometrical division, saying 'there is no more prompt and powerful way of effortlessly making all the parts of France into one body and all the peoples who divide it into one nation'. Rabaut Saint-Étienne, a prominent Protestant and third-estate deputy for Paris *extra-muros*, declared that 'just as Louis XIV said one day of a simple [Bourbon] family pact, "There are no more Pyrenees", so we can say of a solemn pact sworn by 1,200 representatives of the nation, "There are no more provinces"'. Mirabeau, deputy of the third estate of Aix-en-Provence, proposed a compromise solution whereby the boundaries of the new departments would respect as far as possible those of former provinces. Yet it was argued, even then, that provinces were extremely hard to define. France was divided not into provinces but into the diverse and overlapping units of *gouvernements* (military), *bailliages* (judicial), *généralités* and *subdélégations* (administrative), and dioceses (ecclesiastical). In a sense the concept of provinces was elaborated only on the eve of their abolition.

Despite the pressures in favour of a uniform system of administration, there was a strong sense in some quarters that the new framework of departments would severely disrupt existing patterns of loyalty. Malouet, a partisan of a strong monarchy, criticized the reform by arguing that 'the spirit of a province considered in terms of habits, soil, climate, customs, local mores, types of industry, and agriculture is composed of a number of factors which the law is powerless to change and which it must indeed respect'. When the division was applied, protests were legion. Controversy raged at the borders of Normandy and Maine, Poitou and Berry, Burgundy and the Nivernais. There was opposition to the division into departments of Provence, Auvergne, and Franche-Comté. Aix-en-Provence and Marseille were pitted against each other in the race to be capital of the Bouches-du-Rhône department. Some provincialists opted squarely for counter-revolution. One Franc-Comtois noble, in exile in

Switzerland, wrote to the Emperor Leopold II in May 1791 to say that there was a pro-Habsburg groundswell among his peers and that he could have the province back whenever he wanted it. At the same time Comte de Botherel, who had been *procureur-général-syndic* of the Estates of Brittany, denounced the attack on the constitution governing the Breton union with France of 1532 and took to counter-revolutionary conspiracy.

Noble counter-revolution was explained by opposition both to the administrative reform that abolished provincial estates and *parlements* and introduced elected departmental *conseils généraux* and the executive directories that headed them, and to their displacement in the new bodies by a wealthy non-noble class. This propertied and educated élite was the mainstay of moderate revolution, opposed to both court politics and mob rule, and enjoyed a certain autonomy vis-à-vis the central government under the Constituent and Legislative Assemblies. But this autonomy was violently attacked after the Paris Commune of August 1792 began to dictate to the Convention, and particularly when the Montagnards expelled the Girondins from the Convention on 31 May/2 June 1793. This provoked a 'federalist' revolt against the tyranny of the Parisian 'anarchists'. In the departments and cities of the Midi and in regions like Normandy, federalists underlined the point that the Republic was composed of eighty-three free and equal departments, not just Paris. Despite attempts to smear them as partisans of counter-revolution, federalists were in fact revolutionaries who subscribed to the principles of 1789, but not to those of 1793. One of their leaders, the Marseille deputy Barbaroux, had taken part in a mission to suppress the counter-revolution in Arles and had even argued in the Convention just after the founding of the Republic that it must be constituted as a unitary regime, not a federal one on the American model.

The federalist revolt and its ruthless suppression by the Montagnards set up a tension that was evident throughout the nineteenth century between three different ideals. First, there was the view of Parisian revolutionaries that any demand for decentralization was essentially counter-revolutionary. Devolving power to the departments and cities was no better than resurrecting the provinces of the *Ancien Régime*, which were by definition feudal and reactionary. Second, there was the view of provincial notables that administrative centralization left France prey to revolution, since revolutionaries who seized power in Paris disposed of the levers of command to impose revolution on the provinces. Greater decentralization was thus demanded as a necessary antidote to revolution. Third, there was the governmental view, held by imperial, royal, and republican governments alike, that administrative centralization must be secured in order to prevent the triumph of both Parisian revolution and provincial reaction. The centrepiece of this policy was the law of 28 Pluviôse Year VIII (17 February 1800) by which the central government appointed a prefect to serve its interests at the head of each department. The *conseil général* of elected notables met only once a year and was firmly under the control of the prefect. Mayors were also appointed, by the central government in larger towns (over 5,000 inhabitants), and by the prefect in smaller ones. Paris was denied a mayor because of its revolutionary past and was ruled by a prefect of police and the prefect of the Seine. The only moment when this rigid framework loosened and towns, departments, or regions threatened to recover some autonomy was when France suffered defeat and occupation, in 1814/15 and in 1870–1. For this reason, however, governments of all political persuasions were keen to resume the reins of centralized administration as soon as possible.

As Napoleon's armies retreated in 1813, a group of Franc-Comtois nobles under Comte Pierre-Georges de Scey-Montbéliard, who had fled France in opposition to the Revolution, conspired to return Franche-Comté to Austria in the hope that the province would thereby have more autonomy than under French rule. In 1813–14 Franche-Comté in fact enjoyed this status, under the effective government of Scey-Montbéliard. After the French monarchy was restored, Scey-Montbéliard was kept on as prefect, but of only one of the three departments in the province. The Bourbon monarchy, despite the enthusiasm of many of its supporters for the revival of the *Ancien Régime* provinces, decided to retain Napoleon's system of centralized departmental administration in order to prevent the breakdown of what had been revealed to be a worryingly fragile structure.

The partisans of provincial government made their point with force after the fall of Charles X. Refusing the oath to Louis-Philippe they abandoned central government, retired to their country estates and there sought to revive the province, mythically if not in reality. The programme of the Franc-Comtois nobility, as spelled out by *La Gazette de Franche-Comté* in 1831, was 'morally to recreate our ancient county of Burgundy, not to resurrect the political ideas of the Middle Ages but to demand in its name our old liberties, our municipal franchises, our close-knit administration, our frank and noble freedom of speech . . . Under the Empire, under the Spanish, we enjoyed a noble independence; after the French conquest our liberties were respected, but under Parisian centralization, we saw those fall under the humiliating yoke of the bureaucrats.' At the other end of the country an Association Bretonne was founded in 1843, ostensibly to promote modern methods in agriculture and explore Breton archaeology, history, and language, but dominated by Breton nobles who cultivated nostalgia for the separate Breton state that existed before 1532.

The Revolution of 1848 and the working-class uprising of the June Days produced a wider and more concerted campaign on the part of provincial notables for greater decentralization. Comte Louis de Kergolay, a Legitimist who had taken part in the attempt of the Duchesse de Berry in 1832 to restore the old dynasty and was secretary of the Association Bretonne, founded a *Revue provinciale* with Arthur de Gobineau in September 1848. Noting that 'a handful of men, a coup, are enough at a given moment to overthrow the government and rule France by means of the telegraph', Kergolay praised the provincial estates of the *pays d'états* and the provincial assemblies set up in 1787, and criticized the National Assembly of 1848 for not going far enough in its plans for decentralization. Gobineau was less extreme, trying to salvage the federalist ideas of the Girondins from the condescension of history, and was taken on by Alexis de Tocqueville as his *chef de cabinet* in the Foreign Office in 1849. Louis de Kergolay, although he was Tocqueville's cousin, attacked Tocqueville's *The Ancien Régime and the French Revolution* when it came out in 1856 on the grounds that it claimed the *Ancien Régime* monarchy was as guilty as the Revolution for the centralizing drive of modern France.

To demand the administrative resurrection of the provinces during the Second Republic or Second Empire was political pie-in-the-sky. More feasible was the cultivation of the cultural distinctiveness of France's provinces and pressure for decentralization which respected the existing division of France into departments and municipalities. The authoritarian period of the Second Empire in the 1850s saw the publication of a rash of provincial reviews edited by local jurists, clergy, and other professionals which disguised any political agenda behind an enthusiasm for local history, archaeology, science, language, literature, and folklore. Such were the *Revue d'Alsace* launched in 1850, the *Annales du Comité Flamand de France* in 1853, the *Revue d'Aquitaine* in 1856, the *Revue de Bretagne et de la Vendée* in 1857, the *Revue de la Normandie* in 1862, and the *Annales Franc-Comtoises* in 1864. The argument of these reviews was that provincial loyalties and national loyalties were complementary, not contradictory, but that laws alone were not enough to eliminate proud and deep-rooted provincial identities. 'It is not by decrees that a land and inhabitants who have soaked the soil with their blood and sweat can be transformed', announced the first number of the *Annales du Comité Flamand de France*; 'as far as mores, customs and dialects are concerned, there will always be Bretons, Normans, Provençaux, Basques, Burgundians and Picards, Alsatians and Flemings'.

The period of national unification in Europe and the civil war in the United States opened up the whole issue of centralism and federalism and put force behind those in France who, without calling into question the departmental division of 1790, demanded much greater administrative decentralization. In 1863 Jacques-Louis Hénon, mayor of Lyon, denounced the 'virtually irresponsible dictatorship' of prefects under which Lyon and Paris were placed and demanded 'an elected and independent municipal council' for each. In 1865 a group of notables from Nancy published a 'Decentralization Plan' which they had endorsed by leading liberal politicians of all shades, Legitimist, Orleanist, and republican. In order to deflect accusations of counter-revolution they denied that they wished to 'resurrect an independent Lorraine or Franche-Comté'; instead they wanted to 'emancipate the departments'. By this they meant permanent commissions on the Belgian model to sit when the *conseils généraux* were not in session, greater financial autonomy, and their own administrative staff, seconded from the prefecture. Their modest demands did not even extend to demanding the election of mayors by municipal councils, but they did request that the government appoint mayors from among the elected councillors.

The so-called Nancy manifesto found some echo in a government feeling its way towards the liberalization of the Empire. The Liberal Empire ministry of Émile Ollivier in fact set up a commission on decentralization in 1870, chaired by former chief minister and signatory of the Nancy manifesto, Odilon Barrot. Barrot told the commission that decentralization was the best guarantee against the spate of revolutions and changes of regime that nineteenth-century France had witnessed, and that the popular participation in local affairs would develop public spirit in the citizen body. Although the commission voted in favour of the election of mayors by municipal councils, except in Paris and Lyon, the government was reluctant to cede the powers it held lest the major cities fall into the hands of the republican opposition. Moreover the commission's demand that permanent commissions be elected by the *conseils généraux* was not dealt with before the fall of the Empire.

What could not be achieved by reform was achieved by defeat and revolution. During the Franco-Prussian war, in August 1870, republican municipalities were elected in a string of large towns including Lyon, Marseille, and the *arrondissements* of Paris, which lacked a central municipal council or mayor. In the south, thirteen departments broke away to found the Ligue du Midi, a re-edition of the federalist revolt of 1793 to protect the autonomy of southern cities and departments. In Paris in March 1871 revolutionaries seized power and elected a revolutionary government, the Paris Commune. This was imitated in a series of provincial cities, including Lyon and Marseille, Toulouse and Narbonne, Le Creusot, and Saint-Étienne. Provincial notables wanted municipal liberties but they were horrified by the commune movement. They took the view that after yet another Parisian outrage calls for administrative decentralization must be listened to, and they were all powerful in the conservative National Assembly elected in February 1871. Though Thiers, now President of the Republic, was reluctant to surrender the powers of a central government threatened by war, revolution, and civil war, under a law of August 1871 *conseils généraux* obtained their permanent commissions and became little local parliaments chaired by the prefect. Under laws of March 1882 and April 1884, after the Republic was fully secured, municipal councils finally obtained the right to elect their own mayors and were given wider powers under the supervision of the prefect. Because of the Commune, however, a mayor for Paris was entirely out of the question.

Despite the ambition of many local notables to 'emancipate the departments', the department was an artificial creation going back to 1790 which rarely corresponded to any geographical, historic, or religious reality. While nobles nostalgic for the powers their families had exercised under the *Ancien Régime* dreamed of restoring the province, the inhabitants of ordinary rural and urban communities had much more limited horizons. Étienne Bertin, the subject of Émile Guillaumin's *The Life of a Simple Man,* born in 1823 into a peasant family of the Bourbonnais, reflected that 'Beyond the confines of the canton, beyond known distances, were mysterious countries which we imagined to be dangerous and populated by barbarians.' Rural artisans like the stonemasons of the Limousin, notably Martin Nadaud, born in 1815, were less parochial because they went to Paris for long periods to work on building projects. The goal, however, was always to 'return to the *pays*', to marry a local girl, and eventually to settle there.

If the *pays* corresponded to any administrative unit it was most likely to be the *arrondissement.* The *pays* was an ensemble of forty or fifty villages, defined by geography, economic ties, and often religious and political loyalties, which were generally the hinterland of a small town that served as a local market and administrative centre, with its sub-prefect, mayor of some standing, and elected deputy. Very often a single department was made up of a number of *pays* which had totally different identities and were divided by Reformation and Counter-Reformation, Revolution and Counter-Revolution, or by the way in which France had been built up as a nation-state. The Gard, for example, was divided between the Protestant Cévennes, taking their character from the Camisard rebellion of the early eighteenth century, and the Catholic plain. Maine-et-Loire, roughly the same as Anjou, included the Mauges, around Cholet, which joined the Vendée rising in 1793, and the Saumurois, around Saumur, which defended the Republic and behaved as if it were part of neighbouring Touraine. The line between the two went along the valley of the Layon, which divided granite from limestone, *bocage* from openfield, cattle from wheat and vine, religious fervour from indifference, and counter-revolution from republicanism. In the Midi, the Vaucluse was divided into the western part, formerly part of the Comtat-Venaissin, which was not part of France before 1791 and voted royalist in the legislative elections of 1849, and the *arrondissement* of Apt, which had been part of Provence, voted for the Left in 1849 and took up arms in defence of the Republic in 1851. Loyalty to the *pays* did not exclude loyalty to the nation, but so long as most French people continued to live in the countryside or small towns it embodied the French sense of belonging in the most concrete way.

Language and assimilation

France is generally considered to be a civic nation, defined by political will, by contrast to the nations of central and eastern Europe, like Germany, which are seen to be defined by language or ethnicity. How important language was in the constitution of French nationality must nevertheless be examined. Could the French state tolerate the coexistence of rival linguistic groups, so long as political loyalty to the nation was guaranteed? Or did it feel obliged to assimilate these groups into the dominant French culture, in order to be sure of their political loyalty?

In France there existed an official language for public acts and documents from the early sixteenth century. This was also the language spoken in the heartland of France. But Fernand Braudel described France as a country of micro-*pays* and micro-dialects, and in 1793 the Abbé Grégoire calculated that out of a population of 28 million, 6 million were ignorant of the French language and another 6 million were incapable of conversing in it. There were substantial minorities who spoke a very different language: Breton, Flemish, German, Catalan, or Basque; elsewhere, across most of southern France, local inhabitants spoke a dialect of the *langue d'oc*.

Although the French nation was being created in a civic sense, little pressure was felt in the short term to make all citizens speak the same language. The National Assembly decided in 1790 to translate its decrees into minority languages and various patois. But as external and internal crises developed and loyalty to the French Revolution became an issue, so revolutionaries adopted the view that the French language must be imposed as a medium of the Revolution. In a famous report to the Convention on behalf of the Committee of Public Safety on 27 January 1794, Bertrand Barère argued that there was an explicit connection between foreign languages, religious opposition, and counter-revolution. 'Federalism and superstition speak Breton, emigration and hatred of the Republic speak German, counter-revolution speaks Italian and fanaticism speaks Basque,' he declared, 'Let us destroy these harmful and erroneous tongues.' As a consequence he ordered that French teachers be established in all communes where French was not spoken. The Abbé Grégoire

published a report in June 1794 'On the need and the means to eliminate patois and to universalize the use of the French language'. His
argument was that without the universal practice of French, liberty,
equality, and fraternity would not be secure. French was the language
of liberty, using abstract political terms that were simply not available
in familial and familiar patois. French was required to exercise public
office and the exclusion of non-French speakers would perpetuate
inequality. Lastly, since patois was devised by feudalism so that each
domain had its patois and runaway serfs would be easily detected and
caught, its replacement by French was a prerequisite of fraternity.

These reports have been seen by Patrice Higonnet as evidence of
the 'linguistic terrorism' of the French Revolution, a ruthless strategy
to parallel those of dechristianization and the command economy.
Yet extreme rhetoric was evident for only a few months and disappeared after Thermidor. The bark was worse than the bite, for the
schools necessary to spread the French language were never
adequately organized or funded by the Revolution; indeed, elementary education was left to market forces until the Guizot law of
1833. Speaking French was not in this period considered a necessary
condition of being a good patriot. Napoleon's first language was Cor-
sican and he frequently swore in it. He never achieved a full command of French, and while his secretaries could generally provide a
clean copy of official documents, his letters to Marie-Louise were
peppered by mistakes such as 'eccellent', 'mon pays de nécense', and
'ambrasser'. Neither did he require his soldiers to speak French in
order to win battles on behalf of France. His armies were multinational institutions, composed of Italians, Germans, and Poles, and
he once said of the Alsatians, who were French citizens but spoke a
German dialect, that he did not care whether they spoke German, so
long as they charged like Frenchmen.

The French Revolution certainly assisted the spread of French, but
its limits must also be appreciated. The novelist Stendhal wrote in *The
Life of Henri Brulard* that 'a Minister of the Interior who wanted to do
his job should ask for a budget of 2 million francs a year to bring to
the level of instruction of most French people the populations who
live in the fatal triangle between Bordeaux, Bayonne, and Valence. In
these regions people believe in witches, cannot read and do not speak
French.' In 1863 a Minister of Public Instruction ordered a survey
which revealed that the triangle that did not speak French was more

like a rectangle, including all the departments south of a line from Bordeaux to Geneva, together with the eastern frontier and Brittany. He found that of 4 million schoolchildren aged 7 to 13, nearly 0.5 million spoke no French at all while another 1.5 million spoke it but could not write it. Claude Duneton, who argued in 1973 that the patois spoken south of the Limousin and the Alps should be called 'Occitan', pointed out that 'it was not true that French was really the language of the French people. Not in 1880.' Even in 1896, he said, French was a first language for only the 14 out of 39 million people who lived in the big cities and the 'French' provinces of the Île-de-France, Normandy, the Loire, Burgundy, and Champagne; the other 25 million considered it a foreign language.

These inconsistent but eloquent figures suggest either that the French government was indifferent about assimilating the non-French speaking population, or that the various dialects and patois were extraordinarily resistant to French cultural imperialism. Though the principal task of the school required in every commune under the Guizot law of 1833 was to teach French, and stories of children being punished for using patois in the classroom or even in the playground are legion, schools were unable to eliminate usages which were the normal parlance at home and in the local community. French was seen to be the language of the public sphere—of the school, the town hall, the law court—but not of the private sphere. 'It would have occurred to no one to speak French at home,' wrote Claude Duneton of the Limousin, 'it would have been in bad taste, pretentious, ridiculous, as if the head of a household today went on holiday to the United States and came home affecting an American accent.' While Peter Sahlins argued that market relations as well as power relations in Roussillon stimulated the use of French rather than Catalan, Duneton recalls that the lingua franca of the markets, fairs and shops of the Corrèze was Occitan until 1918 at least. The plain fact was that there was no question of *replacing* dialect or patois by French. Most French people were bilingual in their own dialect and also in French, switching from one to the other as the situation demanded. This was the case for rural populations but for local notables too, such as Duneton's doctor who consulted in Occitan, or notaries who discussed matters in Occitan before drawing up the document in French.

It is also true that the French state did not exert real pressure to impose French until the era of unification in Italy and Germany. Just as during the French Revolution the state felt that minority languages harboured counter-revolution, so the drive for national unification made the French state concerned about the loyalty of peripheral populations who did not speak French. The movement for German unification in particular caused Napoleon III's administrators to take a less sanguine view of German-speaking Alsatians than had Napoleon I. In 1859 the Rector of the Academy of Strasbourg reported that 'the propagation of the French language in Alsace is, let there be no doubt, a question of *political* importance. The obstinacy of this large province to remain German is an argument that sustains wild hopes in Prussia and Austria. Alsace will not be fully part of the French Empire until it has adopted without reservation the language and spirit of France.' In the 1860s, for the first time in the nineteenth century, the French school system set about trying to foster French at the expense of German in Alsace.

The campaign of the French state to eliminate minority languages was largely counter-productive. In areas where minority languages were eroded, such as French Flanders, there was no necessary destruction of local or provincial mentality, because the existence of such languages was a sufficient but not a necessary condition of local or provincial identities. Elsewhere, however, French cultural imperialism provoked a cultural revival orchestrated by intellectuals who campaigned to raise the level of local idioms from spoken to written language, claiming an equal status with French, and supported by the establishment of a written literature derived from the oral tradition. This did not involve a challenge to the French state, and the proponents of cultural revival were keen to dismiss all accusations of separatist intent. But it did suggest a view of France that was more decentralized and more accommodating of regional identities.

The first counter-culture to develop was Breton. Jean-François Le Gonidec (1775–1838) was rescued from the scaffold in 1793 and, on the run after the failed counter-revolutionary Quiberon expedition of 1795, took refuge with peasant families and learned Breton. He published a Breton grammar in 1807 and a French-Breton dictionary in 1821. Its second edition in 1847 was produced by Brittany's Grimm, Vicomte Théodore Hersant de La Villemarqué, whose *Barzas-Breiz* of 1839 was a collection of popular Breton songs of love, legend, and faith, as handed down by the bards. Likewise, Charles de Coussemaker (1805–76), a magistrate of Dunkerque and founder of the Comité

Flamand de France, saw France as his 'second homeland' but argued that since the Revolution France had striven to eradicate Flemish culture. His mission was to resurrect the folklore of medieval Flanders, of its freemen, its prosperous cities, and its Burgundian history, and in 1856 he published the *Popular Songs of French Flemings*.

Meanwhile Frédéric Mistral (1830–1914), born into a prosperous farming family in Provence and a law student at Aix-en-Provence when Louis-Napoleon launched his coup in 1851, responded to the new centralization by founding a group of Félibres or men of free faith in 1852, who would rediscover and rewrite the Provençal poetry of the troubadours which predated the annexation of 1481. His love poem *Mirèio/Mireille* (1859) was brought to the attention of Lamartine and Dumas and became the subject of an opera in Paris with music by Gounod in 1864. Mistral was careful to adhere to a cultural agenda, avoiding commitment to political camps. He argued with glorious imprecision in 1870 that 'the Félibrige can only be Girondin, federalist, religious, liberal and respectful of tradition, otherwise it has no *raison d'être*', although his commitment to Catholicism, tradition, and decentralization gave him an obvious affinity with Legitimism. He also avoided the accusation of separatism, declaring that his goal was 'the resurrection of the Provençal country crushed for five hundred years by French centralization', but insisting that loyalty to the Provençal nation in no way detracted from loyalty to the larger *patrie*. Indeed in 1875 he told the Montpellier meeting of the Floral Games, where poets vied for honours, that 'broad patriotism comes from attachment to one's *pays*, to its customs, to one's family . . . if we want to resurrect our poor fatherland, let us promote from city to city and from province to province that which creates patriots: religion, traditions, national memories, the old language of the *pays*'. There was no political separatism in France during this period, only a cultural regionalism that was entirely compatible with national unity.

Nation and race

Despite the fact that the French considered themselves as a civic nation, claims were also made for an ethnic identity just as they were made to a linguistic identity. Whether the French in fact constituted a race was the subject of prolonged controversy. Significantly too, the ethnic debate was a transposition into racial politics of the clash between privileged and unprivileged orders during the French Revolution.

The Revolution witnessed a surge of interest in the Celtic origins of the French people. One use of the flimsy evidence was to underpin the imperial ambitions of Revolutionary-Napoleonic France. Théophile-Malo La Tour d'Auvergne (1743–1800), a distant relation of Turenne who continued his military career in the armies of the Republic and was baptized 'the first grenadier of the Republic' by Napoleon Bonaparte, published his *Origines gauloises* in 1796. This argued that 'our ancestors the Celts' had at one time a vast empire stretching from Spain to Sweden and from Brittany to Moscow. They were known as Scythians or Celto-Scythians by the Greeks and as Gauls by the Romans and their language and customs were said to be preserved by the Celts of Brittany. The Académie Celtique founded in 1807 developed the myth that most peoples of Europe were descended from them, and that the Napoleonic Empire now brought them once again like 'a single great family, under the same federative government'.

The other use of the evidence was less imperialist than revolutionary. It fastened on the Gauls as the Celtic inhabitants of the whole of France and on their subjugation first by the Romans, then by the Franks. In a work published in 1727 Comte Henri de Boulainvilliers had argued that the French aristocracy was descended from the Frankish warriors who conquered the Gauls in the fourth century and set up an elective monarchy answerable to assemblies of nobles. Although since Clovis and Charlemagne the French monarchy had eroded the privileges of the Frankish nobles, Boulainvilliers claimed that their independence vis-à-vis the crown and the exclusion of the third estate from the political process were justified by the Frankish right of conquest. These pretensions were challenged at the Revolution, when ethnic arguments were used to reinforce sociological and juridical ones. In his *What is the Third Estate?* the Abbé Sieyès asked why the third estate 'did not send back to the Franconian forests all those families who hung onto the mad claim that they were descended from the race of conquerors and had succeeded to their rights?' The French people may have been descended from the Gauls and Romans, but this was better than being descended from the 'savages who emerged from the woods, lakes and marshes of old Germany'.

The racial debate faded during the Revolution but returned (in its revolutionary guise) at the Restoration. In 1814 the Comte de Montlosier argued in *On the French Monarchy* that the French were descended from three nations—the Gauls, the Romans and the Franks—but that only the Franks accounted for the 'lustre of greatness, honour and generosity which characterised France from its earliest times'. According to him, the Franks alone remained free men, invented feudalism and assemblies of nobles, and now that the Revolution was over and a monarchical regime was indispensable, only the nobility descended from the Franks could guarantee constitutional monarchy against despotism.

This interpretation served to justify royal authority and aristocratic power. At his coronation Charles X made repeated reference to the baptism and consecration of Clovis, the first king of the Franks, at Reims in 496. It was, however, forcefully attacked by the liberals, notably Augustin Thierry and his brother Amédée. Liberals not only rewrote the history of the third estate in order to justify bourgeois influence, they also rewrote the history of Gauls and Franks in order to combat the arrogance of king and aristocracy. Their heroes were the Gauls who had been subjugated by Romans and Franks but, rather than the Franks, were the source of the best French characteristics. Amédée Thierry, in his *History of the Gauls* (1828) saw in them 'a personal bravery unmatched among ancient peoples, a spirit that is free, impetuous, impressionable, eminently intelligent; but at the same time an extreme fickleness, no constancy, a marked repugnance towards ideas or order and discipline which are so powerful in the Germanic races'. The hero of his tale, portrayed as a great national leader embodying these traits, was Vercingetorix, defeated by the Romans at Alésia and put to death in Rome.

The struggle between Gaul and Frank was sublimated in the highly influential *History of France* (1838–53) by one of Augustin Thierry's pupils, Henri Martin (1810–83). He dedicated the *History* to his 'dear and illustrious master' but also praised Amédée Thierry's *History of the Gauls* as the 'foundation stone of the history of France'. Martin popularized the idea of the 'fusion of races', arguing that the French were 'sons of the Gauls by birth and character, sons of the Romans by education, violently revived by the admixture of German barbarians as the vitality of ancient civilisation was fading'. Further, he argued that 'the soil of Gaul was the theatre prepared by Providence for a nation destined to bind the European alliance and to initiate modern civilisation'. And yet the clever synthesis thought necessary to unite the French nation was not always as popular as the revolutionary idea of struggle between Gauls and Franks continuing to the Revolution and beyond. Martin Nadaud, the stonemason from the Creuse who became an intransigent republican politician, used the struggle of Gauls and Franks to underpin not the conflict between orders but that between republicans and royalists. He began his memoirs by asserting that he was descended from the 'great and powerful Gaulois race that was reduced to slavery by the double conquest of Romans and Franks'. He argued that the Gallic people suffered a 'long and cruel domination' and that eighteen centuries after the Roman conquest a Gaul was thrown into the Bastille for praising 'our chivalrous Gallic fatherland'. While the nobles had been Frankish and monarchist, he said, 'the Gauls always wanted the republic' and finally had their way in the nineteenth century.

The *patrie* and the wider world

The *patrie* in French thought is the fatherland, the ancestral territory for which its descendants are prepared to die, but with the French Revolution it also became a spiritual homeland, the land of liberty, which the French as citizens founded and for which as soldiers they were equally prepared to die. The first moment of trial came on 12 July 1792 when the Legislative Assembly declared the 'patrie en danger' and called all citizens to arms. The army of *sans-culottes* [artisans and shopkeepers] together with peasants, drove back the professional Prussian army at Valmy on 20 September 1792, the day before the Republic was proclaimed. A second moment of trial came on 23 August 1793 as the enemy forced the French armies back on a number of fronts. The Convention then ordered a *levée en masse* requisitioning all French people until the enemy had been expelled from the territory of the Republic. 'Young men will go to fight,' it declared, 'married men will make weapons and transport supplies; women will make tents and uniforms and will serve in hospitals; children will make bandages from old linen; old people will have themselves carried to public places where they will stimulate the courage of the soldiers, hatred for kings, and the unity of the Republic.'

This patriotic upsurge is the stuff of myth but how far did the reality live up to it? In the first place the French armies were never solely made up of volunteers: these fought alongside regular troops and were in fact amalgamated with them after 1793. The appeal for volunteers was never enough and in 1793 and again in 1798 the Republic had to resort to compulsion. Populations living near the eastern frontiers were generally willing to fight, but those in the West were not. For many people the *patrie* was understood in the older sense of a local or regional homeland, no different from the *pays*. And while in the east defending the *patrie* in the newer sense might help to defend the *pays*, in the west conscription to fight for a regime that persecuted the faith and had killed the king was resisted as an attack on the close-knit structures, and Catholic and royalist sentiments of the region. Napoleon brought opposition to conscription under control, instituting the gendarmerie and mobile columns of soldiers to track down draft-dodgers and deserters in the countryside. The massive round-ups of 1810–11 supplied the army that invaded Russia in 1812, although this force was multinational: only 200,000 of the 600,000 soldiers were French.

After the Restoration there was no question of a citizen-army that had revolutionary as well as patriotic impulses. The one organized by the reforms of 1818 and 1832 was a small professional army recruited by drawing lots rather than universal obligation, insulated from society by long-term (six or seven years) service and the inculcation of a military spirit, and trained to fire on rioters and insurgents when necessary. Arguably France did not engage in a major war for half a century because of its revolutionary implications. Not until the Franco-Prussian war, when the Republic came into being after the collapse of the Empire and faced imminent defeat, did the provisional government under Gambetta have recourse to a *levée en masse*. The model of 1792 was on everyone's mind, but what they got was 1793, as the National Guard of Paris refused to accept the humiliating peace terms imposed by Prussia and launched an insurrection. The result was the Paris Commune and a renewed aversion to a citizen-army which, as Thiers said, meant 'putting a gun on the shoulder of every socialist'.

One of the characteristics of French patriotism was a belief that the French were not only serving France but serving humanity as a whole. The French Revolution and the Declaration of the Rights of Man and the Citizen were not only for the benefit of the French but for mankind in general. They presumed that human nature was everywhere the same and had no conception that other peoples were different or could wish for anything else. The gospel of liberation from tyranny, feudalism, and superstition would spread itself, and to distance itself from the expansionist ambitions of French kings the Constitution of 1791 stated that 'the French nation renounces the undertaking of all war with a view to conquest, and will never use its strength against the liberty of any people'. The message was certainly an attractive one. The inhabitants of Avignon and the Comtat-Venaissin, who since the Avignon papacy had been subjects of the Pope, voted to become citizens of the French nation and were welcomed by the National Assembly in September 1791. As the French armies pushed back the Austrians and Prussians in November 1792, the Convention declared 'in the name of the French nation that it will provide fraternity and aid to all peoples who seek to recover their liberty'. In the Rhineland, Savoy, and Nice votes were held in which the populations or their delegates expressed the will to join the French nation, and the Convention duly obliged.

France, however, was not just a beacon of liberty but a power fighting for survival in an extended European conflict. Alongside this ideological imperialism developed the doctrine of the natural frontiers of France which for its own national security it must occupy. 'The boundaries of France are marked out by nature', Danton told the Convention on 31 January 1793 as it debated the future of Belgium, 'We shall reach them at their four points: the Atlantic, the Rhine, the Alps, the Pyrenees.' After the setbacks of the summer of 1793 the Convention began to think in terms not of liberation but of annexation. When victory permitted, in 1795, France annexed Belgium and the Rhineland, without any mention of a plebiscite, integrating them into the departmental system of centralized administration and preparing for their assimilation. Further afield, in the Netherlands, Switzerland, and Italy, under the Directory, there was never any doubt that the French intended to occupy, control, requisition, tax, and conscript for the benefit of the French army and the French Republic, but annexation was concealed behind the fiction of sister-republics, notionally part of the revolutionary fraternity. When French armies were again in retreat in 1799 General Masséna reported that 'Now only the efforts of France can stop Europe from falling back into the barbarism into which her enemies are plunging her.' Napoleon found the ultimate justification for his strategy of European empire: by imposing French rule on other ethnic groups from the Spaniards to the Russians, he was bringing them up to a level of civilization enjoyed by the French nation alone. The civilizing mission allowed the French to neatly resolve the contradiction between the liberating mission and the imperative of conquest.

In spite of the revolutionaries' rejection of the *Ancien Régime* heritage of dynastic conquest, they were under pressure to attain the same greatness as the kings they had overthrown. *Grandeur* was as much an obsession for them as it was for Louis XIV. On the death of Lazare Hoche, who had conquered the Rhineland, in 1797, Marie-Joseph Chénier called him the 'grand général' leading the 'grande armée' of the 'grande nation'. Napoleon promoted himself alternatively as a Roman emperor or as Charlemagne, although his enemies preferred to see him as Genghis Khan or Attila the Hun. Yet France spent most of the nineteenth century in the shadow of defeat, first that of Waterloo, then that of Sedan. National consciousness was perhaps forged less by triumph than by humiliation.

After Waterloo France was driven back to her frontiers of 1790, losing Belgium, the Rhineland, Nice, and Savoy. She had to pay a massive war indemnity, some of which went to rebuilding the barrier fortresses from Nieuport to Namur to lock herself in, and for the next few years suffered an army of occupation 150,000 strong. The historian Ernest Lavisse (1842–1922), a native of Picardy, later recalled his grandmother's stories of how she hid in the woods when the Cossacks came by. The lack of international credibility on the international scene was a fundamental factor behind the political weakness of the restored monarchy. Charles X tried to stave off catastrophe in 1830 by seizing Algiers, and under the July Monarchy France became bogged down in a war to subjugate Algeria. 'Great nations, like great men,' reflected the governor-general of Algeria, Bugeaud, 'must make mistakes with grandeur'.

In 1840 the government of Adolphe Thiers tried to revive Napoleon's glories in the Orient by supporting the pasha of Egypt in his bid to take Syria from his suzerain, the Ottoman Emperor. The coalition of Great Britain, Prussia, Austria, and Russia that had brought down Napoleon immediately re-formed. 'March on the Rhine, tear up the treaties of 1815,' blasted *Le National*, 'tell Germany, Italy, Spain and Poland that you carry the magnet of civilization at the tip of your weapons . . . whether France will retain its rank or not in the world is at stake'. In the event France was obliged to bow to the coalition and climb down. 'The chains of 1815 were suddenly fastened again,' wrote the historian Edgar Quinet who as a boy had met the heroes of Austerlitz and hungered for a national renaissance, 'as if she had lost the battle a second time France was reliving the day after Waterloo.' The repercussions of the crisis in the Mediterranean were felt on the Rhine where the Germans, far from awaiting liberation from the French, went into spasms of nationalism. Quinet riposted that 'the Rhine is a French river, and every time that France has been great she has bathed in its waters. Louis XIV and the Republic, not to mention Charlemagne, have mixed it with our history.' Such assertions, however, only reinforced German determination not to be bullied by France again.

How to recover national greatness without provoking a resurgence of the anti-French coalition was the eternal conundrum. When the Republic was again declared in 1848 many hoped that the great deeds of 1792 would instantly be repeated. The new Foreign Minister Lamartine was even more keen, however, to appease the old enemies. The treaties of 1815, he announced, were no longer valid in the eyes of the Republic, and France was prepared to take military action to safeguard the aspirations of the Swiss and Italians for national self-determination. But he said nothing about helping the Poles and he was determined to lay to rest the spectre of French revolutionary armies rampaging across Europe. 'To return after fifty years to the principle of 1792, to the idea of conquering an empire', he said, 'would be to go not forwards but backwards in time.' A year later, French troops seemed to move backwards in time by restoring the Pope to the Papal States, whence he had been ejected by Italian patriots.

Napoleon III demonstrated a certain flair in recovering greatness while keeping the enemy coalition at bay. He shook off French isolation and orchestrated a diplomatic alliance with Great Britain, Austria, and Prussia against Russia, by spiritualizing the Eastern Question into a rivalry with Russia to protect the Christian subjects of the

Ottoman Empire. He returned to the policy of natural frontiers, acquiring Nice and Savoy from Piedmont as the price of military assistance to the Italians against Austria. He led his troops into the war to liberate Italy along the 'sacred road' taken by his uncle via Marengo, Lodi, Castiglione, and Arcola, and repeating his triumphs at Magenta and Solferino. However, he made a truce with Austria the moment that Prussia, fearing that like his uncle he would cross the Rhine as well, began to mobilize. Although he sidestepped the European coalition, Napoleon unwittingly provoked Prussian military reform and the unification of Germany under Prussian leadership. The Prussian victory over Austria at Sadowa in 1866, which led to a Prussian-dominated North German Confederation, was felt by France to be a national humiliation. The incorporation of south Germany into the new German Empire entailed a war between Prussia and France for the title of greatest European power. Émile Ollivier, who was chief minister in 1870, declared that he was going to war with Prussia with a light heart, taunting the republican opposition which had insisted since 1866 that France had lost its rank as the leading power in Europe and must recover it.

The French entered upon the war of 1870 with immense patriotic fervour. In his memoirs, to defend his reputation, Ollivier quoted a source in the political world who reported that 'you would have to go back to 1792 or 1793 to have some idea of the national *élan*. The enthusiasm of France to avenge so many years of humiliation matched that which was stirred up, eighty years ago, for the defence of our frontiers.' 'No war was ever entered into', wrote Arthur de Gobineau, 'with such a swelling of pride, a more intense joy of battle, a more absolute certainty in military superiority . . . Never was blindness stretched to such a limit.' National pride led to national catastrophe, the fall of the Empire, and the castration of the Republic. Defeat preyed on the French mind until, with American assistance, Germany was defeated in 1918.

Conclusion

For the development of French national sentiment, the defeat of 1870–1 was crucial. It was second only to the French Revolution as a period during which the idea of the nation as the political will to belong to it was refined. After the German annexation of Alsace and Lorraine a controversy broke out between the Berlin historian Theodore Mommsen and the Strasbourg historian Fustel de Coulanges. Mommsen argued that since the Alsatians mostly spoke a German dialect they were part of the German *Volk*. Fustel de Coulanges replied that a nation was based not on race or language but was 'a community of ideas, interests, affections, memories and hopes . . . it is what one loves'. If the Alsatians did not wish to become German, he asserted, they would remain French. This was the context of Ernest Renan's famous Sorbonne lecture of 1882, *What is a Nation?* Extrapolating from the Alsatian case to a general theory he argued that belonging to a nation was an act of political will, a 'daily plebiscite', taken in the light of a common history of striving for glory. In this sense a defeat such as that of 1870 might bind the nation even more firmly, since 'we love in proportion to the sacrifices we have agreed and the pain we have suffered . . . indeed, collective suffering unites more than joy'. Such ideas of the nation were in fact percolating to every classroom in the Republic in the form of the best-selling reader *Le Tour de la France par deux enfants* by G. Bruno, the pen-name of Augustine Fouillée. It is the story of two orphans who leave Phalsbourg in Alsace after its annexation to Germany, in search of their French uncle and a new home. Travelling the length and breadth of France they discover its beauty and fertility, as well as stories of its heroes and heroines. Eventually they find their uncle and settle in the Orléanais to rebuild a France in mourning by cultivating the land. In the last scene the younger boy, Julien, runs into the courtyard of the new-found farm 'in the joy of at last having a *patrie*, a house, a family, as he had wished for so long', and cries, 'I love France!'

7

France and the wider world

Michael Heffernan

Introduction

The history of modern France can be seen as an ideological struggle between competing interpretations of the nation's past, present and future. Opposing political groups developed distinct, usually mutually exclusive, visions of the country, although no single perspective dominated for more than a decade or so in the century after the Revolution. Paradoxically, the failure to invent a transcendent idea of France to which a majority of Frenchmen and women could subscribe provided opportunities for those whose ideas would otherwise have commanded little public support. The belief in a 'greater' imperial France, linked to a large extra-European empire, is a revealing example. The arguments in favour of French overseas expansion won limited support before the 1890s but despite this France established a colonial empire second only to Britain in size and population. How such an empire was established in the absence of substantial political support is the principal theme of this chapter.

France, the Caribbean, and slavery, 1788–1804

Prior to the Revolution, French colonial interests had focused on the Americas but had been repeatedly frustrated by Britain's dominance of the Atlantic. The Seven Years War virtually ended French overseas ambitions with the exception of the Caribbean where Martinique, Guadaloupe, and Saint-Domingue (the French sector of Hispaniola) were amongst the world's most profitable plantation colonies. Saint-Domingue supplied 40 per cent of the world's sugar (*c.*120,000 tonnes) in 1789 and made a sizeable contribution to the £9 million profit the French Caribbean generated in that year (compared to £5 million in the British Caribbean). Fifty per cent of these profits accrued to France itself, particularly the major Atlantic ports of Nantes, Bordeaux, and La Rochelle where a new cadre of super-rich plantation owners emerged. Their wealth was based on the labour of roughly one million African slaves who crossed the Atlantic during the eighteenth century from France's West African enclaves of Gorée and Saint-Louis. By 1789, there were more than 650,000 slaves in the French Caribbean, half a million on Saint-Domingue alone. They formed the demographic foundation of a complex social order which included wealthy plantation owners (*békés*), poorer white farmers (*petits blancs*), white labourers (*engagés*), and the mixed race mulattos. Race was a determining factor in this system but by no means all blacks were slaves. The unindentured African population on Saint-Domingue outnumbered the European population and perhaps 100,000 slaves, 20 per cent of the total slave population, were owned by free Africans in the 1780s.

The nature of the colonial order provoked intense debate in France. The initial anti-slavery criticisms of Montesquieu and the Abbé Raynal inspired Condorcet, Mirabeau, the Duc de Roche-foucauld, and others to establish the Société des Amis des Noirs in 1788, a year after William Wilberforce and his colleagues founded the London Society for the Abolition of Slavery. French planters promptly organized a rival society, the Club Massiac, whose first meeting took place a matter of days after the Bastille was stormed. Although the new National Assembly agreed to leave colonial matters in the hands of local officials and to preserve the existing property regime, the administration of French colonies quickly degenerated into chaos. By the middle of 1790, pitched battles had broken out between whites, mulattos, and blacks on most French Caribbean islands, particularly Saint-Domingue where a mulatto rebellion flared briefly, led by Vincent Ogé. Attempts at reform only created confusion and further anger. Having recognized mulatto political rights on 15 May 1791, the National Assembly revoked this decision three months later. By the summer of 1791, Saint-Domingue was a bewildering patchwork of white and mulatto-controlled areas patrolled by rival gangs such as the republican *pompons rouges* and the royalist *pompons blancs*.

On 21 August 1791, a more organized revolt of runaway slaves erupted in the north of Saint-Domingue led by a 50-year-old former slave-turned-veterinarian named Toussaint Breda. It became the first social revolution in the western hemisphere and the only successful slave revolt in history. The Legislative Assembly in Paris was divided about how to respond to this new threat. Three Civil Commissioners, supported by 6,000 troops, were eventually dispatched to Saint-Domingue in July 1792, in an attempt to restore law and order (based on a new decree that guaranteed the political rights of all non-slaves, regardless of colour) and re-establish the lucrative colonial trade. British and Spanish authorities on neighbouring islands had been providing financial and material support both to Toussaint (who was by now commissioned as a colonel in the Spanish army under his assumed surname of L'Ouverture) and to other counter-revolutionary, royalist gangs. Following the declaration of war between France and Spain in March 1793, Spanish troops invaded Saint-Domingue in an attempt to create a united Hispaniola under Bourbon control, with L'Ouverture's men still nominally associated with their campaign. Two small British forces also landed in the extreme south-west and north-west of the island later that year.

Cut off from metropolitan France and with only half their original expeditionary force still alive, the beleaguered French Commissioners proclaimed the end of slavery on the island in August 1793. A black deputy, Jean-Baptiste Belley-Mars, was sent to Paris to defend this position before the National Convention. The Commissioners' ruling was duly endorsed on 4 February 1794 and extended to all French colonies, a decision partially motivated by the hope that freed slaves would rally to France rather than Britain or Spain. L'Ouverture soon obliged, repudiating his Spanish association and directing his 4,000 well-disciplined men to strike against their former 'allies'. Through the summer and autumn of 1794, republican soldiers and Toussaint's men successfully resisted British, Spanish, and royalist forces in all sectors of Hispaniola as smaller slave revolts erupted all over the Caribbean. In the midst of this turmoil, a small French force recaptured Martinique and Guadaloupe from the British and then conquered Saint-Vincent, Sainte-Lucie, and most of Grenada. In 1796, a huge flotilla of nearly 1,000 British ships and 30,000 men, the largest force ever to cross the Atlantic, set forth to destroy French republican influence in the Caribbean, with further reinforcements dispatched during 1797. Despite this impressive show of strength, the British campaign soon faltered as its troops fell prey to guerrilla warfare and disease, particularly malaria which had reached epidemic levels following the collapse of drainage and irrigation systems. Some 60,000 British soldiers probably expired in the struggle for Caribbean hegemony between 1796 and 1800, by which time the rebellion was entirely controlled by Toussaint, the French Civil Commissioners having returned to France.

Napoleon, now firmly in control in Paris, was increasingly concerned by Toussaint's independent actions and, following a preliminary peace accord with Britain in September 1801, a new 20,000-strong French expedition set forth, under General Leclerc, Napoleon's brother-in-law, to restore order to Saint-Domingue. L'Ouverture was captured on 6 June 1802 and transported back in France where, on 4 May 1802, it was decreed that slavery would once again be recognised throughout the French Caribbean. The decision to restore slavery undermined the last vestiges of the revolutionary idealism of 1789 and undermined Leclerc's tenuous control of Saint-Domingue. The divisions between rival black factions, and between blacks and mulattos, that had hampered Toussaint's capacity to resist Leclerc's initial invasion were quickly forgotten as all groups united against the common, French invader. Toussaint's arrest, and his subsequent death in early 1804, following months of brutal ill-treatment, was symbolically important but only served to encourage the well-trained black commanders who continued his struggle on Saint-Domingue. The arrival of 15,000 French troops in 1803 did little to bolster Leclerc's collapsing authority. The remaining French troops were finally evacuated, ignominiously as British prisoners of war, late in 1803. On 1 January 1804, Saint-Domingue gained its independence as Haiti, an entirely new Amerindian name chosen deliberately to underscore the complete break with the island's colonial and slave past. Perhaps 20,000 French soldiers died on Saint-Domingue (out of a total of some 35,000 throughout the Caribbean).

The foundation of an independent Haiti marked the final collapse of France's attempt to re-establish a presence in the Americas. The French decision in 1803 to sell the 828,000 square miles of territory west of the Mississippi recently acquired from Charles IV of Spain to the USA, for a mere $15 million (a land deal that doubled the size of the infant American Republic and inaugurated a century-long process of westward American expansionism), reflects Napoleon's realistic assessment of France's potential influence in the Americas. Henceforth, Napoleonic imperialism would be a predominantly European ideology concerned with the creation of a land-based continental empire. Extra-European possessions would be seen, in the Napoleonic geographical imagination, as pawns in a geopolitical game designed to reinforce France's political and cultural hegemony in continental Europe.

France, Africa, and Islam, 1798–1851

The other Napoleonic interventions beyond the European theatre emphasize this point. Fresh from his Italian triumph in 1796, a campaign of liberation rather than a military conquest according to French republican propaganda, Napoleon shifted his acquisitive gaze to the south and east, towards Egypt and the Holy Land. A fleet of thirteen ships and over 36,000 troops set forth for Alexandria, at the mouth of the Nile, in June 1798, conquering Malta on the way. Napoleon himself remained in Egypt for fourteen months but his armies stayed on the banks of the Nile until 1801 when they were forced by disease and a British blockade to evacuate the area. The French invasion of Egypt, and its ultimate failure, was inspired by a desire to curb British and Russian ambitions in the Ottoman Empire, to challenge Britain's trade routes to India, and to protect French commercial interests, but was also justified by more complex cultural arguments.

Reared on a rich diet of Enlightenment classicism and revolutionary republicanism, the new generation of French imperial soldiers saw direct historical affinities between modern France and the ancient Mediterranean civilizations of Rome and Greece, a theme endlessly recycled in the melodramatic paintings of Jacques-Louis David, in the stage-managed revolutionary festivals of the early 1790s, and in the symbols and icons selected to embody the new Republican ideals and values. The shift from Republic to Empire in the Ancient World was, it seemed, a preordained historical trajectory, destined to repeat itself in modern France. But where the ancient world had seen Mediterranean republics spawn empires in the Middle East and northern Europe, the modern world would see a new northern European Republic give birth to new Mediterranean and Middle Eastern empires in the very heartland of the Ancient World, now sadly eclipsed and prey to the rapacious exploitation of monarchical powers and corrupt local rulers.

Protected by the occupying French soldiers, 150 handpicked scholars undertook an exhaustive survey of the past and present conditions of the Nile Valley. The objective was the establishment of a new Académie des Sciences in Cairo, modelled on the French Académie in Paris, a modern replacement for the great library at Alexandria established by Alexander the Great. This represented a suitably grandiose idea discussed in the multi-volume *Description d'Égypte* that appeared between 1809 and 1822, the published result of the expedition's scholarly inquiries. The Egyptian expedition and survey heralded a new and distinctively French cultural imperial imagination that was to persist and develop over the next two centuries. It marked a turning point in French, and European, engagement with the Islamic world and marked the birth of modern 'Orientalism' as a scholarly pursuit with a distinct ideological and imperial rationale. By conquering Egypt militarily through force of arms and intellectually through the power of European scholarship, Napoleonic France sought to possess not only the land, resources, and people of Egypt but also the region's inspirational history and civilization in the name of modern republican France.

The final collapse of the Napoleonic regime in 1815 left France with only scattered remnants of its former overseas empire: Guadaloupe, Martinique, Guiana, the islands of Saint-Pierre and Miquelon, Réunion, and a few enclaves on the coast of India. A new global geopolitics was now firmly in place, the outcome of the preceding victory of a British-controlled 'Atlantic system' over the French-controlled 'continental system'. Britain's Atlantic supremacy sustained an extraordinary export boom that underpinned the country's early industrialization. France's short-lived dominance of the continental system did not compensate for the dramatic downturn in French trade with the former American colonies. Whereas French cotton production tripled between 1790 and 1815, Britain's industrial production quadrupled over the same period from an already higher level. At the same time, French ports, the gateway to the world under the *Ancien Régime*, were steadily undermined.

Under the Restoration Monarchy, the very word 'empire' was enough to set alarm bells ringing in Parisian ministerial corridors but there remained a small constituency, including some notable veterans of the Napoleonic armies, who still dreamed of relaunching a new non-European French empire, particularly in Africa. A group of these diehards established the world's first geographical society in Paris in 1821 to encourage French interests in travel, exploration and, by extension, overseas empire in Africa. The quest for the source of the Niger river and the location of the fabled central African city of Timbuctoo were among their central preoccupations. Such scientific concerns were reinforced by hard economic logic. French planters insisted that their profit margins in the remaining Caribbean islands demanded a continued supply of African slave labour. Despite Louis XVIII's personal assurance that he would end slavery in French colonies, some 125,000 Africans crossed the Atlantic to work in the French Caribbean between 1815 to 1831. The desire to reinforce France's position on the West African coast, whence most African slaves originated, inspired some less than successful colonial schemes, notably the attempt to establish new colonial settlements in Senegal in the summer of 1816. The flagship of the convoy transporting 360 pioneering French *colons*, *La Méduse*, ran aground in calm waters off the West African coast and broke up. The terrible plight of the ship's passengers, abandoned by their captain and cast adrift on a flimsy raft, was described in a lurid account by two survivors and immortalized in Théodore Géricault's huge canvas, *The Raft of the Medusa* (1819).

Such reversals did little to advance the cause of a new African empire through the 1820s and it was not until the death knell of the

Restoration Monarchy had been sounded that the argument for an African imperial *démarche* received serious official support. This renewed attention was encouraged by stories of fantastic Algerian wealth, the supposed outcome of centuries of Mediterranean piracy, and also by the need to divert attention from domestic political problems. As a pretext for invasion the French government resurrected a dispute that had erupted three years earlier between the Turkish *dey* in Algiers and the French consul over a supposedly unpaid bill for a grain shipment made to France during the 1790s. A fleet of 635 French ships and 35,000 troops was hastily assembled in June 1830 and duly took possession of the former Turkish Regency of Algiers, beginning more than 130 years of colonial rule in North Africa and transforming France's relationship with Africa and the Islamic world.

The invasion came too late for the doomed monarchy which collapsed a few weeks later. Since Louis-Philippe's new July Monarchy was preoccupied with domestic affairs, it showed little interest in North Africa. Matters were left in the hands of the occupying army. A new unit, the Légion Étrangère, was established in 1831 and stationed at the small Algerian outpost of Sidi-bel-Abbès, to the south of Oran. Initially, French authority was limited to Algiers and its hinterland and the coastal towns of Oran, Bône, Koléa, Azeu, and Mostaganem, all seized in the early months of occupation. The rural areas remained in a state of near anarchy until the arrival of Marshal Bertrand Clauzel as the new governor-general in 1835. Ignoring an official report of the preceding year that recommended only a limited colonization beyond the larger coastal towns (the so-called *occupation restreinte*), Clauzel expanded the sphere of French military authority and captured several inland towns, including Tlemcen, Mascara, Miliana, and Médéa. Following fierce resistance, the fortress city of Constantine was also occupied. In an attempt to make his forces self-sufficient, Clauzel cleared woodland and drained the marshy areas of the Mitidja, south of Algiers. This fertile region—the 'garden' of Algeria—was to become a cherished symbol of France's pioneering colonial spirit. A number of *fermes fortifiées* were established across the region and European settlers, mostly army veterans, were given free land and accommodation to begin a new life as colonial pioneers. By 1835, the first French colonial village, Boufarick, was established. The European civilian population increased steadily through the 1830s from 8,000 in 1833 (with 28,000 troops) to nearly than 38,000 by 1840 (with 66,000 troops).

The expansion of French control during the 1830s met with increasing resistance. Many native Algerians fled from their homes in the fertile coastal belt, or *tell*, and took refuge from the escalating violence in the mountainous interior. The 'liberated' territory they abandoned was promptly acquired by the occupying French army. Various ineffective peace treaties were signed with local Islamic leaders but these were invariably infringed. In November 1839, the principal resistance leader, Abd el-Kader, marshalled sufficient support to declare a full-scale *jihad* against the French invaders. After two years of savage warfare, Marshal Thomas-Robert Bugeaud was installed as the new governor-general in early 1841. A tough, uncompromising soldier of peasant Limousin stock, Bugeaud waged a brutal campaign that claimed countless innocent victims and which saw the wholesale destruction of villages, livestock, and crops. A steadily increasing number of French troops served under Bugeaud; by 1846, a third of the entire army was stationed in Algeria. After six years of bloodshed, Abd el-Kader surrendered in December 1847. Like Toussaint L'Ouverture before him, he was arrested and imprisoned in France though he was subsequently pardoned by Napoleon III in 1852 and lived the remainder of his life in Syria where he became a trusted ally of France in the Middle East.

Large areas of Algerian land were now under French military control. Land seizures reflected not only an indifference to indigenous property rights but also an inability to make sense of landownership regulations. Under Islamic law, privately owned *melk* land represented only a small part of the rural territory. Most land was classified as either *beylick* (controlled by the *dey* and the Ottoman imperial authorities), *habous* (controlled by mosques and other Islamic institutions), or *arch* (communally controlled, tribal land). To most French army commanders, the Algerian agrarian system seemed primitive, wasteful, and inefficient. A standard refrain developed amongst French commanders. Algeria was a region of emptiness and disorder; of past glory but present decay. It was *un pays sans maître* which cried out to be mapped, surveyed, drained, irrigated, and brought into the orbit of modern capital-intensive agriculture.

The existence of these 'new' lands provoked vigorous debate about the possibilities of European colonization in North Africa. More than

300 books and pamphlets were published about Algeria in the 1830s alone. More serious commentators argued the Algerian adventure would prove a costly diversion but others hoped a French presence in North Africa would restore the region's agricultural potential, so skilfully exploited by the classical civilizations of antiquity. This would only be possible, it was argued, after a major influx of European capital and labour. If properly managed, Algeria might become a stepping stone to a new French African empire, an opportunity to extend French language, culture, and influence across a new continent. Bugeaud had clear ideas on the most suitable form of administration in his Algerian fiefdom. His slogan, *Ense et Arato* (the sword and the plough), perfectly encapsulates his policy. Drawing on a Roman imperial model, and on the more recent experience of Russian colonization in central Asia, Bugeaud envisioned an Algerian settler community made up of army veterans. Former soldiers would be acclimatized to the rigours of the North African environment and could be relied upon to defend themselves in an emergency. They would tolerate military administration, the *régime du sabre*, that Bugeaud hoped to preserve in the face of growing pressure to establish local civilian government.

However, this method would never generate a large settler community, as Bugeaud freely admitted and, on 18 April 1841, a new law offered free passage, land and accommodation to incoming civilians, regardless of their point of origin, provided they agreed to work their land for a specified period. By 1845, there were 100,000 European colonists in Algeria. In the mid-1830s, most Europeans lived in or near Algiers; a decade later, the majority were farming land in an expanding network of fortified villages and farmsteads, including 63 new colonial villages. Only 43 per cent of the European immigrants came from France, the rest originated in Spain, Italy, Malta, and various parts of Germany. On 15 April 1845, another decree confirmed the three ancient provinces of Algiers, Oran, and Constantine as French administrative territories and specified three different forms of colonial land to replace the complex mosaic of local land rights. Henceforth, Algerian lands were designated as either *zones civiles* (where Europeans were in the majority), *zones mixtes* (where Europeans were in the minority), or *zones arabes* (where there was no European settlement). Military rule prevailed in the latter two zones though the indigenous population in all areas was to be governed by local colonial officers and their Muslim assistants (*caids*) through a network of *bureaux arabes*. Deprived of virtually all legal rights, native Algerians were subjected to further legislation on 21 July 1847, designed to undermine the migratory nature of the agrarian economy. Based loosely on US attempts to sedentarize native Americans, the new law introduced the system of *cantonnement*. Presented as a liberal act to protect indigenous property rights, the real objective was to ensure maximum control over an otherwise mobile and suspect local population. The result was the 'liberation' of more land for European settlement. At least 60,000 hectares passed from Muslim to European hands in western Algeria in the early 1850s.

Despite the manifest injustices of French expansion, many on the radical Left supported the policy of energetic Algerian colonization. The Saint-Simonians, that priesthood of utopian socialists who flourished briefly under the Restoration and early July Monarchy, had a significant influence on early French colonial thinking in Algeria. Following the now familiar model inherited from the Egyptian intervention, the Ministry of War decided to organize a major scientific survey of Algeria. Like the earlier surveys, this partly reflected the urgent need for detailed geographical knowledge about local topography, climate, and soils. The initial failure to capture Constantine, a reversal that cost the lives of over 1,000 French soldiers, had been blamed on poor reconnaissance and inadequate maps.

After much dithering, about twenty young soldiers and academics were dispatched to Algeria in 1839. Many of these men were products of the École Polytechnique, the spiritual home of the Saint-Simonians since the last days of the First Empire when the movement's eponymous leader, Claude Henri de Saint-Simon, took up residence nearby and began to exert a powerful influence over the young students studying there. The thirty-nine-volume report of the Algerian expedition, published between 1844 and 1867, was an impressive achievement, particularly in view of the escalating warfare in the region at the time. Like the Egyptian survey, this was an all-embracing encyclopaedic description of the region's history, physical environment, and social order. The more eloquent *savants* made a strong case for a coordinated, large-scale programme of civilian colonization, involving immigrants from all over Europe. The French conquest of Algeria, it was argued, was the ideal opportunity to engineer a new and better society on the edge of a new continent; a 'hybrid' civilization combining the best of Europe with the best of Africa.

This was the message of Prosper Enfantin, the self-styled leader of the Saint-Simonians, who was the expedition's chief ethnographer. Although he fell out with his superiors and published his report as an independent volume, his utopian vision was remarkably influential on other members of the expedition and on the wider colonial debate. In Enfantin's view, the chaotic, unplanned European emigration to the New World was sapping Europe's vitality and would end with the wholesale destruction of the indigenous populations of the Americas and Australia. Lessons could be learnt from this disorderly exodus. If wisely planned, the European colonization of Africa would benefit colonizers and colonized alike. North Africa, once the 'granary of Rome', could be returned to its former glory. Contemptuous of Bugeaud's military colonization, Enfantin insisted that French Algeria should have a civilian administration for a civilian population who would bring with them a range of European skills to complement native customs and practices. The two communities should live alongside each other, insisted Enfantin, and eventually intermarry.

The idea that French colonial authority in Africa might develop along different, more enlightened lines than the systems of imperial domination imposed by other European powers won some support on the Left outside of France. Friedrich Engels memorably welcomed France's 'pacification' of Algeria on the eve of the 1848 Revolution as the necessary first step towards the creation of a new social order in Africa. Despite the liberal, even socialist, pretensions of early colonial theorists, most were hopelessly romantic and prone to wild generalizations that were to have disturbing implications. Ernest Carette, a fellow Saint-Simonian on the expedition, insisted that the village-dwelling Berbers of Kabylia were the descendants of the region's original inhabitants who had taken refuge in these upland valleys following the Arab invasions of the seventh and eleventh centuries. The Kabyles had racial, cultural, and even religious affinities with northern Europeans, claimed Carette, as both communities had developed from common roots in the classical Mediterranean civilizations of Antiquity. The nomadic and Muslim Arabs, on the other hand, were representatives of entirely different, Asiatic culture whose religious, cultural, and social practices might be tolerated but never encouraged. This early version of the 'Kabyle' myth, the belief in the 'good' Kabyle and the 'bad' Arab, was to be endlessly reworked throughout the nineteenth century as part of a blatant 'divide and rule' strategy.

The mid-century domestic political upheavals in France altered the pace and nature of the French colonial impact in North Africa. In the wake of the February 1848 Revolution, the new Provisional Government introduced several colonial reforms, including the belated abolition of the slave trade. This was a personal triumph for Victor Schœlcher, whose Société pour l'Abolition de l'Esclavage had campaigned effectively since 1835 backed up by liberal intellectuals such as Victor Hugo, Alexis de Tocqueville, and Alphonse de Lamartine. A quarter of a million slaves were liberated and enfranchised in the Caribbean, while a new port settlement was also established in 1849 at Libreville in the Gabon for former slaves. The decision to ban slavery removed a source of tension between France and Britain but the attempt to police the new consensus produced further antagonism, particularly over the right to search ships suspected of illegally transporting slaves. French shipowners suspected this right was being misused by Britain to reinforce its authority over the open seas.

The other colonial reform introduced in the wake of February 1848 was the decision to make Algeria an integral part of the French Republic, no longer a colony but an extension, beyond the Mediterranean, of France itself. The three Algerian provinces became French *départements* and all Algerian land was re-classified as either civilian or military. In the civilian zones, administration would be conducted by, and on behalf of, Europeans through the same system of prefects, sub-prefects, mayors, and local councils as in metropolitan France. In the military zones, where the great bulk of the Arab and Berber population lived, a *régime du sabre*, or military rule, remained in place. The new constitutional arrangements were partly designed to facilitate rapid civilian colonization. Worried by the simmering discontent amongst France's urban unemployed, a popular anger that had precipitated the Revolution and which threatened to erupt once again if the promises of radical reform were not realized, Alexis de Tocqueville and Alphonse de Lamartine both proposed schemes involving resettlement of the unemployed urban poor. After the violence of June 1848, 50 million francs were hastily set aside to pay for the mass exodus of up to 10 per cent of the Parisian population who were promised free land and accommodation in new, purpose-built agricultural villages in Algeria. Nearly 40,000 Parisians registered for the scheme though only 15,000 eventually made the journey. These unfortunates endured dreadful conditions under military rule, living in tents, temporary barracks, and poorly constructed colonial villages, many situated in the most impractical and unhealthy locations. Despite this disaster, by the end of 1851, in the wake of Louis-Napoleon's *coup d'état*, the European population of Algeria stood at over 130,000, a third of whom were farming land around more than 130 new colonial villages.

The early history of French rule in Algeria set the scene for the subsequent phase of French empire-building in Africa and Asia. The original intervention in 1830 was a desperate and unsuccessful panic-measure designed to bolster a failing domestic regime. Successive governments under the July Monarchy and Second Republic failed to develop coherent or consistent colonial policies and only evinced an interest in North Africa during periods of domestic crisis. The catastrophic attempt to accelerate civilian colonization after 1848 suggests that high-sounding colonial rhetoric often masked a much cruder belief that Algeria was seen as a resettlement zone for France's unwanted urban poor. The absence of clear and realistic policies in Paris played directly into the hands of the occupying French army, whose senior commanders had a vested interest in increasing the area under their authority.

The chaotic nature of French imperial expansion was equally evident in West Africa. During the 1830s and 1840s the territories under French control gradually extended inland from Saint-Louis and other coastal trading posts, along the Senegal and Casamance rivers. The same story was repeated further south in Guinea, along the so-called Rivières du Sud, in the Côte d'Ivoire (despite significant reversals), and in equatorial Africa along the Ogooué and Congo rivers. A key figure in this process was the soldier-explorer Commander Bouët-Willaumez. French explorations in other parts of the world were less successful. The attempt to re-establish a presence in the Pacific, where French Catholic missionaries had been active on several Polynesian islands since the 1820s, including Tahiti, ended once again in frustration. French sailors docked off the previously unclaimed New Zealand in 1840, and made ready to seize the islands for France, only to learn that British seamen had arrived to seal the Treaty of Waitanga with the Maori chiefs a week earlier.

The Second Napoleonic Empire, 1851–1870

During the early years of the Second Empire, the situation in French North Africa continued much as before. By 1856, when the first census containing data on the population was published, there were 170,000 Europeans living in Algeria, many now second-generation immigrants, as well as 21,000 Jews. Half of the European population worked the land but only 5 per cent lived under military rule compared to 90 per cent of the 2.3 million Algerians. However, Napoleon III began to develop a serious interest in North Africa, inspired in part by the Arabophilia of a senior adviser, Ismail Urbain, a former Saint-Simonian. In 1858, the governor-general's position was suppressed and a new colonial ministry with responsibility for all of France's overseas possessions was established instead, headed by the Emperor's cousin, Prince Napoleon-Jérôme. In an attempt to limit the power of the occupying army and protect Muslim property, decrees were passed in 1858 and 1860 that halted the donation of free land and accommodation to incoming *colons* (settlers), thus dramatically reducing the pace of European colonization. In September 1860, Napoleon III embarked on a triumphant tour of Algeria which confirmed his grandiose ideals for a new African *imperium*. Henceforth, he insisted that he was Emperor not only of the French but also of the North African Arabs. In future Algeria would be known as a *Royaume arabe*. To reflect the multinational character of the *colons*, Algeria was explicitly referred to as a European (rather than a specifically French) colony. Under this apparently more benign imperial regime, new schools and hospitals (mostly run by the local Catholic clerics, directed by the fiercely evangelizing Archbishop Lavigerie of Algiers after 1867) were to cater for both European and Algerian peoples alike, though their success with respect to the latter was strictly limited.

These reforms caused concern in the army and, following outbreaks of violence in several parts of the Empire, the Emperor was persuaded to abandon the colonial ministry and reinstall local military rule in Algeria under a new governor-general, Amable Pélissier, the Duc de Malakoff. Pélissier was a disciple of Bugeaud and tried to use the *cantonnement* laws to launch a fresh offensive against Muslim property. But his actions were curtailed by further legislation—the so-called *Sénatus-Consulte* decrees published on 22 April 1863 and 14 July 1865—that prevented the confiscation of Muslim property by the military without proper compensation. Although this further reduced the rate of European colonial expansion, it also facilitated a more capital-intensive development of the existing European areas. Generous land concessions to exploit Algeria's forest and mineral resources had been granted to European companies since the early 1850s, notably the Société Genevoise de Sétif (20,000 hectares in 1853) and the Société de l'Habra et de la Macta (24,000 hectares in 1854). The era of the large colonial company was secured by the award, in 1865, of over 100,000 hectares of land to the Société Générale Algérienne. The development of a capitalist agrarian regime was mirrored by the dramatic transformations in the larger Algerian cities. During the 1850s and 1860s, new European *cités* emerged in Algiers, Oran, Constantine, Bône and Tlemcen. Jostling alongside the ancient *casbahs* of the Islamic citadels, the new European *quartiers* boasted modest versions of the sweeping boulevards and ornate buildings that had become such distinctive features of France's metropolitan urban landscapes.

The Emperor's interest in Algeria was endorsed by elements in the fashionable, and increasingly wealthy, French urban middle class. This was not entirely unprecedented, of course, for the regions bordering the eastern Mediterranean—Chateaubriand's 'land weathered by miracles'—had fascinated generations of French travellers, writers, and painters from the Enlightenment to the early nineteenth-century Romantic era. But the high point of French Orientalism, much of it centred on North Africa rather than the Middle East, came in the 1850s and 1860s. Highly romanticized historical novels, such as Gustave Flaubert's *Salammbô* (1862), set in ancient Carthage, and Eugène Fromentin's lyrical musings about the great desert underbelly of North Africa, *Un été dans le Sahara* (1857) and *Un été dans le Sahel* (1859), enjoyed immense popularity. With the enthusiastic support of the influential art critic Théophile Gautier, equally romanticized Orientalist paintings by Fromentin, Eugène Delacroix, Léon Belly, Gustave Guillaumet, and Théodore Chassériau regularly won prizes at the official *Salons*. This was a complex body of work, to be sure, ranging from the serious and evocative to the quasi-pornographic but certain familiar themes recur: lounging harem women, wild-eyed Arab horsemen, caravans plodding stoically across quasi-biblical desert landscapes, and images of religious devotion, occasionally overspilling into fanaticism and wanton cruelty. In such scenes, the Islamic world was depicted as a place where time stood still. Sometimes frightening and disturbing, North Africa was also a deeply alluring environment, the opposite of the increasingly secular, materialist world of modern, urban France; an arena where European taboos and conventions could be overturned.

Interest in the colonies was also sustained by a new generation of restless, independent-minded explorers who set off to chart the unmapped areas beyond the frontiers of the French Empire. The popularity of travel and exploration in the more exotic parts of the world is indicated by the enormous success of *Le Tour du monde*, an illustrated magazine, devoted to voyages of discovery, published by Hachette from 1860 onwards under the editorship of Édouard Charton. Although most explorers would have dismissed French Orientalism as a shallow metropolitan fad, they too were frequently inspired by a desire to experience a more 'authentic', spiritual arena beyond the safe, bourgeois world of Second Empire France. The idealism of French explorers was encapsulated by Henri Duveyrier, son of a leading Saint-Simonian playwright, who acquired a deserved reputation as an expert on the Sahara following his youthful voyages in the late 1850s. To Duveyrier, the nomadic desert Touareg were the perfect exemplification of 'savage' nobility, a people in many respects superior to corrupt and debased Europeans.

The colonial military authorities in the Empire were understandably annoyed by young explorers wandering around in sensitive areas. But as the colonial army was itself dominated by similarly adventurous spirits, their indignation was somewhat disingenuous. Indeed, senior colonial officers knew only too well that the French overseas empire would scarcely exist had it not been for ambitious young soldiers, intrepid explorers or ambitious 'chancers' seeking a quick profit. Soldiers on the distant outposts of empire quickly learned that official decrees and restraining orders took months to arrive and counted for little 'on the ground'. Here, in the colonial periphery, insubordination and a general refusal to carry out policies defined in Paris were raised to an art form. Objectives were always determined by local imperatives and strategic needs. As each new sector of land was conquered and pacified, so new threats (some real, many imagined) loomed in the territories beyond. It was only ever a matter of time before some incident (often deliberately engineered) became a pretext for further incursions. Once acquired, territory proved virtually impossible to surrender without unacceptable loss of face. Successive generations of Parisian ministers and politicians, few of whom had any enthusiasm for an overseas empire, were reduced to the status of impotent onlookers, offering only embarrassed *post hoc* justifications for already completed conquests: the politics of the *fait accompli*.

The expansion of the French Empire in West Africa during the 1850s and 1860s reflects the failure of political authority. The coastal enclaves at Saint-Louis and Gorée were somewhat vulnerable by 1850 following the abolition of slavery in 1848. Eager to maintain their presence in the region, the French army launched military explorations along the Ogooué valley and its tributaries during the early 1850s, some directed by an ambitious young officer, Louis-Léon-César Faidherbe, an abolitionist disciple of Schœlcher. Faidherbe believed that the Senegal river system could be a launching point of a great central African empire that would eventually extend seamlessly from the French colonies in North Africa. Acting more or less on his own volition, Faidherbe pioneered the exploitation of new cash crops, particularly groundnuts for their oil, while dreaming of a network of railways spreading from Saint-Louis into the African interior. He also pioneered new systems of territorial control which maximized the potential of limited troop numbers by the use of heavily defended forts in a carefully planned network. In 1854, though still a captain in his mid-thirties, Faidherbe became governor of Senegal at the behest of local commercial interests. In 1857, he established another legendary unit of the French army, the *tirailleurs sénégalais*.

A similar story can be recounted in Indochina, scene of a new imperial venture from the late 1850s. This reflected a growing concern in Paris that France was being left behind in the race for Asian markets. Britain had expanded into the Far East from its long-established power base in India, adding Singapore (1819) and Hong Kong (1842) to its Asian empire. Even Spain, Portugal and the Netherlands reaped the benefits of profitable Far Eastern possessions in the Philippines, Macau and Indonesia. France's initial objectives were modest and involved the establishment of a small enclave encompassing an area from Saigon, capital of the south Vietnamese province of Cochin-China (Nam Bo), to the coast. A French presence here, it was reasoned, would afford valuable access to the busy traffic of the South China Seas. The prospect of French business interests cornering a significant portion of the lucrative opium trade was also an important consideration. The Saigon enclave would become, it was hoped, a French Hong Kong. The fact that Catholic missionaries had operated in the city from the seventeenth century provided Napoleon III with what became a familiar self-serving rationale for invasion. Catholic France, it was argued, was the only great power that could offer protection to such small and vulnerable Christian communities. Following exaggerated reports of violence against Christians and a vigorous campaign in support of intervention by French bishops, fourteen gunboats, and 2,500 troops (mostly black Africans), under the command of Admiral Rigault de Genouilly, seized control of Saigon in 1858.

The subsequent expansion of French control into the Vietnamese interior was largely the result of military adventurism riding roughshod over limited original objectives. Within months of landing, forty villages had been occupied along the Saigon river. Four years later, the French army controlled much of Cochin-China. Despite widespread opposition in France (including criticism from otherwise pro-colonial commentators who argued that Indochina would be a costly diversion from the nation's African interests), military explorations and expeditions added more and more Vietnamese territory, particularly along the Mekong river into Cambodia, a trail blazed by Ernest Doudart de Lagrée in the late 1860s. By 1863, a protectorate was declared in Cambodia and in 1867 the remaining portions of Cochin-China were annexed. No official instructions had ever been issued to justify these actions.

The elaborate celebrations marking the opening of the Suez canal in 1869, in the presence of the Emperor and Empress, represented another projection of French cultural and political power. The Suez canal was the culmination of a long-held imperial dream dating back to the first Napoleonic expedition to Egypt. Mathieu de Lesseps, whose son Ferdinand would eventually oversee the canal's construction, had accompanied Napoleon to Egypt in 1798 and had remained for several years after the French armies were evacuated. Mathieu passed on his enthusiasm for a canal linking the Red Sea and the Mediterranean to Ferdinand, who was posted to Cairo as pro-consul during the early 1830s. Here Ferdinand encountered Prosper

Enfantin, the Saint-Simonian prophet later so influential in Algeria, who was engaged in a fruitless attempt to establish an Académie d'Égypte while also seeking to raise interest in the idea of a canal. Inspired by the charismatic Enfantin, de Lesseps devoted the next thirty years of his life to selling the idea to politicians and financiers across Europe. There was little enthusiasm for the project before the early 1860s, but the idea of realizing this long-held dream appealed to Napoleon III's sense of grandeur. French commercial and political interest in the Middle East had intensified since 1860, the latter reinforced by the Emperor's insistence that France, 'the eldest daughter of the Church', would henceforth protect the Christian communities throughout the region. With the support of the Emperor, de Lesseps was able to secure the necessary backing. The opening of the Suez canal was seen as an unalloyed triumph, a manifestation of France's benign intentions towards Africa and Asia. Frédéric Auguste Bartholdi's Statue of Liberty, eventually presented to the USA to mark the centenary of the American republic in 1876, was originally designed to stand at the entrance to the Suez canal to symbolize Europe spreading enlightenment to Africa and Asia.

Interest in France's overseas empire increased during the Second Empire, though the engine generating imperial expansion remained in the possession of independent-minded soldiers rather than metropolitan politicians. Some colonies were still seen as little more than dumping grounds for those rejected by the new Napoleonic order. French Guiana, the 'dry guillotine', had been used as a penal colony since the Revolution and it was to a small island off this swampy coastline, the notorious Devil's Island, that the Emperor banished his political opponents from 1852. The following year, French naval officers attempted to make good their failure in New Zealand by claiming the substantial Pacific island of New Caledonia for the Second Empire. After a decade of uncertainty, it was decided that this too would be a penal colony, a revealing illustration of the regime's fear of domestic political opposition.

Metropolitan imperialism, 1871–1880

For all this effort, the French overseas empire in 1870 was still tiny by comparison with Britain's. Informed public opinion had little interest in expanding the empire and very few political leaders felt that the nation's destiny would ever be significantly influenced by the non-European territories. Insofar as empire was ever seriously debated, a familiar anti-colonial argument had dominated amongst both liberals and conservatives. Overseas empire was seen as the British way. Having lost its battle with Britain in the eighteenth century, France had no choice but to accept its status as a European power with only limited overseas ambitions. Moreover, why should France waste precious resources of capital and labour on overseas empire when there was an insufficient supply of either to develop the country's European territory? How could the country ever compete as a colonizing power with other European nations that had large, 'surplus' populations in relation to available land? Without labour and capital reserves, colonies brought no economic benefit. The analysis of Jean-Baptiste Say was frequently invoked: empires were inherently antithetical to free trade, fundamentally mercantilist and corrupted 'natural' trading arrangements. Sheltered behind protective tariffs, colonial trade reduced economic innovation and survived only by relying on oppressive capital–labour relations, notably slavery. Colonies could only be maintained by autocratic, rather than democratic, rule.

As we have seen, counter-arguments in defence of imperial expansion were frequently advanced, but these were rarely characterized by hard-nosed political realism. During the last months of the Second Empire, however, two serious and prophetic challenges were mounted to the anti-colonial orthodoxy. The first, *La France nouvelle* (1868), by Anatole Prévost-Paradol, was a spirited denunciation of the complacency and decadence beneath the superficial glamour of Second Empire France. The country's failure to match the demographic vigour of other European nations was, according to Prévost-Paradol, a manifestation of a deeper moral and cultural malaise. Far from undermining the case for overseas expansion, the absence of domestic vigour reinforced the need for more colonies. If a new, expanded empire could be established based on a common set of

French cultural values and political traditions, then France's demographic problems could be solved overnight. A 'greater France' would emerge whose 'natural limits' were no longer the old European mountain and river borders. This 'new France' would be a more complex, global, and imperial space where all peoples, regardless of colour, religion, or custom, would be equal citizens. It would be a new empire of 'one hundred million Frenchmen'. France should not be seen as a fixed geographical entity, hemmed in by its European frontiers. Rather, it should be seen as an evolving process, a transcendent idea open to anyone willing to contribute. The various forms of cultural imperialism that emerged over subsequent decades—encapsulated by terms such as civilizing mission, assimilation and association—were all variations on this simple idea. This was a radical argument, to be sure, for it directly rejected the idea, proposed by theorists of racial polygenesis such as Arthur de Gobineau and others, that different 'races' were arranged in a natural hierarchy and could never be intermingled as equals. While Gobineau saw racial miscegenation, particularly in Europe's burgeoning cities, as the principal cause of moral and physical degeneration, Prévost-Paradol claimed precisely the opposite. The blending of different races in a common political project was the only cure for France's current decay.

The second major defence of overseas empire was written in 1869 by a young economist, Paul Leroy-Beaulieu, for a competition launched by the Académie des Sciences Morales et Politiques to stimulate discussion of modern colonial systems. Leroy-Beaulieu's winning entry, subsequently expanded as *De la colonisation chez les peuples modernes* (1874), was a historical survey of Europe's colonial systems and an attempt to theorize how a given colony might be developed to its maximum capacity. The book's principal objective, however, was the development of a distinctive French colonial policy that would be at once intellectually compelling and politically attractive. For Leroy-Beaulieu, there was no necessary contradiction between empire and free trade. Say's critique was dismissed as outdated and relevant only to the mercantilist colonies of the *Ancien Régime*. Modern trading empires were no longer closed systems and were now facilitating, rather than corrupting, international commerce. Limited protective tariffs were useful in the short or medium term, however, and far from diminishing trade and innovation, such measures allowed fragile colonial economies to develop. French imperial expansion was too important to be left to independent-minded army officers, claimed Leroy-Beaulieu, and a more considered, scientific approach was needed. The first objective should be the intensive development of the country's existing colonies rather than further, reckless expansionism. There were three kinds of colony, he argued, colonies of settlement, commercial colonies, and plantation colonies. Colonies of settlement had only limited value for France though those colonies that had been intensively colonized, notably Algeria, would certainly have a special role in any future French overseas empire. Commercial and plantation colonies, on the other hand, were ideally suited to France as neither required large-scale civilian colonization. Leroy-Beaulieu later inclined towards more expansionist policies, but he never wavered from a belief that an overseas empire was a vehicle for democracy and liberty. His elaborate economic defence of imperialism rested ultimately on moral, political, and cultural foundations. Only by looking outwards, he concluded, would France avoid further damaging warfare in Europe.

Prévost-Paradol and Leroy-Beaulieu were not the only prophets of empire at the end of the 1860s, for similar views were expressed no less eloquently by liberal journalists such as Jules Duval, Henri Verne, and Paul Gaffarel. All of these writers were recognizable offspring of First Empire cultural imperialists and Saint-Simonian idealists. Their relatively obscure texts would probably have been quickly forgotten had not the *annus horribilis* of 1870–1 shattered the complacency and decadence that all these authors lamented. In the aftermath of this terrible year, their heady mixture of nationalism, republicanism and imperialism struck a chord with a growing number of patriotic Frenchmen and women anxious to rejuvenate a defeated nation. Suddenly, colonial arguments that had previously fallen on deaf ears sounded much more convincing. Having lost territory and prestige in Europe, France would need to look beyond the old continent if it wanted to regain both. The change in popular attitudes to the empire did not happen overnight and never amounted to a complete transformation. Gradually, however, the centre of gravity of French colonialism began to shift from the colonies and from the army to the metropolitan centre where a small, but vocal group of middle-class and mainly republican businessmen, academics, civil servants, and politicians began to organize themselves into various colonialist clubs and societies. Some of these organizations were scientific, notably the geographical societies. The fellowship of the strongly pro-colonial Paris Geographical Society, established fifty years earlier, more than doubled between 1870 and 1875 (from 600 to 1,353) and peaked at 2,500 in the mid-1880s, the new members coming mainly from the liberal professions, banking, commerce, and trade. Other colonial societies emerged during the early 1880s to play a more overtly political and commercial role on behalf of French business interests in different parts of the existing empire and in those areas of the world that seemed ripe for further French expansion. Examples include the Comité de l'Afrique Française, the Comité de l'Asie, the Comité de l'Océanie Française, and the Comité de l'Orient. This amorphous constellation of interest groups, sometimes misleadingly called the Parti Colonial, operated as a loosely structured pressure group, guided by rising political figures such as Eugène Étienne, the deputy for the Algerian town of Oran, who was subsequently to serve as both the Minister of War and the Interior. Senior republican political leaders, notably Léon Gambetta and Jules Ferry, were also converted to the imperial cause.

The new breed of metropolitan colonialists were never large in number but they more than made up for this with their evangelical zeal. The chronic instability of the early Third Republic played directly into their hands. Operating in the interstices of political power, though rarely at the heart of government, French colonialists were able to wield an influence out of all proportion to the popular support, either within government or in society as a whole. Their success, at least in promoting the relatively straightforward business of imperial expansion, was in part due to the willingness of colonialists to suspend ideological disputes that would otherwise have divided them. Unlikely colonial alliances were regularly established, therefore, between diehard anticlerical republicans and committed Catholics. As the anti-Catholic politician Léon Gambetta famously remarked: 'anticlericalism is not an article for export'. The pro-colonial Jules Ferry, architect of the resoundingly secular network of state primary schools in France, seemed to detect no contradiction between his domestic educational policies and his willingness to celebrate the 'civilizing' role of the 500 French Catholic schools that existed in the Middle East in the late 1870s. Such compromises do not mean that the colonial lobby never developed a coherent or agreed policy, however, as different colonial societies often advocated contradictory, if not mutually exclusive, programmes. The tension between those campaigning for a larger African empire and those supporting a greater presence in Asia was never resolved. It should also be noted that while the colonial lobby offered effective, and at times decisive, support for campaigns to acquire new overseas territory through the 1870s and 1880s, it was less successful in changing French patterns of investment and trade. The chronic failure of French government and business to invest in the empire was largely unaffected by the resurgence of imperial expansion. Less than 10 per cent of the country's trade and overseas investment ended up in the French colonies at the end of the nineteenth century. Most French overseas investment was directed towards the Ottoman Empire, Russia, and Latin America.

The growing influence of the colonial lobby in France during the 1870s and 1880s can be illustrated by reference to Algeria. The events of 1870–1 had provided an ideal opportunity for opponents of French rule to reassert themselves. Despite his Arabophile rhetoric, Napoleon III's reforms had a similar impact in Algeria as in France itself. Agriculture had become more capital-intensive and the region's towns had expanded significantly as centres of population, industry, and commerce. The main beneficiaries were the wealthier *colons* and the commercial interests in France which controlled most of Algeria's industrial capacity and imported the bulk of its agricultural produce. With their traditional, often nomadic way of life under threat, the Algerian majority became increasingly susceptible to environmental crises. By the mid-1860s, the Arab and Berber population had reached three million only to fall sharply by almost one million in just five years, the result of several catastrophes of near biblical proportions: a widespread famine led to cholera, typhus, and smallpox epidemics. The impact of these disasters was worsened by a major earthquake and a plague of locusts that destroyed newly planted crops. When the Second Empire fell, a series of uprisings broke out across Algeria, beginning in the upland areas of Kabylia in 1871. The rebellion was eventually suppressed, though only after another brutal campaign involving massacres on both sides. The tribes found guilty of instigating the revolt were obliged to pay indemnities and surrender their lands. The surviving leaders of the Kabyle rebels were either executed or sent to New Caledonia along with 4,000 Parisian Communards, including the remarkable Louise Michel. The so-called 'red virgin of the Commune' established schools for Melanesian children and, unlike her fellow deportees, actively supported a subsequent rebellion against French rule that erupted on the island in 1878.

A complex range of Algerian reforms were brought forward by the unsteady Third Republic in the wake of the revolt, some liberal, others punitive. The Jewish population was granted full French citizenship, but the *bureaux arabes* were suppressed and the *Sénatus-Consulte* decrees were repealed, paving the way for yet another assault on Muslim lands. The large influx of refugees from Alsace-Lorraine, now part of the German Empire, posed a problem for the authorities in Paris and, once again, the 'empty' lands of Algeria seemed an obvious solution. Some 100,000 hectares were set aside and work began on a new network of colonial villages. By 1874, 877 families from Alsace and Lorraine had been resettled in Algeria. Conditions were still difficult but the lessons of earlier colonization schemes had been learned and the majority of the new arrivals established themselves with more or less success. Encouraged by this episode, the veteran *colon* and deputy for Algiers, Auguste Warnier, forced through new legislation, the so-called *Loi Warnier* on 26 July 1873, that opened a new era of state-sponsored colonization or *colonisation officielle*. Free land and accommodation were made available to incoming *colons*, regardless of their national origin, along with an unenforceable stipulation that concessions be farmed for five years.

The law recognized only private, individual property rights and effectively outlawed collective, tribal property. Over 2 million hectares of Algerian land passed to European ownership in the twenty years following the Warnier law. The European population of Algeria was still only 260,000 in 1872, but by the end of the 1880s there were over half a million Europeans. Still less than one in six of the total population, European colonists owned over 85 per cent of the cultivable Algerian land. Migrants from the countryside flocked to the unsanitary and already overcrowded Muslim quarters in the main towns. While the European quarters assumed the elegant appearance of affluent districts in any late nineteenth-century French provincial city, Muslims were condemned to live in deteriorating urban conditions. Needless to say, the reforms of the Third Republic in Algeria demonstrate that the pioneering colonialist arguments of Prévost-Paradol and Leroy-Beaulieu were only selectively deployed. The idea of an empire where race would count for nothing and all citizens would have equal rights was the first casualty in the attempt to translate colonial theory into colonial policy.

Having reasserted its authority in Algeria, the French army set about launching a new era of imperial expansion in Africa, with the support of the colonial lobby in France. Tunisia, still theoretically part of the Ottoman Empire, was an obvious target. Endemic corruption had impoverished the region's once prosperous peasantry and precipitated a major rebellion against Ottoman rule in 1864, led by Ali Ibn Gdaham. France, Britain, and the new Italian state vied with one another for influence in the area as social and economic conditions worsened still further. In 1878, following Russia's defeat of the ailing Ottoman Empire, a French request to administer Tunisia was accepted, despite Italian opposition. Little happened for three years, however, until a border skirmish precipitated a full-scale intervention in May 1881. Tunisia was declared a Protectorate and, by the middle of 1882, the entire region had been brought under French military authority with a French Resident, Paul Cambon, installed alongside the traditional ruler, the *bey*. To the west of Algeria, beyond the snowy peaks of the Rif and High Atlas mountains, Morocco remained a place of mystery and imagination for French colonialists until the end of the century. Despite sporadic explorations, the major push into Morocco would not take place until the early years of the twentieth century.

By the 1880s, the French army controlled great swathes of the West African interior and newly established French trading companies plied a lucrative trade in hardwoods and other primary products. Resistance to these incursions intensified through the 1870s and 1880s, notably in the Islamic Mandinka Empire where Samory Touré waged a long and bloody campaign against French troops under Louis-Gustave Binder, governor of the Côte d'Ivoire from 1883. As the French gradually gained the upper hand, however, the scene was set for further exploration and expansion to the north-west, along the Niger river towards Timbuctoo and into the Sahel regions of Mali, Upper Volta and Niger during the closing years of the century. The story of French expansion into equatorial Africa conforms to the same pattern. During the 1870s and the 1880s, this most impenetrable part of the 'dark continent' became associated with the exploits of Pierre Savorgnan de Brazza, an Italian aristocrat who studied at the French naval academy and assumed French nationality in 1874.

Brazza's explorations of the Ogooué and Congo basins in three expeditions—1875–7, 1879–82, and 1883–5—were relayed back to an eager French public, particularly through the ever-popular *Le Tour du monde*. The rivalry between the European colonial powers in Africa reached a peak in these unclaimed and unexplored regions of the equatorial belt. Lured by the promise of huge profits from hardwoods and rubber, Britain, France, and Belgium jostled for comparative advantage to the north and south of the Congo river. The establishment of the International African Association in 1876, ostensibly to diminish international tension in the area and encourage scientific exploration, turned out to be a front for Léopold II's ambitions for a vast Belgian empire in Central Africa. Brazza, the French champion, and Henry Morton Stanley, a Welsh-born, American-raised Englishman in the employ of the Belgian king, were bitter rivals.

At the time of the Berlin Conference in 1884–5 (a gathering of colonial powers to delimit the European spheres of influence in Africa), both France and Belgium laid claim to enormous areas to the north and south of the Congo respectively. The intensity of Franco-Belgian rivalry was to be forever reflected on the map, France establishing its inland capital, later to become Brazzaville, on the north bank of the Congo directly opposite the Belgian capital, Léopoldville (modern Kinshasa), on the south bank. As the expanse of blue spread across the map of Africa, several colonialists began to consider how these new lands might be forged into a cohesive geopolitical structure, an integrated African empire bound together by networks of canals, roads, and railways. Inspired by de Lesseps's success, French entrepreneurs proposed equally grandiose feats of engineering in other parts of Africa during the 1870s and 1880s. Captain François Roudaire claimed that a series of infertile saline depressions (*chotts*), stretching westwards in a widening arc from the Gulf of Gabès in Tunisia deep into the Algerian Sahara, were below sea level and might easily be flooded with water from the Mediterranean by means of a series of canals. The *chotts* were the remnants of the Sea of Triton, claimed Roudaire, where ancient ships once rode at anchor. Recreating the 'mer intérieure' would transform the region's climate, facilitate commercial agriculture and make the desert bloom. Roudaire's dream came to nought but a few years later, an engineer from Montpellier, Alphonse Duponchel, argued that a railway should be driven across the Sahara linking French colonies in North and West

Africa. If the Americans could drive a railroad across their continent and if the English could dream of a Cape-to-Cairo route across the 'red' parts of Africa, then France had a duty to bind together the different parts of its African domain with a 'blue' band of iron. This idea, which was to be periodically resurrected down to the 1950s, also foundered but not before hundreds of thousands of francs had been wasted on disastrous military explorations to chart a course for the railway. Two expeditions were led in 1880 and 1881 by Colonel Paul-Xavier Flatters, the second ending with the massacre of all involved.

Conclusion

The creation of France's overseas empire demonstrates the power that small and otherwise marginal interest groups could exert in an era characterized by the failure to create a political consensus. Although the major phase of French imperial expansion was to occur after the mid-1880s, it is important to consider the roots of a distinctively French imperial *mentalité* in the decades after 1789. A third of today's French citizens are first-, second-, or third-generation immigrants. Although many trace their ancestry to European countries, many more have roots in the country's former colonial territories. Modern, multicultural France reflects the country's long engagement with the non-European world. Despite the dishonourable claims of those who seek to deny immigrants their full rights as French citizens, the invigorating presence of such people in post-colonial France bears witness to the persuasive arguments developed by earlier generations who saw their country in the most expansive terms: as a 'greater France' rooted in Europe but never limited by the European arena. The difficult process of building a new, post-colonial France in a new, multicultural Europe depends, I would argue, on understanding all phases in the country's colonial past. The fact that 14 million US citizens, 7 million Canadian subjects (over a quarter of the Canadian population), and more than a million Caribbean islanders are of French descent, and speak versions of the French language, is further testimony to France's historic status as a global power.

Conclusion

Malcolm Crook

1880: the advent of post-revolutionary France?

The Eiffel Tower, that most famous of metropolitan landmarks, was erected in Paris in 1889 to commemorate the first centenary of the French Revolution. Designed to serve as a gateway to the International Exhibition organized in the same year, it was then the tallest building in the world. Although originally intended to be a temporary construction it has become the most celebrated monument in the French capital. Yet few tourists, standing in its shadow on the Champ de Mars, scene of the first anniversary of the Revolution in 1790, may be aware that this site of memory is freighted with so much historical meaning. The *tour Eiffel* was designed to represent scientific progress and human mastery of nature; it can also be regarded as a symbol for the Third French Republic, which emerged as a provisional regime, yet has endured ever since. In 1880, according to the historian François Furet, 'the Revolution had finally come into port'.

Was France really entering a post-revolutionary era after its great century of upheaval? The triumph of the Republic over its adversaries should not be exaggerated. The church of Sacré-Cœur, whose great white basilica rivals the Eiffel Tower on the skyline of Paris, was already being built on the heights of Montmartre on the opposite bank of the River Seine. Sacré-Cœur signified a different vision of France for it was conceived as an act of contrition for defeat and rebellion in 1871, and it also represented an acknowledgement of the divinity rather than a statement of human self-confidence. Construction had commenced during the 1870s, while royalists commanded a majority in the Chamber of Deputies, when Marshal MacMahon, Duc de Magenta, and the Duc de Broglie had respectively become President and Prime Minister of the nascent Third Republic. Aristocratic elements recalling the *Ancien Régime* thus retained a potent presence almost one hundred years after its collapse. Had a more suitable royal personage been available to serve as pretender to the throne, a restoration of the monarchy might have followed the downfall of the Second Empire, just as it had the First. The Third Republic survived as much by default as by design.

Nor was the Church condemned to extinction in the same way as the Throne. Republicans were anxious to combat its influence precisely because they recognized a powerful, even resurgent opponent, not the ailing enemy that some have depicted. Contrary to received opinion, the nineteenth century in France was a period of religious revival as much as a time of decline. In 1878, for example, there were as many priests as there had been a hundred years before, when the population of France had been scarcely smaller. Monarchical and imperial regimes had proved decidedly sympathetic and encouraged the Church to play an important role in education and poor relief. Moreover, recent developments might be turned to religious advantage: the use of railways could be used for pilgrimages to a remote site like Lourdes, while the growth of literacy and a popular press were employed to disseminate a Christian message.

Efforts to consolidate the Third Republic after its official enactment in 1875 were manifest in a series of symbolic measures specifically designed to overawe this sort of opposition. In 1879, revolutionary history repeated itself, this time as triumph, when the National Assembly returned to Paris, after a decade at Versailles amidst the faded glories of the monarchical past. The following year the 'Marseillaise' was adopted as the national anthem, and the 14 July as a national *fête*, to join the *tricolor* as the national flag. The 'Republic of the Dukes' had given way to the 'Republic of the Republicans', as MacMahon resigned in face of hostile majorities in Assembly and Senate, and town halls across the land. Now the Church paid for its alliance with the royalists, as a new 'religious war' broke out, not unlike the strife of a century earlier. This time,

Republican leaders were determined to capture the minds of future generations with the creation of free, compulsory, and secular primary education.

Yet it is only with the benefit of hindsight that we can say the Republic had finally arrived to become the definitive form of government in France. It had an inauspicious birth and difficult infancy, and there would be further crises before the century was out, notably the challenges presented by General Boulanger or the Dreyfus Affair. There was no way of knowing that the upheaval of 1871, the most bloody of all the revolutions which had occurred in the capital since 1789, had effectively closed the cycle of Parisian revolution. The violent suppression of the Commune certainly aided the creation of a conservative Republic. The Left was physically destroyed for the moment, but though the revolutionaries had been annihilated, the revolutionary message remained. By no means all political opponents were reconciled to working within the republican framework in future, as syndicalists on the Left, and nationalists on the Right, were to demonstrate. Barricades would reappear in the following century and, even today, as Robert Tombs has remarked, France remains a country where the unpredictable is always possible.

Yet the Third Republic, democratic and secular, survived and represented an outstanding exception among the great states of Europe, all of which retained monarchy and none of which had introduced male universal suffrage in any meaningful fashion. France had pioneered modern political culture since 1789, though the process involved a long and often painful apprenticeship, albeit a varied and exciting one. After the 1870s, however, more than 80 per cent of the huge French electorate regularly turned out to nominate members of the Chamber of Deputies. It is true that the national assembly, and in particular its government ministries, continued to be dominated by wealthy notables, but the landed magnates were in retreat. Meanwhile, at the local level, reform of municipal government in 1884 ensured the participation of more humble elements in society on some 40,000 elected councils.

To be sure, contradictions remained embedded in the republican regime and one of the most noteworthy was the conservatism of its gender relationships. Political participation was restricted to males and women would have to wait until the middle of the twentieth century to receive the vote; the first country in the world to award the franchise to all men was one of the last in Europe to treat females in a similar fashion. The paradox of a democratic yet patriarchal culture has attracted a good deal of attention of late. The Republic adopted a feminine icon, but Marianne had few more rights than Marie, the traditional symbol for Catholics: both were confined to the private sphere as second-class citizens. Republicans were reluctant to legislate on behalf of their sisters out of fear that enfranchising women would reinforce reactionary elements in politics. Yet men on the Left also shared the patriarchal preoccupations of those on the Right in so far as efforts to raise the sluggish French birth rate encouraged them to regard women chiefly as childbearers.

An advanced, male-dominated political culture had been nurtured in a society that remained predominantly rural and peasant-based. Indeed, commentators in the past have always emphasized the backwardness of French economic and social development, especially in comparison with its industrializing neighbour across the Channel. The English historian Alfred Cobban even went so far as to characterize nineteenth-century France as a period of 'stagnation without stability'. Yet current writers are more anxious to stress the advances that were made and suggest that the 'French way' was not necessarily inferior to the British model. It might be going too far to suggest that France was an 'early developer' rather than a 'late comer' but, judged on a per capita basis, growth rates were comparable with other developing economies. Beneath the superficial continuity of a nation of smallholders there was adaptation to a market economy. Obstacles to growth served as stimuli to invention and the high quality of artisanal production compensated for its lesser quantity. The process was a gradual rather than a revolutionary one, perhaps with lower social costs for those involved, and it was certainly incomplete in 1880, but no one was left untouched by it.

As this volume has constantly demonstrated, it is dangerous to try to generalize about a country as vast and varied as France: General de Gaulle had good cause to despair of mastering a people who, as he put it, produced more than 300 different types of cheese. The state thus served as a guarantor of unity, as well as order. The pressures for uniformity may well have backfired, encouraging a stubborn and defensive localism as a result. Regionalism certainly remained pronounced, though criticisms of Eugen Weber's famous study *Peasants into Frenchmen* have accumulated, not least regarding the concentration of his analysis upon those peripheral provinces where development was less marked. A focus on the more literate parts of France, which were served by better communication networks, reveals a rather higher degree of integration. It is worth emphasizing that provincial loyalties were constructed and invented just as much as national affiliation, in some cases to serve as a justification for conservatism and anti-republicanism. Equally, some of the areas most committed to the Republic were in the least developed regions of France, such as the Centre and South-West, where small peasants predominated and French remained a second language.

Despite its enduring diversity, the Third Republic no longer represented the rich and populous 'great nation' of the revolutionary and Napoleonic periods. The relative weight of France in Europe was declining sharply, though its presence overseas was simultaneously expanding. With a population of around 30 million in 1800 France had been well endowed with inhabitants, but thereafter growth slowed: in 1836 the total was only 33 million, and after 1871 it was no more than 36 million. The French death rate was falling, but so too was its birth rate, at an unusually rapid rate. Though it was bemoaned at the time, some commentators have viewed this factor more positively as a herald of twentieth-century patterns of fertility. Equality of inheritance, established everywhere during the Revolution and maintained by the Napoleonic Code, has usually been held responsible for limiting the size of French families in the nineteenth century. Whatever the cause, there were good demographic reasons to compensate for this shortfall by looking overseas, besides encouraging immigration from adjacent European countries. This helps to explain why colonialism was not strongly opposed on grounds of principle and why there was no real challenge to the suppression of freedom elsewhere just as it was being consolidated within the metropole. France amassed colonies on a scale second only to Britain; the Rights of Man seemed to be confined to home consumption, rather than for export.

Despite the acquisition of Nice and Savoy under the Second Empire, French domestic territory in 1880 was scarcely greater than it had been in 1788. Alsace-Lorraine was annexed by the newly unified German state, whose population began to overhaul that of France at precisely the same moment. Defeat by Prussia in 1871 was a watershed, for it concluded a long period of French hegemony on the continent and heralded the promotion of Germany to that supreme status. The notion that this great reversal of fortune was fore-shadowed in 1815 is ill-founded, for nineteenth-century France continued to maintain a large, conscript army. After the defeat of Russia in the Crimean War of the mid-1850s, with a second Napoleon at the helm, the rest of Europe was rightly fearful. The peace signed at Paris in 1856, at the conclusion of this conflict, appeared to reassert French domination of the continent. Indeed, most observers confidently expected the French army to win the war of 1870–1 (an illusion that was tragically shared by the French themselves). In future, faced by an industrializing and expanding Germany, France would struggle to emerge victorious, even with the assistance of powerful allies. For the past 200 years other countries had been forced to establish coalitions in order to defeat the French, but now the tables were decisively turned in the opposite direction.

National sentiment became defensive and pessimistic after 1870. During the century that followed France would need to adapt to its diminished status as a military power. The transition would prove a difficult one, for inflated pretensions in this regard were hard to abandon. Yet France succeeded in maintaining great influence in both Europe and the world despite the loss of its former hegemony. This leadership was expressed not only in political, but above all in intellectual and artistic terms. French remained an international language in a way that is difficult to imagine now that Anglo-American culture has seized the upper hand. Paris in particular acquired a reputation as the acme of modernity, as a great centre of excellence for the literary and visual arts. Of course, some recognition must be given to the reconstruction of the capital under Louis-Napoleon, whose Second Empire is generally accorded a more positive role in the development of France than earlier generations of historians were willing to grant. The great exhibition of 1889, for example, which left the Eiffel Tower as a lasting monument, was consciously modelled on its imperial predecessors.

The triumph of the Republic after 1880 was, of course, registered in historiographical as well as political terms. When a Chair of the French Revolution was established at the Sorbonne, during the following decade, it might have seemed that the subject would cease to be a source of great controversy and simply become a matter for academic study instead. Yet, as the bicentenary one hundred years later demonstrated, a scholarly consensus regarding the nature of revolutionary France, 1780–1880, remains as elusive as ever. The century of upheaval explored in this volume thus continues to excite controversy and to attract some of the most innovative historical writing; in this regard, at least, the Revolution is far from over.

Further reading

The French Revolution and Napoleon, 1788–1814

The best, short introduction is Jeremy D. Popkin, *A Short History of the French Revolution* (Englewood Cliffs, NJ, 1995), which also examines the Napoleonic period. General histories abound, but William Doyle, *The Oxford History of the French Revolution* (Oxford, 1989) is a magisterial survey. David Andress, *French Society in Revolution, 1789–1799* (Manchester, 1999) is not as 'social' as the title might suggest, but it offers a solid, short account. Donald G. Sutherland, *France 1789–1815: Revolution and Counterrevolution* (London, 1985) is a demanding, but rewarding survey which emphasizes provincial complexities. The controversial origins of the Revolution are admirably assessed in William Doyle, *Origins of the French Revolution* (Oxford, 1999) and T. C. W. Blanning, *The French Revolution: Class War or Culture Clash?* (Basingstoke, 1998). Georges Lefebvre, *The Coming of the French Revolution* (trans., Princeton, 1988), Alfred Cobban, *The Social Interpretation of the French Revolution* (Cambridge, 1999), and François Furet, *Interpreting the French Revolution* (Cambridge, 1981) are milestones in the ongoing debate. P. M. Jones, *Reform and Revolution in France: The Politics of Transition, 1774–1791* (Cambridge, 1995), Timothy Tackett, *Becoming a Revolutionary. The Deputies of the French National Assembly and the Emergence of a Revolutionary Culture (1789–1790)* (Princeton, 1996), Jeremy D. Popkin, *Revolutionary News: The Press in France 1789–1799* (Durham, NC, 1990), Malcolm Crook, *Elections in the French Revolution: An Apprenticeship in Democracy, 1789–1799* (Cambridge, 1996), and Isser Woloch, *The New Regime: Transformations of the French Civic Order, 1789–1820s* (New York, 1994) examine the transition to the political culture of the Revolution, which has produced four volumes of essays from Colin Lucas et al. (eds.), *The French Revolution and the Creation of Modern Political Culture* (Oxford, 1988–94). George Rudé, *The Crowd in the French Revolution* (Oxford, 1959) and Richard Cobb, *The Police and the People: French Popular Protest 1789–1820* (Oxford, 1970) cover a now unfashionable topic. Hugh Gough, *The Terror in the French Revolution* (Basingstoke, 1998) is a fine survey of another deeply controversial subject, while Martyn Lyons, *The Directory* (Cambridge, 1975) and Malcolm Crook, *Napoleon Comes to Power: Democracy and Dictatorship in Revolutionary France, 1795–1804* (Cardiff, 1998) explore the neglected, later years of the Revolution. Martyn Lyons, *Napoleon Bonaparte and the Legacy of the French Revolution* (Basingstoke, 1994), Jean Tulard, *Napoleon, the Myth of the Saviour* (trans., London, 1984), Geoffrey Ellis, *Napoleon* (Harlow, 1997), and Isser Woloch,

Napoleon and his Collaborators: The Making of a Dictatorship (New York, 2001) introduce the Bonapartist dictatorship. T.C.W Blanning, *The French Revolutionary Wars 1787–1802* (London, 1996), David Gates, *The Napoleonic Wars 1803–1815* (London, 1997), and Alan Forrest, *Soldiers of the French Revolution* (Durham, NC, 1990) cover the vital military dimension. For individuals, see John Hardman, *Louis XVI: The Silent King* (London, 200), David P. Jordan, *The Revolutionary Career of Maximilien Robespierre* (New York, 1985), and or Norman Hanson, *Danton* (London, 1978). Colin Jones, *The Longman Companion to the French Revolution* (Harlow, 1988) is an essential work of reference.

Upheaval and continuity, 1814–1880

Useful broad surveys of nineteenth-century France include Robert Tombs, *France 1814–1914* (Harlow, 1996), Martin S. Alexander (ed.), *French History since Napoleon* (London, 1999), Pamela M. Pilbeam, *Republicanism in Nineteenth-Century France, 1814–1871* (Basingstoke, 1995), and François Furet, *Revolutionary France 1770–1880* (Oxford, 1992). The legacy of Napoleon is treated in R. S. Alexander, *Bonapartism and the Revolutionary Tradition in France: The Fédérés of 1815* (Cambridge, 1991). Aspects of the Left during the Restoration are presented in Alan B. Spitzer, *The French Generation of 1820* (Princeton, 1987). The Right is neatly summarized in James Roberts, *The Counter-Revolution in France 1787–1830* (London, 1990). The 1830 revolution and the July Monarchy are covered by David Pinkney, *The French Revolution of 1830* (Princeton, 1972), Pamela Pilbeam, *The 1830 Revolution in France* (London 1994), H. A. C. Collingham, *The July Monarchy: A Political History of France 1830–1848* (Harlow, 1988), and Pamela Pilbeam, *The Constitutional Monarchy in France 1814–48* (Harlow, 1999). The 1848 Revolution and the Second Republic are surveyed in Roger Price, *The French Second Republic: A Social History* (London, 1972). An important work is Mark Traugott, *Armies of the Poor: Determinants of Working-Class Participation in the Parisian Insurrection of June 1848* (Princeton, 1985). See also Roger V. Gould, *Insurgent Identities: Class, Community and Protest in Paris from 1848 to the Commune* (Chicago, 1995). Resistance to the dismantling of the Second Republic is ably analysed in Ted W. Margadant, *French Peasants in Revolt: The Insurrection of 1851* (Princeton, 1979), John M. Merriman, *The Agony of the Republic: The Repression of the Left in Revolutionary France 1848–51* (New Haven, 1978), and most recently and comprehensively by Peter McPhee, *The Politics of Rural Life: Political Mobilization in the French Countryside 1846–1852* (Oxford, 1992). On the Paris Commune and the early years of the Third Republic, Robert Tombs, *The Paris Commune 1871* (Harlow, 1999) is indispensable and Philip Nord, *The Republican Moment: Struggles for Democracy in Nineteenth-Century France* (Harvard, 1995) is instructive. Early socialism is the theme of

Pamela Pilbeam, *French Socialists before Marx: Workers, Women and the Social Question in France* (Teddington, 2000). The presence of women in insurrections is surveyed in David Barry, *Women and Political Insurgency: France in the Mid-Nineteenth Century* (Basingstoke, 1996), and displayed in Gay L. Gullickson, *Unruly Women of Paris* (London, 1996). Contemporary observers include Karl Marx, *The Class Struggles in France 1848–1850* in Karl Marx, *Surveys from Exile. Political Writings: Volume 2*, ed. David Fernbach (London, 1992) and Alexis de Tocqueville, *Recollections* (New York, 1971). Those who variously drew, painted and made lithograph cartoons of their fellows are well represented in David S. Kerr, *Caricature and French Political Culture, 1830–1848: Charles Philipon and the Illustrated Press* (Oxford, 2000) and Petra ten-Doesschate Chu and Gabriel P. Weisberg, *The Popularization of Images: Visual Culture under the July Monarchy* (Princeton, 1994). Contemporary novels that deal with social and political conflict include Stendhal, *Scarlet and Black* (Harmondsworth, 1971), Hugo, *Les Misérables* (Harmondsworth, 1980), Flaubert, *Sentimental Education* (Harmondsworth, 1964), and Zola, *The Debacle* (Harmondsworth, 1971).

State and religion

The first volume of Adrien Dansette's *Religious History of Modern France* (New York, 1961) is still worth reading. Ralph Gibson, *A Social History of French Catholicism, 1789–1914* (London, 1989) summarizes the more recent literature. The metaphor of religion as a sacred canopy is discussed in Peter Berger, *The Sacred Canopy: Elements of a Sociological Theory of Religion* (New York, 1967). For those who read French, Gérard Cholvy's *Être chrétien en France au XIXe siècle, 1790–1914* (Paris, 1997) is succinct and up to date. John McManners has recently published a massive study, *Church and Society in Eighteenth-Century France*, 2 vols. (Oxford, 1998) covering the period up to 1789. His brief survey, *The French Revolution and the Church* (London, 1969) remains a useful introduction, splendidly updated by Nigel Aston, *Religion and Revolution in France 1780–1804* (London, 2000). Timothy Tackett, *Religion, Revolution, and Regional Culture in Eighteenth-Century France: The Ecclesiastical Oath of 1791* (Princeton, 1986), is the definitive study of a crucial issue. For a local study, see Suzanne Desan, *Reclaiming the Sacred: Lay Religion and Popular Politics in Revolutionary France* (Ithaca, NY, 1990). Attempts to create a civil religion are analysed in Mona Ozouf, *Festivals and the French Revolution* (Cambridge, Mass., 1988). For general studies of religious minorities see Paula Hyman, *The Jews of Modern France* (Berkeley, Calif., 1998) and André Encrevé, *Les Protestants en France de 1800 à nos jours: histoire d'une réintégration* (Paris, 1985). For religious experimentation see Nicole Edelman, *Voyantes, guérisseuses et visionnaires en France, 1785–1914* (Paris, 1995), which provides material on Spiritualism. For the development of civil religion see Maurice Agulhon, *Marianne into Battle: Republican Imagery and Symbolism in France, 1789–1880* (Cambridge, 1981), D. G. Charlton, *Secular Religions in France, 1815–1870* (New York, 1963), Jacqueline Lalouette, *La Libre Pensée en France, 1848–1940* (Paris, 1997), and Matthew Truesdale, *Spectacular Politics: Louis-Napoleon Bonaparte and the Fête Impériale, 1849– 1870* (New York, 1997). Austin Gough, *Paris and Rome: The Gallican Church and the Ultramontane Campaign 1848–1853* (Oxford, 1986) contributes to an older tradition of institutional church history. For life at parish level see Edouard Pierchon's memoir, edited by Guy Tassin, *Un village du Nord avant la mine: chronique d'Edouard Pierchon, curé d'Haveluy au XIXème siècle* (Paris, 1996). Catholic nuns are studied by Sarah Curtis, *Educating the Faithful: Religion, Schooling, and Society in Nineteenth-Century France* (De Kalb, Ill., 2000). For links between the political and cultural history of religion, see Sheryl Kroen, *Politics and Theater: The Crisis of Legitimacy in Restoration France, 1815–1830* (Berkeley, Calif., 2000) and Edward Berenson, *Populist Religion and Left-Wing Politics in France* (Princeton, 1984). Claude Langlois explores the battles between Church and state in 'Catholics and seculars', in Pierre Nora (ed.), *Realms of Memory: Rethinking the French Past, i: Conflicts and Divisions* (New York, 1996). Ruth Harris, *Lourdes: Body and Spirit in the Secular Age* (New York, 1999) brilliantly reconstructs and contextualizes the origins of the famous shrine. Other works on the religion of ordinary people include: Alain Corbin, *Village Bells: Sound and Meaning in the Nineteenth Century French Countryside* (New York, 1998); Judith Devlin, *The Superstitious Mind: French Peasants and the Supernatural in the Nineteenth Century* (New Haven, Conn., 1987); Raymond Jonas, *France and the Cult of the Sacred Heart: An Epic Tale for Modern Times* (Berkeley, Calif., 2000); Thomas Kselman, *Miracles and Prophecies in Nineteenth-Century France* (New Brunswick, NJ, 1983); and the same author's *Death and the Afterlife in Modern France* (Princeton, 1993).

Class and gender

Among the important theoretical works on class formation is Ira Katznelson and Aristide R. Zolberg (eds.), *Working-Class Formation: Nineteenth-Century Patterns in Western Europe and the United States* (Princeton, 1986), which includes excellent articles on the French working class. See also extracts in Patrick Joyce (ed.), *Class* (Oxford, 1995). Less theoretical but extremely useful is Steven Laurence Kaplan and Cynthia J. Koepp (eds.), *Work in France: Representations, Meaning, Organization, and Practice* (Ithaca, NY, 1986). The classic work on French artisans and the legacy of 1789 is William H. Sewell, Jr., *Work and Revolution in France: The Language of Labor from the Old Regime to 1848* (Cambridge, 1980). See also Cynthia Truant, *Rites of Labor: Brotherhoods of Compagnonnage in Old and New Regime France* (Ithaca, NY,

1994). On the interrelationship between industrialization, gender, and family among workers, see Elinor Accampo, *Industrialization, Family Life, and Class Relations: Saint Chamond, 1815–1914* (Berkeley, 1989) and Tessie Liu, *The Weaver's Knot: The Contradictions of Class Struggle and Family Solidarity in Western France, 1750–1914* (Ithaca, NY, 1994). The best recent book on women and work is the study by Judith Coffin, *The Politics of Women's Work: The Paris Garment Trades, 1750–1915* (New Jersey, 1996). Roger Magraw's two-volume *A History of the French Working Class* (Oxford, 1992) offers an extraordinary synthesis of secondary literature. For the bourgeoisie, see David Garrioch, *The Formation of the Parisian Bourgeoisie, 1690–1830* (Cambridge, Mass., 1996) and Carol E. Harrison, *The Bourgeois Citizen in Nineteenth-Century France: Gender, Sociability, and the Uses of Emulation* (Oxford, 1999). The latter integrates gender and social class, as do Robert A. Nye's *Masculinity and Male Codes of Honor in Modern France* (Oxford, 1993) and Bonnie Smith's *Ladies of the Leisure Class: The Bourgeoises of Northern France in the Nineteenth Century* (Princeton, 1981). For theory about gender, Joan Scott's essays in *Gender and the Politics of History* (New York, 1988) offer an excellent introduction, while Joan B. Landes pioneered new interpretations of the French Revolution and gender with *Women and the Public Sphere in the Age of the French Revolution* (Ithaca, NY, 1988). See also Lynn Hunt, *The Family Romance of the French Revolution* (Berkeley, Calif., 1992) and Dominique Godineau, *The Women of Paris and their French Revolution* (Berkeley, Calif., 1998). Claire Goldberg Moses, *French Feminism in the 19th Century* (Albany, 1984), remains the standard work, but see also Karen Offen, *European Feminisms, 1700–1950: A Political History* (Stanford, Calif., 2000). Sharon Marcus, *Apartment Stories: City and Home in Nineteenth-Century Paris and London* (Berkeley, Calif., 1999) offers an important corrective to standard interpretations about public and private spheres. Joshua Cole, *The Power of Large Numbers: Population, Politics, and Gender in Nineteenth-Century France* (Ithaca, NY, 2000) analyses the influence of demographic statistics on redefining the family and gender roles. The role of consumerism in shaping both class and gender identities is explored in Leora Auslander, *Taste and Power: Furnishing Modern France* (Berkeley, Calif., 1996) and Rosalind H. Williams, *Dream Worlds: Mass Consumption in Late Nineteenth-Century France* (Berkeley, Calif., 1982). Finally, an excellent synthesis is provided in Michelle Perrot (ed.), *A History of Private Life: From the Fires of Revolution to the Great War* (Cambridge, Mass., 1990).

Town and country

Some of the themes of this chapter are explored further by James R. Lehning, *Peasant and French: Cultural Contact in Rural France during the Nineteenth Century* (Cambridge, 1995). General accounts which consider the changing relations between town and country are Peter McPhee, *A Social History of France 1780–1880* (London, 1992); Roger Magraw, *France 1815–1914: The Bourgeois Century* (London, 1983); and Roger Price, *A Social History of Nineteenth-Century France* (London, 1987). Many of the best studies of urban and rural France are monographs of particular communities. Among the best studies of towns and cities are John M. Merriman, *The Red City: Limoges and the French Nineteenth Century* (New York, 1985); and *The Margins of City Life: Explorations on the French Urban Frontier, 1815–1851* (New York, 1991). There are fine studies of regions and villages by Maurice Agulhon, *The Republic in the Village: The People of the Var from the French Revolution to the Second Republic* (Cambridge, 1982); Alain Corbin, *The Village of Cannibals: Rage and Murder in France, 1870* (Cambridge, Mass., 1992); Gay Gullickson, *Spinners and Weavers of Auffay: Rural Industry and the Sexual Division of Labour in a French Village 1750–1850* (Cambridge, 1986); Peter Jones, *Politics and Rural Society: The Southern Massif Central, c.1750–1880* (Cambridge, 1985); James R. Lehning, *The Peasants of Marlhes: Economic Development and Family Organization in Nineteenth-Century France* (London, 1980); and Liana Vardi, *The Land and the Loom: Peasants and Profit in Northern France 1680–1800* (Durham, NC, 1993). Among the studies of urban–rural relations of particular periods across the century are Richard Cobb, *Reactions to the French Revolution* (Oxford, 1972); Peter Jones, *The Peasantry in the French Revolution* (Cambridge, 1988); Peter McPhee, *The Politics of Rural Life: Political Mobilization in the French Countryside, 1846–1852* (Oxford, 1992); Ted W. Margadant, *French Peasants in Revolt: The Insurrection of 1851* (Princeton, 1979); Peter Sahlins, *Forest Rites: The War of the Demoiselles in Nineteenth-Century France* (Cambridge, Mass., 1994); and Charles Tilly, *The Vendée* (Cambridge, Mass., 1964). Religion is expertly surveyed by Ralph Gibson, *A Social History of French Catholicism, 1789–1914* (London, 1989); and education by François Furet and Jacques Ozouf, *Reading and Writing: Literacy in France from Calvin to Jules Ferry* (Cambridge, 1982). The recollections of Emile Guillaumin have much to say about relations between town and country: *The Life of a Simple Man* (London, 1982).

Province and nation

Useful introductions to the study of and debates surrounding French national identity and nationalism are Fernand Braudel, *The Identity of France*, 2 vols. (London, 1988–90), Roger Brubaker, *Citizenship and Nationhood in France and Germany* (Cambridge, Mass., 1992), and Hans Kohn, *Prelude to Nationalism: The French and German Experience, 1789–1815* (Princeton, 1967). On the question of administrative centralization and decentralization there are Alan Forrest and Peter Jones (eds.), *Reshaping France: Town, Country and Region during the French Revolution* (Manchester, 1991); Marie-Vic

Ozouf-Marignier, *La Formation des départements: la représentation du territoire français à la fin du XVIIIe siècle* (Paris, 1989); Sudhir Hazareesingh, *From Subject to Citizen: The Second Empire and the Emergence of French Democracy* (Princeton, 1998); and Louis M. Greenberg, *Sisters of Liberty: Marseille, Lyon, Paris and the Reaction to the Centralized State, 1868–71* (Cambridge, Mass., 1971). The question of language and national and local identity is dealt with by Michel de Certeau, Dominique Julia, and Jacques Revel, *Une politique de la langue: la Révolution française et le patois* (Paris, 1975) and Stephen L. Harp, *Learning to be Loyal: Primary Schooling and Nation-Building in Alsace and Lorraine, 1850–1940* (De Kalb, Ill., 1998). On myths of a French race see Krzysztof Pomain, 'Francs et Gaulois', in Pierre Nora, (ed.), *Les Lieux de mémoire iii: conflits et partages* (Paris, 1992), and Eugen Weber, 'Nos ancêtres les Gaulois', in his *My France: Politics, Culture, Myth* (Cambridge, Mass., 1991). Questions of attitudes to foreigners and national greatness are dealt with variously in Norman Hampson, 'The French Revolution and the Nationalisation of Honour', in M. R. D. Foot (ed.), *War and Society* (London, 1973); Jacques Godechot, *La Grande Nation* (2nd edn., Paris, 1983); Jean-Paul Bertaud, *La Révolution armée: les soldats-citoyens et la Révolution française* (Paris, 1979); John A. Lynn, *The Bayonets of the Republic: Motivation and Tactics in the Army of Revolutionary France, 1791–1794* (Chicago, 1984); Peter Sahlins, *Boundaries: The Making of France and Spain in the Pyrenees* (Berkeley, Calif., 1989); Michael Rapport, *Nationality and Citizenship in Revolutionary France: The Treatment of Foreigners, 1789–1799* (Oxford, 2000); two articles by Stuart Woolf, 'French Civilization and Ethnicity in the Napoleonic Empire', *Past and Present*, 124 (1989), and 'The Construction of a European World View in the Revolutionary-Napoleonic Years', *Past and Present*, 137 (1992); Paddy Griffith, *Military Thought in the French Army, 1815–1851* (Manchester, 1989): and Richard Holmes, *The Road to Sedan: The French Army, 1866–1870* (London, 1984).

France and the wider world

The best recent work in English on the French overseas empire is Robert Aldrich, *Greater France: A History of French Overseas Expansion* (London, 1996). On French involvement in the Americas and the Caribbean during the late eighteenth and early nineteenth centuries, see Yves Benot, *La Révolution française et la fin des colonies* (Paris, 1988) and *La Démence coloniale sous Napoléon* (Paris, 1991). C. L. R. James, *The Black Jacobins: Toussaint L'Ouverture and the San Domingo Revolution* (London, 1938) remains an inspiring read, though Robin Blackburn's *The Overthrow of Colonial Slavery 1776–1848* (London, 1988) is the best recent analysis. David Eltis, *Economic Growth and the Ending of the Transatlantic Slave Trade* (Oxford, 1988); Lawrence C. Jennings, *French Reaction to British Slave Emancipation* (Baton Rouge, La., 1988);

James F. Searing, *West African Slavery and Atlantic Commerce: The Senegal River Valley, 1770–1860* (Cambridge, 1993); and Robert-Louis Stein, *The French Slave Trade in the Eighteenth Century* (Madison, 1979) are excellent on the French role in the Atlantic slave trade before and after the Revolution. On the Napoleonic intervention in Egypt, see Henry Laurens et al., *L'Expédition d'Égypte, 1798–1801* (Paris, 1989); on the subsequent French involvement in Egypt and the Middle East, William I. Shorrock, *French Imperialism in the Middle East* (London, 1976) and, for a challenging account, Timothy Mitchell, *Colonizing Egypt* (Cambridge, 1991). Among the works in English on the early decades of French colonial rule in Algeria, the relevant chapters in Charles-Robert Ageron's succinct *Modern Algeria: A History from 1830 to the Present* (London, 1991) should be consulted, together with John Ruedy, *Modern Algeria: The Origins and Development of a Nation* (Bloomington, Ind., 1992). On French West Africa, there are Christopher J. Harrison, *France and Islam in West Africa, 1860–1960* (Cambridge, 1988), Alexander S. Kanya-Forstner, *The Conquest of the Western Sudan: A Study in French Military Imperialism* (Cambridge, 1969), and the relevant chapters in Michael Crowder, *West Africa under Colonial Rule* (London, 1968). On French Indochina, see Pierre Brocheux and Daniel Hémery, *Indochine: la colonisation ambiguë, 1858–1954* (Paris, 1995) and on the Pacific, the relevant passages in Robert Aldrich, *The French Presence in the Pacific 1842–1940* (London, 1990). The intellectual response to the French overseas empire from the mid-nineteenth century onwards has been a major recent theme: for example, William B. Cohen, *The French Encounter with Africans: White Responses to Blacks, 1530–1880* (Stanford, Calif., 1980), James E. McClellan III, *Colonialism and Science: Saint-Domingue and the Old Regime* (Baltimore, 1992), Lewis Pyenson, *Civilizing Mission: Exact Sciences and French Overseas Expansion, 1830–1940* (Baltimore, 1993), and, more generally, Edward Said's hugely influential *Orientalism* (London, 1978). The impact of the overseas empire on the French economy is brilliantly surveyed in Jacques Marseille, *Empire colonial et capitalisme français: histoire d'un divorce* (Paris, 1984).

Chronology: Revolutionary France 1788–1880

1783 End of American War

1786 Finance minister Calonne produces reform package

1787 Assembly of Notables meets at Versailles; dormant provincial estates reconvene; Calonne dismissed and Brienne takes over; Notables dissolved

1788 (May) Lamoignon remodels Parlements; (June) 'Noble' revolt in provinces; (Aug.) Louis XVI agrees to call Estates-General for 1789; (Sept.) Parlements restored; demand for traditional format for Estates; (Dec.) number of deputies for third estate doubled

1789 (Jan.) Sieyès, *What is the Third Estate?*; (Mar.) elections to Estates-General commence; (May) Estates-General meets at Versailles; (June) creation of National Assembly; royal session fails and all deputies join National Assembly; (July) Necker dismissed and Bastille is stormed on 14 July; municipal revolution in towns; Great Fear in countryside; (Aug.) abolition of feudalism and privilege; Declaration of the Rights of Man and the Citizen; (Oct.) Louis XVI and Assembly move to Paris following people's march to Versailles; (Nov.) church property nationalized; (Dec.) creation of departments

1790 (May) Sections of Paris created; (June) titles of nobility abolished; (July) Civil Constitution of the Clergy passed by Assembly; Feast of the Federation celebrated on 14 July; (Nov.) Oath to Civil Constitution imposed on the clergy

1791 (Mar.) dissolution of artisan guilds according to *Loi Allarde*; (June) king's attempted escape: the flight to Varennes; (July) demonstration for Republic on Champs de Mars in Paris; (Aug.) slave rebellion breaks out in Saint-Domingue; (Sept.) Gouges, *Declaration of the Rights of Woman*; inhabitants of Avignon and Comtat vote to join the French state; Louis XVI accepts Constitution (of 1791); National Assembly dissolves; (Oct.) new Legislative Assembly convenes; (Nov.) decrees against émigrés and refractory priests (vetoed by king)

1792 (Apr.) declaration of war against Austria; (June) Prussia declares war on France; (July) decree of 'Country in Danger' in response to threat of invasion; (Aug.) Paris sections demand dethronement of king; Tuileries palace stormed; king overthrown; (Sept.) fall of Verdun produces panic; September massacres in Paris; elections for a fresh assembly, the National Convention; victory at Valmy reduces military pressure; Convention meets and proclaims Republic; (Dec.) trial of the king begins in Convention

1793 (Jan.) condemnation and execution of Louis XVI; (Feb.) war declared on Britain and Dutch Republic; decree conscripting 300,000 men; (Mar.) war declared on Spain; Revolutionary Tribunal established; revolt breaks out in the Vendée; (Apr.) creation of Committee of Public Safety; (May) revolts in Marseille and Lyon; anti-Girondin uprising begins in Paris; (June) Girondins purged from Convention; 'Federalist' revolt spreads to Bordeaux; New Constitution (of 1793) accepted by Convention; (July) Robespierre joins Committee of Public Safety; final abolition of feudal dues; (Aug.) decree of *levée en masse*; rebel Toulon surrenders to the British fleet; (Sept.) Law of Suspects introduced; 'maximum' on prices decreed; (Oct.) Girondins sent for trial; Republican calendar introduced: beginning of Year II; government will be 'revolutionary until the return of peace'; new Constitution, accepted by popular vote, is suspended due to crisis; (Dec.) Law on Revolutionary Government; Vendéans defeated and Toulon recaptured

1794 (Feb.) abolition of slavery; (Mar.) arrest of radical Hébertistes; (Apr.) Danton executed; (June) Festival of Supreme Being at Paris; executions accelerate with Law of Prairial; Republican armies win victory at Fleurus; (July) fall and execution of Robespierre; (Aug.) Law of Prairial repealed and revolutionary government reorganized; (Nov.) Jacobin Club of Paris closed; (Dec.) surviving Girondins reinstated to Convention and 'Maximum' is abolished

1795 (Jan.) Holland occupied; (Feb.) armistice in Vendée; freedom of worship restored; (Apr.) Germinal uprising in Paris; treaty concluded with Prussia; integration of Belgium into the Rebublic; (May) 'White Terror': prison massacres at Lyon and Marseille; further, but final, popular uprising in Paris; Revolutionary Tribunal abolished; (June) death of Louis XVII in prison; Declaration of Verona from Louis XVIII; (July) émigré invasion in Brittany defeated; peace treaty with Spain; (Aug.) Constitution of the Year III approved in popular vote; (Oct.) decree of 'two-thirds' provokes right-wing uprising in Paris; (Nov.) new parliamentary Councils meet and executive Directory is established

1796 (Apr.) invasion of Italy; Bonaparte conquers northern Italy; (May) arrest of Babeuf and fellow conspirators

1797 (Feb.) return to metallic currency; (Apr.) parliamentary elections produce right-wing triumph; (May) right-winger elected to executive Directory; (Sept.) *coup d'état* of Fructidor: right-wing deputies purged; right-wingers removed from Directory; (Oct.) Peace of Campo Formio with Austria

1798 (Feb.) Pope overthrown: Roman Republic proclaimed; (Mar.) parliamentary elections return left-wing deputies; (May) *coup d'état* of Floréal: left-wingers excluded from parliament; Bonaparte sets out for Egypt; (Aug.) French fleet destroyed in battle of the Nile; (Sept.) Jourdan law on conscription; (Oct.) uprising in Belgium against French rule

1799 (Mar.) Austria resumes war against France and Russia joins the anti-French coalition; military defeats follow with France expelled from Italy; (June) Sieyès becomes a member of the executive Directory; (July) Law of Hostages, emergency measures in response to crisis; (Aug.) right-wing uprisings in the West and around Toulouse; (Oct.) Bonaparte returns from Egypt; (Nov.) *coup d'état* of Brumaire: Directory replaced by a Provisional Consulate; (Dec.) New Constitution (Year VIII) implemented and put to popular vote; Bonaparte becomes First Consul

1800 (Feb.) prefects created to administer departments; (Mar.) closure of the lists of émigrés; judicial reorganization; (June) French triumph at battle of Marengo; (Dec.) attempted assassination of Bonaparte: the 'infernal machine'

1801 (Feb.) Peace of Lunéville with Austria; (July) Concordat signed with papacy

1802 Peace of Amiens with Britain; Chateaubriand, *The Genius of Christianity*; Proclamation of Concordat on Easter Sunday; creation of the Legion of Honour; popular vote on Bonaparte becoming Consul for Life

1803 Resumption of war between France and Britain

1804 Execution of the Duc d'Enghien; Napoleonic Code enacted; vote on creation of Empire; Emperor Napoleon I crowns himself at Notre-Dame, in presence of Pope

1805 Italy reorganized under French control; battle of Trafalgar confirms British command of the sea; Napoleon wins battle of Austerlitz; third anti-French coalition collapses

1806 Republican calendar withdrawn; Napoleon's brothers become kings of Naples and Holland; Prussia declares war on France but is defeated at Jena

1807 Russia rejoins the war, then makes peace with Napoleon at Tilsit

1808 France invades Spain and provokes popular uprising; creation of imperial nobility; organization of the Imperial University to oversee all education

1809 Austrians defeated at Wagram and make peace

1810 Napoleon marries Marie-Louise, daughter of the Austrian Emperor, having divorced Josephine

1812 Defeat in Spain; food and anti-conscription riots in France;

Napoleon invades Russia, and reaches Moscow, but is forced to retreat

1813   Formation of new anti-French coalition and defeat for Napoleon at Leipzig

1814   (Apr.) Napoleon abdicates; Restoration of Louis XVIII; (May) Treaty of Paris between France and allied powers; (June) Constitutional Charter issued; (Sept.) Congress of Vienna opens

1815   (Mar.) Napoleon returns from Elba for the 'Hundred Days'; (June) Battle of Waterloo; Napoleon's second abdication follows defeat; Second Restoration and White Terror; (Aug.) Ultra-royalist *chambre introuvable* elected; (Nov.) Second Treaty of Paris reduces France to frontiers of 1790

1816   Dissolution of Ultra-dominated *Chambre Introuvable* and fresh legislative elections

1820   Murder of Duc de Berri; law of 'Double Vote'

1821   Death of Napoleon on Saint Helena ; Villèle government

1822   Four Sergeants of La Rochelle conspiracy

1823   French invasion of Spain to restore Bourbon monarchy

1824   Ultra-royalist election victory; death of Louis XVIII; accession of Charles X

1825   Sacrilege law and indemnification of émigrés; coronation of Charles X at Reims

1827   National Guard dissolved; passage of Forest Code; legislative elections

1828   Resignation of Villèle; Martignac forms government

1829   Balzac begins publishing *The Human Comedy*; Polignac becomes chief minister of ultra-royalist government

1830   (June) legislative elections produce huge liberal gains; conquest of Algiers; beginning of French Empire in North Africa; (July) Four Ordinances; 'Three Glorious Days' of revolution in Paris; (Aug.) Charles X abdicates; Louis-Philippe becomes 'King of the French People'; (Sept.) riots in provinces; Stendhal, *Scarlet and Black*; Delacroix, *Liberty Leading the People*

1831   Casimir Périer becomes chief minister; laws on election of municipal councils and National Guard; legislative elections with wider franchise; revolt in Lyon

1832   Cholera outbreak in Paris; popular unrest at funeral of General Lamarque

1833   Guizot's Education Law

1834   Law against Associations; further revolt in Lyon; Rue Transnonain massacre follows uprising in Paris

1835   Fieschi bomb plot to assassinate Louis-Philippe; press Laws restrict publications

1836   Louis-Napoleon attempts to raise the garrison in Strasbourg

1839   Society of Seasons' uprising, led by Blanqui; Louis Blanc, *The Organization of Labour;* Cabet, *Voyage in Icaria;* Louis-Napoleon, *Napoleonic Ideas*

1840   Napoleon's body is returned from Saint Helena and interred at Les Invalides in Paris; Louis-Napoleon tries to raise a rebellion at Boulogne; Guizot forms a government; Proudhon, *What is Property?*

1842   Tahiti becomes a French protectorate

1843   France annexes Dahomey and the Ivory Coast

1846   Legislative Elections result in victory for Guizot; onset of economic crisis

1847   Banquet Campaign commences, aimed at franchise reform

1848   (Feb.) revolution in Paris; Guizot resigns; Louis-Philippe abdicates; Second Republic proclaimed; universal manhood suffrage decreed; (Mar.) radical demonstration Paris; (Apr.) election of Constituent Assembly, with conservative majority; (June) popular uprising in Paris is crushed. General Cavaignac becomes head of government; (Nov.) Constitution of Second Republic; (Dec.) election of Louis-Napoleon as President

1849   Elections to Legislative Assembly; good showing by left-wing *democrate-socialistes;* unrest in Paris and Lyon; French army restores papal power in Rome

1850   Falloux Law on Education gives Catholics right to set up schools; left-wing by-election victories; suffrage restrictions introduced

1851   *Coup d'état* establishes dictatorship for Louis-Napoleon; republican insurrection in south and centre of France; popular vote, or plebisicite, approves coup

1852   Constitution creating Second Empire accepted in another plebiscite; legislative elections return only three republicans

1853   Haussmann becomes Prefect of the Seine

1854   Outbreak of Crimean war against Russia

1856   Peace of Paris successfully concludes Crimean war; Tocqueville, *The Old Regime and the French Revolution*

1857   Conquest of Algeria completed

1858   Bernadette Soubirous experiences a vision of the Virgin Mary at Lourdes

1859   France and Piedmont declare war on Austria; French occupy Saigon

1860   Treaty of Turin cedes Nice and Savoy to France; constitutional reforms introduced

1862   Hugo, *Les Misérables*

1864   Industrial Relations law recognizes right to strike; French protectorate established over Cambodia

1867   Right to question ministers granted to Legislative Body; World Fair in Paris

1868   Greater freedom of press and legalization of public meetings

1869   Flaubert, *Sentimental Education*; election of thirty republicans; Ollivier becomes head of government; opening of Suez Canal, the work of French engineer de Lesseps

1870   (May) plebiscite on further constitutional reform, to create so-called 'Liberal Empire'; (July) outbreak of Franco-Prussian war; (Aug.) invasion of France; army besieged at Metz; (Sept.) Louis-Napoleon surrenders at Sedan; Republic declared at Paris: Government of National Defence established; (Oct.) Paris besieged and government withdraws to Tours

1871   (Jan.) Parisians fail to lift siege; armistice signed with Prussians; (Feb.) election of National Assembly; monarchist majority elects Thiers as head of government; (Mar.) Peace of Frankfurt: France cedes Alsace-Lorraine to German Empire; uprising in Paris leads to proclamation of Paris Commune; revolts in provincial towns, including Lyon, Marseille and Toulouse; (May) Bloody Week and end of Commune; (Aug.) Thiers confirmed as President of the Republic

1873   Death of Napoleon III in England; resignation of Thiers; appointment of MacMahon as President; decision to build Sacré-Cœur at Montmartre; German army of occupation leaves France on payment of indemnity

1875   Wallon amendment; constitutional laws passed founding Third Republic

1876   National Assembly dissolved and Republicans triumph in elections; first workers' congress held in Paris

1877   Gambetta denounces clericalism; MacMahon dissolves National Assembly, but republicans win subsequent elections

1878   Renewal of municipal councils favours Republicans

1879   Senate elections return republicans; MacMahon resigns as President, to be succeeded by republican Grévy; National Assembly returns to Paris; foundation of French Workers' Party by Guesde

1880   Limited amnesty for those involved in Paris Commune; law abolishing official rest on Sundays; national holiday established on 14 July

1881   Liberty of assembly and freedom of press legislated; Tunis becomes a French protectorate

1882   Free, compulsory and secular primary education established; Renan, *What is a Nation?*; French occupy Hanoi

1884 Municipal councils given the right to nominate their own mayors; law permitting divorce; French intervention in Tonkin; French invade Madagascar

Map section

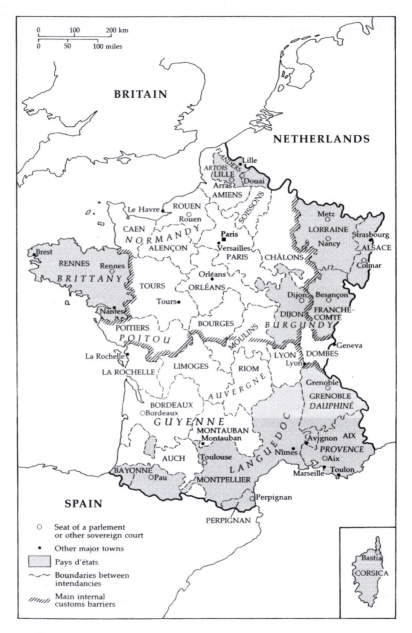

Map 1 France at the end of the Old Regime

Map 2 The departments of France in the Revolution

Map 3 Napoleonic France and Europe

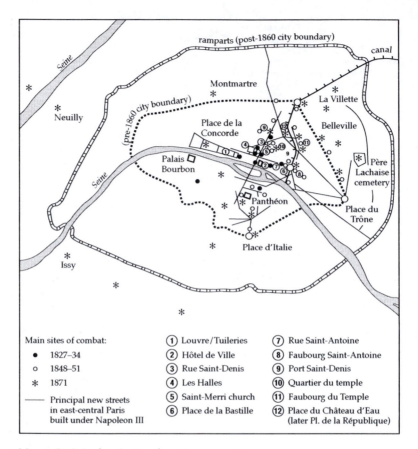

Main sites of combat:

● 1827–34

○ 1848–51

✳ 1871

—— Principal new streets
in east-central Paris
built under Napoleon III

① Louvre/Tuileries

② Hôtel de Ville

③ Rue Saint-Denis

④ Les Halles

⑤ Saint-Merri church

⑥ Place de la Bastille

⑦ Rue Saint-Antoine

⑧ Faubourg Saint-Antoine

⑨ Port Saint-Denis

⑩ Quartier du temple

⑪ Faubourg du Temple

⑫ Place du Château d'Eau
(later Pl. de la République)

Map 4 Paris in the nineteenth century

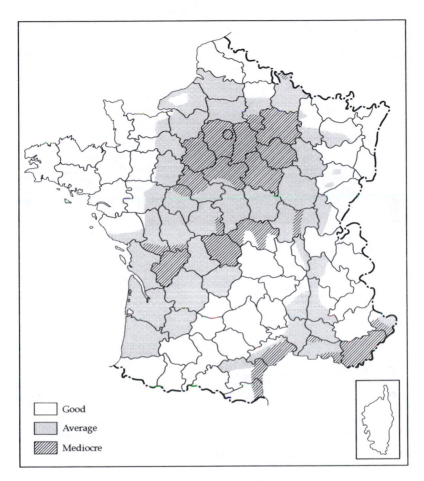

Legend:
- Good
- Average
- Mediocre

Map 5 Religious practice in nineteenth-century France

Wholly French-speaking departments

Map 6 French speakers in the mid-nineteenth century

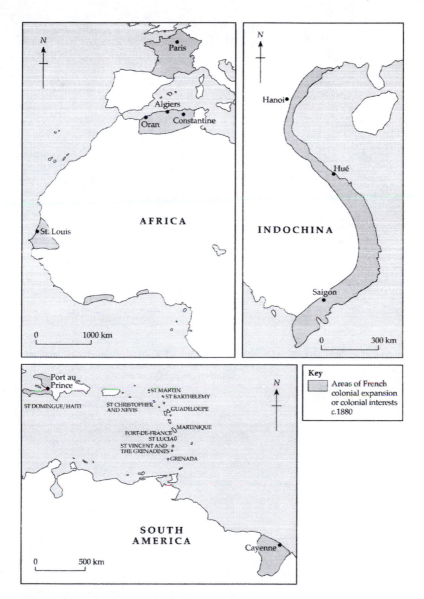

Map 7 The French Empire in the nineteenth century

Index

Pacific 191, 197
Paine, Thomas 14
Pantheon (Paris) 91
Papal States 73
Parent, Jean-François 77, 86, 88
Paris 1, 10, 11, 13, 14, 16, 19, 24, 28–9, 31,
    41–2, 43, 44, 45–7, 51, 57, 59–60, 67,
    69, 74, 82–3, 87–8, 90–1, 99, 109,
    112, 123, 125, 126, 129–30, 133, 135,
    137, 140, 141, 148, 150, 152, 153, 157,
    158, 159, 161–2, 184, 191, 195, 204,
    207, 208, 212
Paris Commune (1871) 1, 43, 46, 51, 56,
    59–60, 89–90, 118, 162, 172, 202,
    209
Paris, Comte de 49
Paris Geographical Society 201
parish priests 13, 18, 21, 22, 25, 27, 39,
    65–6, 68, 69–70, 75–8, 125, 139, 208
parishes 124
parlements 11, 12
Parliament of Industry (1848) 55
Parti Colonial 201
party of Order 138
patois 6, 164–6
patrie 151, 171–2
patriotism 172–4
pays 124, 151, 163, 164, 168
pays d'états 155–6, 160
Peace of Amiens (1802) 32
Peace of Paris (1856) 212
peasants 13, 14, 15, 16, 17, 21, 44, 97, 101,
    106–8, 115, 120, 123, 127, 128–30, 131,
    135–6, 141, 143–4, 171, 209–10
Pélissier, Amable, Duc de Malakoff 192
penal colony 197
Perdiguier, Agricol 46
Père Lachaise cemetery (Paris) 82–3
Périer, Casimir 103
Perpignan 124, 134
phalanges 55
Phalsbourg 177
Philippines 195
philosophes 97
phylloxera 145
Picardy 125, 126, 174

Piedmont 53, 176
Pierchon, Abbé 76–7, 88
pilgrimages 76, 79–80, 90, 208
Pius VII (Pope) 31, 32
Pius IX (Pope) 73, 88
plebiscite 24, 30, 33, 43, 53, 153, 154, 173,
    177
poetry 168
Poitou 157
Poland 34, 175
Poles 175
police 46, 132
political clubs 114
Polignac, Prince de 40
Polynesia 191
Pont-de-Montvert (Lozère) 130, 146
Pont-Neuf (Paris) 153
Pontmain 80–1
population 37, 96, 109, 115, 118–9, 123,
    134, 139–40, 144, 150, 164, 192,
    198–9, 203, 208, 211
Portugal 195
positivism 86
prefects 31, 34, 46, 57, 132–3, 159, 161,
    190
press 11, 17, 30, 40, 41, 42, 44, 51, 53, 56,
    114, 147, 154
Prévost-Paradol, Anatole 198–9, 200,
    203
Printemps store (Paris) 115
prostitution 106, 117, 135
Protestants 18, 67, 73, 157, 163
Proudhon, Pierre-Joseph 112, 117–8
Provençal 168
Provence 11, 13, 80, 155–6, 157, 168
Provence, Comte de (later Louis
    XVIII) 25
provincial assemblies 155–6, 158
provincial identity 124, 125, 210–1
provincial reviews 160–1
Prussia 19, 27, 34, 43, 89, 118, 128, 167,
    171, 172, 173, 175, 176, 211
'public sphere' (see also 'separate
    spheres') 11, 108, 117–8, 119–21
Pyat, Félix 89
Pyrenees 135, 157, 173